ISLANDERS IN THE EMPIRE

THE ASIAN AMERICAN EXPERIENCE

Series Editors
Eiichiro Azuma
Jigna Desai
Martin F. Manalansan IV
Lisa Sun-Hee Park
David K. Yoo

Roger Daniels, Founding Series Editor

A list of books in the series appears at the end of this book.

JOANNA POBLETE

Islanders in the Empire

Filipino and Puerto Rican Laborers in Hawai'i

UNIVERSITY OF ILLINOIS PRESS
URBANA, CHICAGO, AND SPRINGFIELD

© 2014 by JoAnna Poblete
All rights reserved
Manufactured in the United States of America
C 5 4 3 2 1

⊗ This book is printed on acid-free paper.

Library of Congress Cataloging-in-Publication Data
Poblete, JoAnna
Islanders in the empire : Filipino and Puerto Rican laborers in Hawai'i / JoAnna Poblete.
p.   cm. — (Asian American experience)
Includes bibliographical references and index.
ISBN 978-0-252-03829-7 (hardback) — ISBN 978-0-252-09647-1 (e-book)
1. Migrant agricultural laborers—Hawaii—History. 2. Migrant agricultural laborers—Government policy—United States—History—20th century. 3. Migrant labor—Government policy—United States—History—20th century. 4. Puerto Ricans—Hawaii—History—20th century. 5. Filipinos—Hawaii—History—20th century. 6. Puerto Ricans—Legal status, laws, etc.—United States—History—20th century. 7. Filipinos—Legal status, laws, etc.—United States—History—20th century. 8. Labor mobility—United States—History—20th century. I. Title.
HD1527.H3P63   2014
331.5'440896872950969—dc23   2013046538

To my loved ones on earth and up above

Contents

Acknowledgments ix

*Introduction: Defining U.S. Colonial Experiences:
The Long History of U.S. Expansionism 1*

1. *Letters Home: The Failure of Puerto Rican Recruitment 25*
2. *Flexible and Accommodating: Successful Recruitment
   and Retention of Filipinos 47*
3. *Indefinite Dependence: U.S. Control
   over Puerto Rican Labor Complaints 75*
4. *Tensions of Colonial Cooperation:
   Philippine Authority over Labor Complaints 95*
5. *Conflicting Convictions: Filipino Ethnic Minister Interactions
   with the Plantation Community 121*
6. *Limited Leadership: Roles of Puerto Rican
   Labor Agents in the Plantation Community 139*

*Conclusion: Current Struggles
against U.S. Colonialism and Empire 163*

Notes 173

Selected Bibliography 199

Index 217

Acknowledgments

For more than ten years of my life, I have been lucky to work with many amazing people to develop, create, and publish this project. I was fortunate to gain critical funding for this multisite research effort from a variety of programs and institutions, including the UC Pacific Rim Research Program, the UCLA Institute of American Cultures/Asian American Studies Center, the UCLA Center for Southeast Asian Studies, UCLA Affiliates (especially Roz Livingston), the UCLA History Department, and the University of Wyoming Office of Research and Development.

From my multiple research trips across the globe in the past decade, I must thank the following archivists and scholars for their unending support and assistance: in Hawai'i, Joan Hori, Dore Minatodani, and the entire staff at the Hawaiian/Pacific Collection at the Hamilton Library at the University of Hawai'i at Mānoa; Marilyn Reppun, Vivian Guiterrez, John Barker, and other staff at the Mission Houses Museum; Gina Vergara Bautista, Patricia Lai, and others at the Hawai'i State Archives; Roderick Labrador, Jonathan Okamura, Tia Reber, and Dean Saranillio for providing vital connections and assistance in the islands throughout my work on this project.

In Puerto Rico, I must thank Amílcar Tirado, Pedro J. Rivera Guzmán, and the Instituto de Estudios del Caribe; Maria Dolores Luque and her staff at the Centro de Investigaciones Históricas; and the staff at the Colección Puertorriqueña at la Biblioteca, all at la Universidad de Puerto Rico Río Piedras. I must also thank Juan Carlos and other archive staff members at the Archivo General de Puerto Rico, as well as Rudy and Sonia Mendez in San Juan. None of these contacts would have been made without the support of César Ayala.

In the Philippines, I am grateful for the assistance of Yolanda E. Jacinto, Prudenciana C. Cruz, and the entire staff of the Filipiniana division at the National Library of the Philippines, as well as Waldette Cueto and her assistant Bhal at the American Historical Collection at Ateneo de Manila University. In the United States, Joseph D. Schwarz at the National Archives at College Park and the staff at the National Archives Pacific Branch in San Bruno, California, were invaluable.

I also encountered many generous and welcoming individuals throughout my research experience in the Hawaiian Islands. I thank each person who took the time to "talk-story" with me about his or her experiences at Hawai'i sugar plantations. I am especially grateful for the hospitality of and extra effort made by Dr. Fred Soriano and Gus and Marion Villanueva on the island of Hawai'i. Eleanor Morita, Jiro Sumada, and Junko Nowaki also went out of their way to help me contact folks on the island.

I also need to recognize the two major scholars of Puerto Ricans in Hawai'i. Norma Carr not only shared her fabulous oral history collection with me, but she graciously invited me to stay at her home many times. Blase Camacho Souza and her daughter Michelle were also very supportive of my work. Nélida Perez and Kimberlly Irizarry graciously allowed me to take an early look at Blase's collection of materials at the Archives of the Puerto Rican Diaspora before it was fully cataloged at the Centro de Estudios Puertorriqueños at Hunter College. Pedro Hernandez spearheaded image acquisition for me.

At the University of Wyoming, I truly want to thank Ronald Schultz, Michael Brose, Phil Roberts, Kelly Visnak, Keith Wresinkski, Bill Gern, Andy Hansen, Jeffrey Means, Douglas Johnson, and Leif Cawley for their advice and support through the last stages of publication. I am also forever grateful for the support and encouragement of Phil Christman, Faye Caronan, Nicole Choi, Emily Hind, Jennifer Ho, Jennifer Hayashida, Isadora Helfgott, Lucy Mae San Pablo Burns, Robin Derby, Ashley Lucas, Rongsong Liu, Laura Halperin, Gladys Nubla, Carolina San Juan, Lilia Soto, Mary Talusan, and Judy Wu. Last, but not least, Henry Yu has been a great advisor and colleague.

At University of Illinois Press, I am so grateful for the enthusiastic and tireless work and support of Martin Manalansan, Vijay Shah, Laurie Matheson, Dawn Durante, Tad Ringo, Julie Gay, and the rest of the editors and staff. I am grateful to have found an amazing publishing home. Finally, many thanks to my family and friends who endured the ups and downs of my academic pursuits. Your personal support and love have gotten me through many challenges, and I hope this work can inspire others to keep pursuing their own ambitions.

ISLANDERS IN THE EMPIRE

Introduction:
Defining U.S. Colonial Experiences

THE LONG HISTORY OF U.S. EXPANSIONISM

In 1901, Puerto Rican Alberto E. Minvielle played overlapping and contradictory roles as a hospital assistant, interpreter, and general helper for the Ola'a plantation on the east side of the island of Hawai'i while also unofficially leading Puerto Rican laborers at this location and contributing articles to the Puerto Rico–based Spanish-language newspaper *La Correspondencia*. Two decades later, during the 1924–25 labor strike in the Hawaiian Islands, Flaviano M. Santa Ana spoke on behalf of Filipino laborers at the same plantation while simultaneously working as a member of the plantation special police, tasked with maintaining order during strike times. His conflicting responsibilities as labor spokesperson and plantation security became further complicated by his position as a Protestant minister. How did these two individuals come to fill these multiple roles?

The larger political-legal context of their regions of origin directly influenced both men's careers. The complexity of their social roles was intimately tied to the liminal status that both Puerto Rican and Filipino laborers in Hawai'i held as a result of the ambiguous politics of U.S. imperialism in all three regions. The United States had gained possession over the two former Spanish colonies, as well as Guam, after the War of 1898 and the subsequent Treaty of Paris. In 1904, the Supreme Court ruled that the people who resided in these former Spanish territories were not aliens of the United States but citizens of their respective regions under U.S. control. The justices, however, refused to deliberate whether these groups were consequently citizens of the United States, stating, "We are not required to discuss [whether] . . . the cession of Porto Rico accomplished the naturalization of its people; or . . . that a citizen of Porto Rico, under the act of 1900, is necessarily a citizen of the United States."[1] The Court's unwillingness to comment on the exact U.S. citizenship of these populations resulted in an ambiguous political-legal status that unfolded slowly during the early decades of U.S. rule. Unlike foreigners, Filipinos and Puerto Ricans were fully subject to U.S. authority. Yet unlike citizens, they did not have access to full constitutional protections.[2]

Neither citizens nor foreigners, Filipinos and Puerto Ricans also did not have independent government officials representing them in the Hawaiian Islands. Literate both in their native languages and in English, Minvielle and Santa Ana became two of the best options for local leadership in the Puerto Rican and Filipino labor community in the islands. They also represented two of a handful of individuals who could translate employer and government expectations to these non-English-speaking groups of migrant workers. Such factors resulted in Minvielle and Santa Ana's handling of various, contradictory responsibilities on the east side of the island of Hawai'i.

Despite their legally identical classification by the Treaty of Paris and the Supreme Court, Filipinos and Puerto Ricans have generally not been linked to each other in academic scholarship.[3] *Islanders in the Empire* comparatively analyzes how U.S. authority and policies toward both Puerto Ricans and Filipinos have differentiated the labor and migration processes of these populations from foreigners and citizens in the second colonized space of Hawai'i.[4] Minvielle and Santa Ana's stories represent two of many distinct experiences that Puerto Ricans and Filipinos faced in these Pacific Islands.

To better compare the experiences of these two groups, I have developed the category of *U.S. colonial*. This category highlights the liminal and subordinate political-legal status of multiple groups who have come under direct U.S. authority. During different periods and in various locations, native peoples such as American Indians, Chicanos in the Southwest, Alaska Natives, Native Hawaiians, Puerto Ricans, Filipinos, Chamorros in Guam, American Sāmoans, and U.S. Virgin Islanders have occupied subservient positions to the interests of the U.S. federal government and U.S. businesses.

Such dependents, or wards of the United States, have historically existed as a result of U.S. expansionism or the extension of U.S. rule over areas beyond its official borders. Starting with the displacement of American Indians during the early American colonial period and continuing in the twenty-first century with U.S. presence in areas like American Sāmoa and the U.S. Virgin Islands, the United States government has repeatedly taken charge of regions outside its jurisdiction. While some scholars believe overseas expansion marks a qualitative break from earlier domestic expansion, an analysis of U.S. colonial experiences on both sides of this divide demonstrates the larger, consistent government policy of colonialism throughout U.S. history.[5]

The concept of U.S. colonial specifically explores the transitional period for each subjected group, from independent peoples to either incorporated entities of the United States or sovereign groups. Some U.S. colonials forcibly became full-fledged citizens whose lands became states of the union, such as Native Hawaiians and Chicanos in the Southwest. Others remain in an in-between U.S. colonial space, having U.S. citizenship but no full incorporation into the nation, like Puerto Ricans and American Sāmoans. Others gained independence and sovereignty from the United States, such as Filipinos. The political-legal status of each group was ultimately based on the utility of each people and their lands to United States government and businesses.[6] The concept of U.S. colonials explores the treatment and experiences of these groups during their particular periods of liminal political-legal status.

Even though the specific relationship of each U.S. colonial group with the United States has varied, and each set of people has been subject to U.S. rule for different amounts of time, the category of U.S. colonial can facilitate a comparative analysis of imperial experiences across time and geographic locations.[7] The concept of U.S. colonial also connects the imperial experiences of a vast range of subjected peoples *to each other*, exposing the long-term and widespread imperial actions of the United States in multiple places over diverse peoples during varying eras. U.S. expansionism has occurred since the beginning of the country's existence and persists today in different parts of the globe. Such a pattern needs to be acknowledged and integrated into the general study of U.S. history. The concept of U.S. colonial can help such a shift in historical narrative.

To develop an understanding of general U.S. colonial experiences, this book explores the migration and labor histories of two specific groups: Filipinos and Puerto Ricans. This work looks closely at how these wards of the United States interacted with government structures and businesses at the ground level as they labored in the U.S. Territory of Hawai'i. The in-between political-legal status of U.S. colonials resulted in unique work and mobility experiences that sometimes benefited and other times disadvantaged Puerto Ricans and Filipinos. One major opportunity involved *open colonial mobility*, or the exemption of U.S. colonials from U.S. immigration restrictions. This ability to move freely from one area of U.S. jurisdiction to another resulted in distinctive recruitment and retention efforts by the sugar industry in Hawai'i, known as the Hawaiian Sugar Planters Association (HSPA).[8] Filipinos and

Puerto Ricans accessed exclusive employment programs and policies that other workers in the islands never obtained.

One drawback to open colonial mobility involved the lack of official leaders to manage their affairs and concerns in Hawai'i. This shortage became a decisive influence on U.S. colonial life. Without an effective local government representative in the islands, Puerto Rican and Filipino work and living issues could be easily ignored or mishandled. Because they moved *intra-colonially*, or from a colonized home region to another colonized location, their labor complaints were usually funneled through government bureaucracies in Washington, D.C., and their home regions. This hierarchical administrative process could take up to one year for the government to address a single grievance. In contrast, foreign laborers and citizens in Hawai'i had access to officials residing in Honolulu to quickly resolve their daily issues. The absence of local government leadership made Puerto Ricans and Filipinos heavily reliant on community mediators, like Minvielle and Santa Ana, to deal with their everyday affairs. While foreign migrants and citizens also worked with neighborhood leaders, U.S. colonials were dependent on these local middlemen for services that foreign consul generals or citizen-elected representatives usually handled. Thus U.S. colonial status resulted in divergent labor and migration processes from citizens and foreigners at the same time and place.

While not quite foreigners, Filipinos and Puerto Ricans also did not enjoy the advantages of full citizenship.[9] According to Article 9 of the Treaty of Paris, "The civil rights and political status of the native inhabitants of the territories hereby ceded to the United States shall be determined by the Congress."[10] The U.S. government held complete authority over these subjected groups and could determine which rights U.S. colonials could access, known as plenary power. However, the legislature never had total control over the actions of U.S. colonials. Even though Puerto Ricans and Filipinos were wards of the United States, contract (or indentured) labor was banned in 1900. No one could be forced to work in Hawai'i. U.S. colonials and others only participated in labor migration when they believed such movement would result in personal and community advancement. While under U.S. rule, colonized individuals could and did prioritize open colonial, or intra-colonial, mobility.

This mobility contrasted with the desire of foreign populations to participate in the U.S. economy of the period. The first half of the twentieth century was a time of strict anti-immigration legislation in the United States.[11] These rules did not apply to U.S. colonials, who, as wards of the country, had the exceptional lawful ability to travel wherever they wanted within U.S. jurisdiction whenever they chose. Consequently, U.S. colonial migrant laborers engaged in significantly different migration patterns from those of foreign workers. As scholars such as Matthew Guterl and Christine Skwiot, as well as Marilyn Lake and Henry Reynolds, have discussed, the end of slavery and contract labor in the nineteenth century led to a crisis of labor acquisition, particularly for agricultural plantations. Since only free labor was acceptable into the twentieth century, Western capitalist nations had to figure out how to obtain and sustain low-paid manual workers within the confines of the new moral labor code of the modern era. U.S. colonials provided one way for the United States government to gain access to cheap low-skilled migrant laborers.

As part of the endeavor to describe U.S. colonial experiences, this study also highlights specific ways the United States government regulated U.S. colonials. The imperial policies of the United States were not monolithic but mutated according to each region's precise relationship with and significance to the United States. Such variance in legal and institutional procedures toward different groups of U.S. colonials became crucial to the success of U.S. territorial expansion before, during, and after the early twentieth century.[12] From 1898 to 1917, Filipinos and Puerto Ricans had the same ambiguous legal status as wards of the U.S. Congress. But unique political issues and economic concerns in each region eventually led to a divergence of political-legal statuses between the two groups.

Federal officials did not want to fully incorporate Puerto Rico into the United States. They were also not willing to relinquish U.S. dominance and control in this important gateway to the Caribbean and Latin America. Puerto Ricans eventually became U.S. citizens with limited access to full citizenship rights in their home region and a strong, ethnic-based nationalism that developed in reaction to continued U.S. rule. Filipinos, on the other hand, eventually became foreigners to the United States, heavily steeped in pro-U.S. ideologies and structures. While imperialist and anti-imperialist groups in the United States debated the type of authority the United States would wield in the Philippines, neither group viewed the geographically distant and dark-skinned populations of the Philippines as acceptable U.S. citizens.[13] The divergent treatment of Filipino and Puerto Rican colonials illustrate two instances of how U.S. colonialism has historically persisted, adapted, and reacted to find effective ways to gain control, maintain authority, and prevent resistance in each specific region.

Islanders in the Empire explores the overarching process and function of U.S. imperialism, the general impact of ambiguous legal status on U.S. colonials, and the particular experiences of two different colonized groups at a specific time and place. This text is a socio-legal labor history that focuses both on the creation of migration and employment policies, as well as the influence of those programs on the everyday lives of individuals. At one level, this book examines U.S. government administration and business strategies toward Filipinos and Puerto Ricans in Hawai'i. This work also connects the actual function of these practices with the personal experiences of U.S. colonials, like Minvielle and Santa Ana. These men engaged with imperial structures and processes at the ground level on a daily basis. Multiple points of analyses provide a rich, multifaceted narrative about the ways two distinct groups of colonial labor migrants worked within and outside government and labor systems.

Also dealing with issues of citizenship, migration, and labor, this project adds another layer of understanding to the encounters of work migrants who occupy in-between political-legal statuses. In addition to Mae Ngai's category of alien citizens, who had theoretical legal rights but continued to face daily social discriminations, the concept of U.S. colonials in this study explores the explicit and formal forms of subjugation that colonized laborers experienced from U.S. government and businesses as liminal U.S. colonials. In this in-between status, Puerto Ricans and Filipinos engaged in fundamentally different migration patterns, as well as government and labor processes, from foreigners, citizens, and each other.

Intra-Colonial Experiences

Puerto Rican and Filipino experiences in the Territory of Hawai'i complicate and enrich the story of U.S. colonial experiences because these groups were *intra-colonials*: colonized people living in a second colonized place. Outside their home region, as well as the colonizer's home region, Puerto Ricans and Filipinos resided five thousand miles from centers of imperial power. Physically distant from their homeland, they had no official local support network to champion their issues.[14] These U.S. colonials also had no claims to indigenous rights or privileges, unlike Native Hawaiians, who became U.S. citizens after their region became a U.S. Territory by force in 1900. Without local government leaders to help them maneuver through the particular imperial structures created for an unfamiliar colonized location, their concerns had to travel through a slow, global hierarchy of command in their home regions, Washington, D.C., and the Hawaiian Islands.

Yet this bureaucratic distance also conferred on them a degree of flexibility, choice, and immediate control over their everyday lives not available to micromanaged indigenous colonized peoples. The experiences of intra-colonials in the Pacific consequently differed from those of U.S. colonials residing in the colony or the metropole. Filipinos and Puerto Ricans living in their home regions faced assimilationist Americanization programs at all levels of society, including English-language-based education systems, pro-U.S. economic policies, and American-style government structures. Filipinos and Puerto Ricans living on the nativist and racist U.S. continent faced race riots, vigilante violence, and discriminatory marriage and housing regulations.[15] In Hawai'i, the need for these groups as plantation labor for the powerful sugar industry tempered racial animosity and supported their migration rights.

The concept of intra-coloniality is a new direction for scholarship on U.S. colonialism, particularly studies of Puerto Rico and the Philippines. To add to existing works on government policies and identity politics, this study compares the influences that intra-colonial mobility had on more than one group of U.S. colonials at the same time and place, demonstrating both similarities and differences in U.S. colonial experiences.[16]

Intra-colonialism, however, is not unique to the United States empire. Indian subjects of Great Britain migrated to work on other British Pacific, Caribbean, and American territories. According to historian Lomarsh Roopnarine, these groups, like U.S. colonials, used "emigration to better their lives, resist domination, reproduce and reinvent their culture, adapt and turn adverse circumstances to their advantage. . . . [They] understood the pros and cons of the plantation system and manipulated it with minimum disadvantage to themselves under everyday forms of resistance."[17] However, these Indian British colonials also migrated during the nineteenth century as indentured workers. This distinction in labor status differentiated the legal ties that British colonial workers had to plantations from those of wage-labor U.S. colonials in the twentieth century. While independent recruiters in Puerto Rico made large profits, they did not wield immense control over U.S. colonial workers like *kanganies*, or Ceylon recruiters of Indians for work in Ceylon. Even though there were no government restrictions on the movement of Indian migrants, the manipulative kangany system resulted in oppressive conditions. Indian laborers had technical freedom of mobility, with only one-month contracts binding them to employers. However, their dependence on kanganies for transport, food, and lodging during the migration process bound them to labor agents for longer periods.[18] In Hawai'i, Puerto Rican and Filipino U.S. colonial laborers had more flexibility to leave plantations due to the ban on contract labor at the time. Indian British colonial indentured laborers of the nineteenth century consequently did not have the same degree of mobility and flexibility as U.S. colonials in the twentieth century.[19]

The study of intra-coloniality also pushes migration history to expand the concept of transnationalism.[20] While Puerto Ricans and Filipinos in Hawai'i maintained various connections with their home region, these intra-colonials were not foreigners who moved from one independent nation to the United States. As U.S. colonials, they could move freely within United States jurisdiction. Immigration restrictions at U.S. borders did not apply to Puerto Ricans and Filipinos. Adam McKeown discussed the development of international border control and identification at the end of the nineteenth century and how the movement of people became more regulated and standardized throughout the globe in the twentieth century. During such international homogenization of migration policies, the ability of U.S. colonials to move freely back and forth circumvented border controls. Such intra-coloniality represented the increasingly rare "privilege of moving across borders" without an entry visa.[21] The mobility of colonials during a period of increasing immigration restrictions demonstrates that despite the growing prioritization of the individual and state power in migration policies, the economic needs for migration into the twentieth century also played a key role in fostering colonial movement, an alternative experience to the increasingly restricted travel of foreigners. Acknowledging the existence, importance, and uniqueness of U.S. intra-colonial experiences moves analyses of labor migration beyond conventional citizen/foreigner binaries, greatly enhancing our understanding of a wider range of situations facing migrant laborers in the United States.

Looking beyond regional and century boundaries also highlights connections with other global empires.[22] The U.S. government has historically denied the imperial nature of its expansionism. According to Greg Bankoff, "Americans were both new to empire and late to the colonial game. They were anxious to demonstrate that their rule was both qualitatively different from that of the European powers in the region and administered for the benefit of the indigenous population."[23] Government officials and academics alike have focused on the country's encouragement of liberal principles abroad, such as representative government and capitalistic individualism, as reasons why U.S. absorption of other peoples and lands should not be seen as colonial.[24] In contrast, empires, like the British and the French, have acknowledged their roles as exploiters and extractors of people and lands outside their official borders.[25]

Some scholars have also dismissed U.S. involvement in places like the Philippines and Puerto Rico as true signs of U.S. empire or colonialism.[26] These regions and other U.S. possessions and territories are seen as minimal in the larger scheme of U.S. history. *Islanders in the Empire* pushes these scholars to acknowledge and accept that these experiences are not minor anecdotes but central aspects of U.S. history. By connecting the experiences of indigenous peoples abroad to the continental U.S. empire, there can be a greater understanding of the imperial form and function of the U.S. government.

Other scholars have studied the interconnected nature of Western empires during the nineteenth century. Julian Go and Anne Foster discussed how the U.S. government developed international practices in accordance to global empire building of the time, particularly the tactics of the British and the French.[27] Paul Kramer also explained how U.S. officials often "found themselves on imperial pathways already charted and inhabited by the English."[28] Such similarities resulted in U.S. imperial leaders frequently comparing or modeling themselves to this specific empire. Overall, the U.S. government played one part in the larger global phenomenon of empire building in the late nineteenth century.

Christopher Schmidt-Nowara argued that U.S. colonialism actually had more in common with Spanish imperialists due to the U.S. government's rule over the same regions of former Spanish empire.[29] This observation is ironic, since U.S. leaders and yellow journalism newspapers in the early twentieth century often used anti-Spanish rhetoric to promote their more liberal and democratic reasons for exerting colonial control in the Philippines and Puerto Rico.[30] Carol Hess explained how the United States government portrayed itself as the better ruler due to its society's race and principles.[31] The U.S. government planned to protect helpless Caribbean and Pacific natives from the evil Spanish. Regardless of this Black Legend about Spain, U.S. expansionism was neither exceptional nor unique. Border crossing in both the continental United States and abroad was part of a larger international process of colonialism and empire that peaked during the nineteenth century. Actions of U.S. imperialism in both the continental United States and overseas were not separate experiences on the fringes of U.S. diplomatic or legal studies: all of these activities were central and consistent aspects of imperial federal government policy and action throughout the nation's history.

U.S. Colonialism in Hawai'i, the Philippines, and Puerto Rico

At the turn of the twentieth century, the United States developed an overseas empire. While the United States had already purchased Alaska from Russia in 1867, the country further expanded its authority beyond continental North America when it annexed the Hawaiian Islands in 1898. That same year, the war with Spain and the subsequent Treaty of Paris gave the U.S. Congress control over Puerto Rico, the Philippines, and Guam. These regions differed from earlier acquisitions because they involved new types of political-legal relationships with the United States. Although these new possessions were all dominated by the United States at the turn of the century, the legal policies toward each area were inconsistent and quickly became differentiated throughout the first half of the century.

Before the War of 1898, the 1787 Northwest Ordinance mandated that every U.S. territorial acquisition eventually become a state of the union.[32]

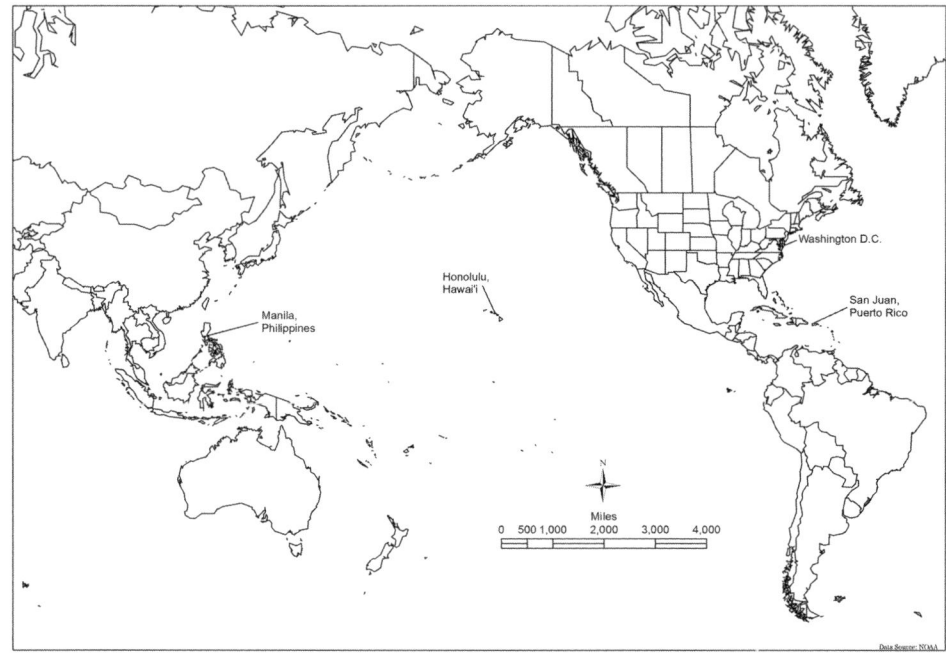

Pacific-centered map of the world.

Hawai'i became a territory in 1900 with the expectation of future statehood. Puerto Rico, the Philippines, and Guam, in contrast, became unincorporated territories under the direct control of the U.S. Congress with no promise of statehood. This systematic variability in U.S. colonialism found Supreme Court sanction in the 1901 *Downes v. Bidwell* decision, which affirmed multiple ways that Puerto Rico and the Philippines could "be introduced into the sisterhood of States or be permitted to form independent governments."[33] Congress could thereby leave the categorization of newly acquired regions ambiguous for an indefinite period, during which the same Congress held ultimate jurisdiction, or plenary power, over these regions.

Colonial policies in Hawai'i, Puerto Rico, and the Philippines differed according to each region's particular relationship with the United States. Historically, Hawai'i functioned as a political, social, and economic borderland where United States and European traders, businessmen, and missionaries interacted with the island monarchy and people.[34] Late-eighteenth-century trade with the west started to break down conventional Hawaiian social relations between *maka'āinana* (commoners) and *ali'i* (the chiefly class) while spreading new diseases, such as tuberculosis and measles, which reduced the native population by 90 percent—from about four hundred thousand in 1778 to about forty thousand by the turn of the twentieth century.[35] The education system created by Protestant missionaries converted the Hawaiian language from an oral tradition passed down from generation to generation to a written language in Western characters.

In the mid-1800s, U.S. missionaries and businessmen steadily convinced the Hawaiian monarchy to subsume customary communal, spiritual, and land-based ways of life to Western structures and ideals, such as capitalism and a constitutional system. Further change came in 1848, when Anglo-American advisors to King Kamehameha III encouraged him to enact the *māhele*, or the division and distribution of land among different levels of Hawaiian society and government, facilitating the privatization of land and the expansion of Anglo-American sugar and pineapple agribusiness in Hawai'i. These shifts were further encouraged by the virtual end of sugar beet farming in the U.S. South as a result of Civil War violence. The Hawaiian Islands became the main source for United States sugar production and, increasingly, a strategic military presence in the Pacific during the twentieth century.

Wanting total legal control in the islands, an imperial complex of U.S. military, government, and business leaders overthrew Queen Lili'uokalani in 1893 and supported the annexation of Hawai'i in 1898. Anglo-American efforts to completely overtake and transform the previous way of life in Hawai'i were completed when the islands became a U.S. Territory in 1900. Territorial status turned more than forty thousand Native Hawaiians into U.S. citizens without their consent.[36] With the importation of laborers and investors for the growing sugar industry, Native Hawaiians quickly became a minority percentage of the population with little control over the politics and economics of their islands, a status which continues today. The sugar industry and the recruitment of non-Hawaiian laborers to the islands furthered the colonization of Native Hawaiians, denying their rights to self-determination and dispossessing these native peoples of their land.[37]

The U.S. Territory of Hawai'i functioned like a colony of the United States from 1900 to 1959. The U.S. Congress and Supreme Court could pick and choose which laws would apply in the islands. Congress often allowed exceptions to the application of federal legislation in the territory if a law threatened U.S. business and military interests. Anglo-American leaders in Hawai'i also asked for exemptions from then-popular race-based restrictions on labor and migration, portraying the region as a unique and exceptional social, political, and economic situation. Since the islands were presented as having fundamentally different labor and migration needs from the rest of the United States, territorial laws should reflect such differences. Anglo-American leaders of the imperial complex in Hawai'i promoted the region's subordinate colonial position within the larger U.S. federal government structure for their own economic advantage.[38] The territorial governor, meanwhile, was selected by the U.S. president and could be changed at any time for any reason, a situation that ensured enthusiastic compliance with pro-U.S. policies in the islands. The continued importance of the islands to the U.S. armed forces during and after World War II, as well as pressures from settlers in Hawai'i, encouraged the U.S. government to fully incorporate the region into the United States as the fiftieth state of the union in 1959.[39]

Like Hawai'i, the Philippines provided the United States with a strategic military position in the Pacific and a fruitful location for sugar production. Before the U.S. government gained jurisdiction over the Philippines in 1898, Spain colonized the archipelago for more than three hundred years, beginning in 1521.[40] The Spaniards transformed this region's multiple independent island kingdoms into one geopolitical unit. Catholic friars and local landed elites cooperated to dictate the social and economic lives of the general population. Drawing upon a long tradition of anti-imperial insurgency in the Philippines, Andres Bonafacio and Emilio Aguinaldo started the final revolution against Spain in 1896.[41] Filipinos triumphed over the Spanish and declared their independence on June 12, 1898. But this claim was ignored by Western powers because the United States was also engaged in a military conflict with Spain at the same time.[42] On December 10, 1898, Spain ceded the Philippines to the United States for $20 million. The colonization of Filipinos continued with U.S. rule in the archipelago, which gave the United States a stronger military position in the Pacific, easy access to Asian trade, new natural resources, and cheap labor. However, Filipinos were barred from U.S. citizenship. Anti-imperialists in the United States, fearing the effect that the incorporation of more than 7.6 million Filipinos would have on the country's Anglo stock, rallied against the Philippines becoming a full-fledged member of the union.[43] Such anti-imperialist concerns were assuaged by official Anglo-American promises that U.S. officials would maintain legal authority over the Philippines only long enough to train Filipinos in proper Western standards of government, economy, and civility.[44] Accordingly, Filipinos were taught to idolize and emulate the new colonists via educational, economic, and political systems modeled after the United States and run in English.

Starting in 1913, the appointed Anglo-American governor general of the Philippines, Francis Burton Harrison, started to encourage Filipinization, or the transition of Philippine government positions from Anglo-Americans to

Filipinos.⁴⁵ Some Filipinos found the phased handover of institutional authority too slow. Philippine independence movements grew in strength at the same time that intense Anglo-American animosity and violence toward Filipinos developed in the U.S. West Coast during the Great Depression of the 1930s.⁴⁶ Pressure from both groups resulted in the 1934 Tydings-McDuffie Act, which granted the Philippines commonwealth status in 1935 and the promise of independence in ten years. Filipinos consequently changed from U.S. nationals to foreigners, subject to immigration restrictions and limited to a fifty-person quota for entry to the United States. They could elect their own governor, but U.S. federal officials still maintained final approval over all Philippine government policies and decisions. Even after final independence was granted in 1946, the last U.S. military base in the Philippines did not close until 1992. After the attacks of September 11, 2001, the U.S. government worked with the Philippine government to reestablish military forces in the archipelago.⁴⁷ Trade interests in the United States also continue to receive special concessions. While no longer an official part of the United States, the Philippines still prioritizes and protects the interests of the U.S. imperial complex in the archipelago, reflecting the persistent colonial relationship between this region and the United States.

Puerto Rico, like the Philippines and Hawai'i, also served as an advantageous location for the business and government interests of the U.S. imperial complex in the twentieth century. A colony of Spain since 1508, Puerto Rico provided an important gateway to the Caribbean and to Latin America, remaining as a significant Spanish outpost until 1821.⁴⁸ Before Spanish presence, Taíno Indians populated this set of Caribbean islands. In the sixteenth century, Spaniards imported African slaves to produce specific agricultural products—sugar, ginger, cattle, tobacco, cocoa, and coffee—for Spanish consumption. Elites from Spain and their children born in Puerto Rico, known as creoles, governed the islands. Catholicism became widespread, with the Church providing social welfare services such as education and medical care for the general populace. In the nineteenth century, when the Spanish government tightened its control over Puerto Rico, local elites began to oppose Spanish authority, culminating in the 1868 armed rebellion *El Grito de Lares*. Despite Spanish defeat of the rebels, Spain granted Puerto Rico more representation within the Spanish colonial administration, then political and administrative autonomy in 1897.

Eight days after the semi-autonomous Puerto Rican government started, U.S. troops landed on the southern coast of the main island on July 25, 1898, as part of their war with Spain. In the same few days, leaders of the anti-Spanish group, the Puerto Rican Revolutionary Party, submitted a manifesto to the U.S. government requesting U.S. citizenship and complete local self-governance. This petition claimed that Spanish rule had not prepared them for independence. United States officials agreed that Puerto Ricans needed guidance, but did not grant their request for U.S. citizenship, instead treating Puerto Rico (like the Philippines) as a legal possession of the United States. Puerto Rico, in much the same fashion as Hawai'i and the Philippines, was then run like a colony for the benefit and profit of the U.S. imperial complex, with imposed United States–style educational, economic, and political structures, official use of English, and economic policies molded to fit U.S. trade needs. As time went on, many Puerto Rican industries shifted to U.S. control, resulting in profits filtering out to the United States instead of remaining in the Caribbean.[49] There was also a distinct imperial and Progressive Era focus on family issues in Puerto Rico, with U.S. colonizers supporting policies to strengthen the institution of marriage or—more controversially—to sterilize "unfit" females.[50]

Unlike Filipinos, the United States government classified Puerto Ricans as white due to the infusion of Spanish blood in the population. According to historian Ileana Rodriguez-Silva, Puerto Rican leaders in turn-of-the-twentieth-century society portrayed their population, especially workers, as white or raceless to gain power and influence under U.S. authority after the War of 1898.[51] Some groups promoted the idea of Puerto Rico as a racially harmonious place to prove the region's ability for self-governance. Consequently, the categorization of Puerto Ricans as white in Hawai'i was likely not shocking to these labor migrants.[52] Citizenship in the United States ultimately became more acceptable for presumed white Puerto Ricans than for dark-skinned Filipinos.

Despite such categorization, the United States would not commit to a full incorporation of Puerto Rico and Puerto Ricans. Beyond the 1901 Insular Cases, the 1900 Foraker Act and the 1917 Jones Act provided the only guidance for Puerto Rico's political-legal status during the first half of the twentieth century.[53] The Foraker Act established a U.S. civil government in Puerto Rico. The Jones Act granted U.S. citizenship to Puerto Ricans, but maintained Puerto Rico as an unincorporated territory of the United States. By giving Puerto Ricans citizenship, the U.S. government justified its continued indefinite political control over the region.

During the 1950s, in reaction to increasingly aggressive demands from different Puerto Rican groups for statehood or independence, the U.S. Congress allowed Puerto Ricans to develop their own constitution. As a compromise among political factions, Puerto Rico became a commonwealth of the United States in 1952. This status meant Puerto Ricans gained political and economic control over their islands, but the United States maintained authority over defense, transportation, communications, immigration, foreign trade, and other affairs. Puerto Ricans obtained one nonvoting member in the House of Representatives, but its people could not vote for the U.S. president. Those living in Puerto Rico did not pay federal income taxes but did pay social security taxes. They received federal welfare benefits, served in the military, and were subject to the draft. Puerto Rico maintains this same colonial status today. Multiple referendum votes have proposed changing the status of Puerto Rico from a U.S. Commonwealth to either a state of the union or an independent nation. No consensus has developed.[54]

While Puerto Rico, the Philippines, and Hawai'i all have continual colonial connections to the United States, the levels and degrees of overt and subtle imperial control have varied greatly. The diversity of colonial tactics in each region catered to the specific circumstances and protests that developed in each subjugated space. This flexible imperialism has been central to successful expansionism throughout U.S. history, while giving rise to local variants that provide imperial agendas with examples of the supposedly exceptional nature of U.S. colonialism.

But U.S. imperialism did not wield total control over its subjects. While Hawai'i became a fully incorporated state of the union, active Native Hawaiian sovereignty movements were and are today demanding independence from the United States. Many Puerto Ricans flout U.S. linguistic norms by using primarily Spanish and resisting statehood. In contrast, while the Philippines has been legally independent from the United States since 1946, the region still experiences the lingering effects of its colonial relationship, especially in its current economic and security policies. These histories and other stories of past and present U.S. colonial groups may seem disparate. But each set of experiences stems from a common process of federal government expansionism throughout the centuries. Different aspects of the U.S. imperial complex have encouraged the U.S. government to expand its authority across the continent and globe. Without an acknowledgement of this prolonged pattern of U.S. colonialism beyond its official borders, well-informed policies for current and future wards of the United States will be difficult to develop.

Labor Needs of Sugar Plantations in the Territory of Hawai'i

The destruction of the continental U.S. sugar industry during the Civil War made Hawai'i, where Anglo-American missionaries and businessmen had already established a foothold, the next-best supplier for this commodity. Founded in 1835, the cane industry in the islands became one of the most efficient producers of sugar in the world due to increased demands for production during the war and the Reciprocity Treaty of 1875, which allowed the duty-free import of sugar from these Pacific Islands to the United States.[55] In an average year, over seventy-five thousand people worked on about thirty-five plantations generating close to $77 million dollars' worth of sugar every twelve months.[56]

Sugar work was physically intense. Weeding between the cane, or *hoe hana*, involved hoeing for hours at a time. *Hole hole*, or the removal of sharp, jagged-edged, dried leaves from the cane stalks, frequently injured workers. *Kālai kō*, or the cutting of ripe cane stalks, involved stooping down and exerting all one's force to chop down the thick stems. All of this activity on the ground generated clouds of red dirt, which stung when inhaled due to the glassy bits of volcanic ash in the soil. Such work, pursued year-round, required a large and consistent pool of laborers who worked under very regulated and strict circumstances: six-day weeks, ten-hour days, 5:00 A.M. wake-ups, and plantation police storming through camps to make sure every laborer left to work the cane.[57]

Since the sugar industry could not rely on the drastically reduced Native Hawaiian population, who refused to engage in the difficult work on plantations, the HSPA constantly searched for a large source of workers for labor-intensive cane cultivation. Sugar leaders were willing to ignore nativist continental U.S. sentiment, recruiting laborers from all over the globe: South Pacific Islanders, Chinese, Portuguese, Norwegians, Germans, Japanese, Spanish, Russians, Koreans, Puerto Ricans, Filipinos, as well as Italians and blacks from the southern United States. Consequently, as Candace Fujikane and Jonathan Okamura have stated, "extensive Asian settlement in Hawai'i was made possible by American colonial efforts to secure a labor base for a settler plantation economy."[58]

The sugar industry in Hawai'i functioned as a total colonial institution in the islands.[59] Founded in 1882 as a cooperative, then expanded and renamed the Hawaiian Sugar Planters' Association in 1895, the HSPA was officially known as "a voluntary, nonprofit, incorporated association organized for the maintenance, advancement, improvement, and protection of the sugar industry in Hawaii and for the support of a sugarcane research station. Companies engaged primarily in the business of growing sugarcane and manufacturing sugar were plantation members of the Association. Individuals directly connected with the direction, management, or operation of the sugar companies were individual members."[60] As part of the influential

Anglo-American leadership in the islands since the 1840s, members of the HSPA supported the overthrow of the Hawaiian monarchy in 1896, which eventually led to the annexation of Hawai'i in 1900. As the industry grew to its peak of one million tons in 1932, with the assistance of supportive government tariff and trade policies on sugar exports, the HSPA also dominated all aspects of worker lives, dictating labor schedules, actions, and consumption. Ethnic groups were strictly segregated in their work assignments and living quarters, discouraging horizontal relationships across nationalities.[61] Highly invested in the economic and immigration policies of the Territory of Hawai'i, the HSPA was a major player in the U.S. imperial complex in the region from the late nineteenth through the twentieth century.[62]

The difficult nature of sugar cane agriculture often resulted in workers expressing their dissatisfaction with plantation conditions. Members from all ethnic groups submitted worker complaints, joined in labor strikes, and left sugar plantation jobs for work in other industries and areas of the U.S. empire. During the first half of the twentieth century, there were major labor strikes in 1900, 1905, 1906, 1909, 1917, 1920, 1924, and 1937.[63] Between 1929 and 1932, more than fourteen thousand employees left plantation work; a slightly larger number of laborers replaced them. The sugar industry was always in search of a source of abundant, stable, and diligent workers.

Sugar production in Hawai'i reflected some of the academic findings about general plantation work and life. The success of most plantations relied on access to cheap and plentiful land and labor.[64] To manage extensive numbers of manual laborers, Marc R. Matrana and Juan Guisti-Cordero found that plantations were "highly organized with a strict chain of command."[65] Discipline was key to efficient agricultural production. However, the employer-worker relationship could not thrive on force alone. According to Joseph Reidy, "Sugar cane production was deeply influenced by the dynamic of mutual dependence between planters and seasonal laborers."[66] While post–Civil War field hands relied on plantations for wages, these free-wage laborers could and did stop work when overburdened. They could choose to move to other plantations or take spontaneous vacations. Since plantations relied on large labor pools for its daily function, agricultural leaders often tolerated minor demonstrations of worker resistance. However, labor strikes, like one in Louisiana in 1874, were usually "met by ruthless force."[67]

Overall, "as scientific managers, planters sought the most cost-efficient way" to raise products like sugar.[68] The sizable workforce was always a costly expense for plantation owners across the globe. Some managers consequently offered free plantation housing and certain social benefits to create a core, stable labor pool. Intensive for-profit agricultural industries typically

18   Introduction

functioned through paternalistic structures where the plantation owner and field bosses mixed ideas of protection and care of workers with subordination, control, and violence in the face of resistance.[69] In the end, these massive farming endeavors usually greatly enriched plantation owners while keeping field hands dependent on difficult low wage manual labor for economic survival.[70] All of these aspects were present in sugar plantations in the Hawaiian Islands.

In addition to Hawai'i, sugar plantations also existed in the nineteenth and twentieth centuries throughout the Caribbean, the continental United States, and different parts of the Pacific and Southeast Asia. Scholars such as César Ayala and Sidney Mintz examined the economic, political, and cultural motivations and subsequent effects of plantation development in Puerto Rico. Walton Look Lai's work and the anthology by Manuel Moreno Fraginals discussed the political influences on labor migration for plantations in the Caribbean. Filomeno Aguilar, Luis Figueroa, Brij Lal, and Kathleen Mapes analyzed how workers and local elite at the ground level wielded varying levels of choice within plantation systems in the Pacific, the Caribbean, and the midwestern United States. Moon-Kie Jung and Moon-Ho Jung dealt with the racialization of plantation workers in Hawai'i and Louisiana, respectively. *Islanders in the Empire* builds on these studies by examining the degree of control among intra-colonial workers and local leaders.

Open colonial mobility could shape migration patterns as well as plantation policies. Similar to indentured Indian laborers in Look Lai's research on sugar plantations in the British West Indies, the political-legal status of Puerto Rican and Filipino U.S. colonials resulted in targeted movement and specialized programs.[71] Both U.S. colonials and Indian British colonials migrated to work on sugar plantations in other parts of their respective empires. Multiple government priorities in the home region, sugar colony, and metropole influenced the recruitment and policies toward all of these colonial workers. As we will see in chapter 1, Puerto Ricans, as did Indians, had difficulty with the journey to the sugar colonies. Like Filipinos in chapter 2, Indians migrated due to the promise of free return passage. In the end, indentured Indian labor faced harsher conditions than Filipino U.S. colonial free labor.

While the actual function, structure, organization, and discipline involved in sugar plantations was similar in Hawai'i and other locations, the existence of a sugar association, or cooperative with the high level of political influence as the HSPA, was unique among sugar plantations of the period. As long as a worker fulfilled the conditions of three-year labor agreements, the HSPA followed through on the promise to pay for passage back to the Philippines. British Caribbean planters, in contrast, often tried to get out of paying for costly return transport to India. The HSPA was more accommodating to openly mobile wage-labor U.S. colonials than British Caribbean sugar companies that exerted more social and economic control over indentured laborers. The form and structure surrounding British colonial contract work limited Indian mobility more than the free-labor status of U.S. intra-colonial workers. The HSPA was a unique entity that mixed corporate priorities with state interests in the management of the sugar industry in Hawai'i.

The Chapters: An Overview

The Ola'a sugar plantation on the island of Hawai'i is the starting point and constant reference for this work. This particular location constituted one of the largest plantations in the Hawaiian Islands. In addition to the existence of a comprehensive collection of plantation documents, this site is also the first place where both Puerto Rican and Filipino intra-colonial laborers began work in the Pacific and maintained constant populations throughout the period of study. As one of the most complete compilations of historic materials from one of the largest plantations in the islands, the Ola'a archive provides an excellent baseline for generalizations about sugar plantation experiences in Hawai'i.

The first part of *Islanders in the Empire* focuses on Puerto Rican and Filipino intra-colonial movement to the second colonized place of Hawai'i. Chapters 1 and 2 include a description of the work and living problems these intra-colonial labor migrants faced. Scholars such as Ninna Nyberg Sorensen and Karen Fog Olwig have discussed how people engage in mobile livelihoods to improve or enhance their lives.[72] Since U.S. colonials could not be forced to go or stay in one place by their employers, recruitment and retention programs had varying levels of success. During the first half of the twentieth century, Puerto Ricans went to the islands only from 1900 to 1901 and again in 1921. Filipinos enthusiastically worked on sugar plantations from 1910 through the 1930s. What accounts for this difference?

Chapters 1 and 2 examine the precise nature of the hardships and risks for these two populations. In the case of Puerto Rico, the recruitment endeavor failed because poor living and working conditions on plantations, coupled with local authorities' failure to improve matters or to provide laborers with money to return to the Caribbean, led to successful anti-recruitment campaigns at home. In the Filipino case, improved recruitment strategies resulted in a long-term and widespread flow of labor.

20   *Introduction*

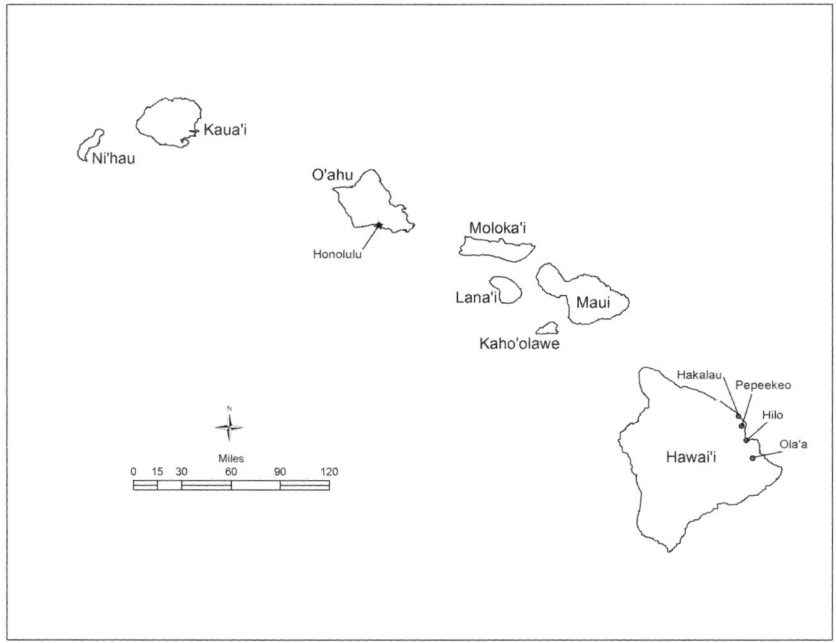

Map of Hawai'i

Chapter 1 describes how independent labor companies used promises of higher wages and better living conditions to entice legally mobile Puerto Ricans to leave for Hawai'i and fill the vast labor needs of the islands. After arriving in the Pacific, many dissatisfied Puerto Ricans wrote home to discourage further recruitment to the region. As U.S. colonials, they expected better treatment from the self-proclaimed benevolent U.S. government. So despite continual federal encouragement for the recruitment of Puerto Ricans to Hawai'i throughout the twentieth century, these U.S. colonials resisted further intra-colonial movement to the islands due to the poor living and working experiences of the first groups of laborers to Hawai'i. While legally mobile during a period of anti-immigration restrictions, Puerto Ricans could not be convinced or forced to migrate to Hawai'i.

Chapter 2 discusses the more effective recruitment and retention strategies that the HSPA developed specifically for Filipino U.S. colonials. Learning from the mistakes of Puerto Rican recruitment, the HSPA successfully attracted legally mobile Filipinos to Hawai'i by offering free return passage after three years of work, as well as family-and-friend employment and re-unification programs. Intra-colonial Filipinos became the only laborers in

Hawai'i to access such liberal recruitment policies. With access to and support for open colonial mobility, these U.S. colonials willingly moved to work on plantations in the islands. Overall, both Filipino and Puerto Rican U.S. colonials had the opportunity to engage in migration processes and labor programs that foreigners and citizens could not. The HSPA created multiple specific policies for Puerto Ricans and Filipinos to encourage their steady and open colonial migration to the islands.

These findings coincide with Seth Garfield's argument that migratory flows "are determined not only by market forces but also by state policies that encourage or inhibit migration and by the cultural predilections of those who formulate or are targeted by these policies."[73] Such multiple factors contributed to negative intra-colonial experiences of Puerto Ricans and positive migration patterns for Filipinos to the islands. The political and social interests of Puerto Rican elite conflicted with the economic interests of the HSPA, resulting in failed recruitment. In the Filipino case, the political, economic, and social goals in the Philippines and Hawai'i merged to make this group of intra-colonials the largest and most successful labor group for the region's sugar plantations throughout the first half of the twentieth century.

Like the detailed analysis of legal structures by Sally Merry and Jonathan Osorio, as well as the essays in Christina Duffy Burnett and Burke Marshall's anthology, the second section of *Islanders in the Empire* closely examines government structures to provide a new perspective on labor migrant issues. Chapters 3 and 4 explain the specific intra-colonial government communication hierarchies Puerto Ricans and Filipinos faced as colonized people in a second colonized place. The grievances of U.S. colonials followed a much different process from those of citizens, foreigners, and each other. While citizens and foreigners had representatives living and working in Honolulu to handle their issues, intra-colonials had no effective government representative in the islands.

Instead, during the first part of the twentieth century, appointed Anglo-American officials in their home regions and Washington, D.C., supervised the greivances of Puerto Rican and Filipino U.S. colonials. Their complaints had to travel from Hawai'i to their home region to Washington, D.C., then back to the Territory of Hawai'i and the HSPA. This circuitous global and hierarchical grievance process closely managed and controlled Puerto Rican and Filipino U.S. colonials. While both groups had to deal with long-distance complaint procedures, the jurisdiction over intra-colonial labor issues diverged over time. In later years, Filipino leaders indoctrinated in U.S. ideas and standards started to gain more control over this process. Puerto Ricans, however, always remained subject to the governance of Anglo-American officials.

Chapter 3 examines how, unlike other labor groups in Hawai'i, Puerto Rican intra-colonials never had a dedicated local government representative. This leadership vacuum resulted in both negative and positive effects on this community in Hawai'i. When Puerto Ricans had complaints about life in the islands, they had to submit their grievances to a slow, cumbersome, and apathetic bureaucratic colonial communication hierarchy in their home region, Washington, D.C., and the Territory of Hawai'i. The absence of an effective regional representative in the Pacific meant Puerto Rican intra-colonial needs were often ignored or disregarded.

However, the lack of an official leader in the islands also gave Puerto Rican migrants a degree of independence in their daily lives. Without a government representative in the area assigned to oversee them, these intra-colonials often chose to move around plantations, out of the sugar industry, and eventually on to the continental United States to circumvent the harsh economic and social conditions in the islands. Many ignored the wishes of the HSPA for them to become stable and loyal long-term workers at one specific plantation. As liminal U.S. colonials without the same access to government representatives as other labor groups, Puerto Ricans could both benefit and suffer from the absence of a local official to act as either their supervisor or advocate.

Chapter 4 analyzes the Philippine resident labor commissioner position that Filipino U.S. colonials in Hawai'i lobbied for and acquired in 1923. While similar in function to consul generals who handled foreign labor issues in Hawai'i, this Filipino leader was still part of the U.S. colonial government hierarchy. Unlike foreign officials, he often prioritized U.S. economic, political, and social interests over those of Filipino workers in the islands. Even though intra-colonial Filipinos gained a local government representative, their working and living conditions did not drastically improve, as the commissioner cooperated with the desires of the sugar industry and the U.S. imperial complex. Workers consequently chose not to trust the commissioner or cooperate with his programs.

In the end, both kinds of government involvement in Filipino and Puerto Rican labor complaints differed significantly from how the government handled foreigners and fully incorporated citizens. The federal government maintained ultimate political-legal control over distant intra-colonials; however, the absence of effective local government representatives also resulted in more flexibility and less supervision over the daily activities of intra-colonials. At a basic level, Puerto Ricans and Filipinos in Hawai'i had a degree of independence in their actions. While directives on how to behave could be created by government or business officials, no authorities resided in the islands with the influence to enforce such expectations.

The third section of *Islanders in the Empire* focuses on the unofficial ways U.S. colonials dealt with labor issues on Hawai'i sugar plantations. Like Lisa Mar's Chinese Canadians or Gunther Peck's immigrant laborers in the continental United States, Filipinos and Puerto Ricans relied on local community leaders who could speak their native language to help negotiate regional policies, daily issues, and moments of crisis. Filipinos looked to Protestant ethnic ministers and labor organizers, while Puerto Ricans mostly depended on local labor agents. All these unofficial leaders provided translation, negotiation, and community-mediation services that were usually handled by the consul generals of foreign laborers or the elected representatives of U.S. citizens. Because U.S. intra-colonials did not have access to these same kinds of local government officials, Filipino and Puerto Rican ethnic mediators like Santa Ana and Minvielle played more central roles in the everyday lives of these groups than those of foreigners or citizens in the Territory of Hawai'i.

Chapter 5 discusses the multiple roles that Philippine Protestant ethnic ministers, like Santa Ana, filled in Hawai'i plantation communities. At Ola'a, Filipino pastors working for the Hawaiian Evangelical Association (HEA) became middlemen for migrant laborers, sugar plantation management, and the Protestant church. Each group looked to these religious men to help them interact with each other. At one point, Santa Ana had obtained such trust and respect, or symbolic capital, from all three groups that he served as a pastor for the Filipino community, as well as a hired mediator for the plantation.[74] Such diverse roles often resulted in suspicion over the true loyalty of these mediators. These men constantly worked hard to convince both Filipino workers and the HEA that their loyalties lay with them over the HSPA. The association of these men with the dominant religious institution in Hawai'i also caused Filipino workers to question the true intentions of these pastors. In the end, these middlemen served important roles for all three groups, especially Filipino U.S. colonials. However, their positions of power were always tenuous and questioned.

Chapter 6 describes the intermediary position labor agents such as Minvielle played between intra-colonial Puerto Ricans and the sugar plantation industry in the islands. Like Filipinos, Puerto Ricans also relied on local leaders to translate and convey their issues to plantation managers. Since few Puerto Ricans at the Ola'a plantation understood English, both workers and plantation leaders looked to these independent labor mediators to bridge the language barrier between Anglo-American leadership and intra-colonials. When Puerto Rican migration to the islands ended after a year and a half and the Hawai'i sugar industry ceased paying them, these profit-oriented labor liaisons stopped providing services for these U.S. colonials. Without these middlemen, Puerto Ricans in Hawai'i lost a critical source of leadership, advocacy, and assistance. Such an absence resulted in the consistent disregard of Puerto Rican intra-colonial issues in Hawai'i and a subsequent invisibility of this ethnic group in the islands through today.

Despite the differences in the level of local leadership available for Filipinos and Puerto Ricans in the Territory of Hawai'i, both Filipino ethnic ministers and Puerto Rican labor agents became important advocates and mediators for these intra-colonials *and* sugar plantation management at the same time and place. This section demonstrates how, in the absence of effective government representatives, community ethnic mediators were some of the few trusted leaders and best options for local leadership for Filipino and Puerto Rican intra-colonials living thousands of miles away from their home region.

Islanders in the Empire concludes by discussing continuing contemporary struggles with U.S. colonialism in Puerto Rico and the Philippines. Some Puerto Ricans are actively pushing for a change in Puerto Rico's political-legal relationship with the United States. In the Philippines, some activists are rallying for the return of the bells of Balangiga, a war spoil from the U.S.-Philippine War in 1901. Despite claims that the United States has never or is no longer engaging in colonial pursuits, both of these issues demonstrate the continuing colonial nature of the U.S. federal government.

Each chapter examines the unique migration policies and labor practices toward Puerto Rican and Filipino U.S. colonials and the ways these intra-colonials interacted with such circumstances on a daily basis. Puerto Rican and Filipino mobility patterns, work negotiations, and forms of community leadership diverged from those of foreign laborers and full-fledged citizens due to their in-between political-legal status. These experiences also highlight the consistent imperial character in United States government policies and actions through the years.

1. Letters Home

THE FAILURE OF PUERTO RICAN RECRUITMENT

On August 7 and 8, 1899, the San Ciriaco hurricane swept through Puerto Rico with winds up to one hundred miles per hour. Twenty-eight days of torrential rain caused approximately thirty-four hundred fatalities, massive flooding, and at least $7 million dollars in agricultural damage. Tens of thousands of people lost their homes and means of livelihood. Not only was the 1899 coffee crop destroyed, but critical shade trees, coffee bushes, and topsoil were also blown away. It would take at least five years before coffee would be profitable again in Puerto Rico.

Before the hurricane, the industry was already declining due to a drop in bean prices. Many landowners started collecting the smallest of debts from their laborers, heightening the impact of agricultural production losses at all levels of society. As Pablo Vilella Pol explained, "The disaster has immersed all citizens in the most terrible misery without distinction between classes . . . since the landowner lacks the most elementary things to maintain his family, the proletarian and working classes are in an even sadder situation."[1] All groups in Puerto Rican society were facing major economic and social problems at the turn of the twentieth century. According to Kelvin Santiago-Valles, the Puerto Rican working class during this period faced a combination of starvation, inflation, unemployment, and land dispossession that resulted from early U.S. economic policies in the region.[2] To cope with such harsh conditions, exacerbated by the hurricane, many from the poorer classes engaged in criminality and social violence such as arson, stealing cattle or food, and rioting against the elite.

While economic downturns, colonial meddling, and natural disasters were not new to Puerto Rico, this chain of events happened in a new context—the islands had just become a colony of the United States. Even though the political-legal status of these former Spanish colonial subjects was not officially determined until the 1904 Supreme Court ruling in *Gonzales v. Williams*, Puerto Ricans were able to circumvent U.S. immigration restrictions and travel to the Territory of Hawai'i to work on sugar plantations after 1898.[3] Such movement promised an improvement in living conditions that historically motivated mobile livelihoods, or the seeking of life enhancements through moving to a new area. Blase Camacho Souza believed her family came to Hawai'i because "they were looking for a place that would give them a job. They came because of the . . . natural disasters, the hurricane that had wiped out a lot of the coffee fields."[4] Their ambiguous legal status as U.S. colonials also gave Puerto Ricans the ability to escape desperate economic conditions in their homeland and migrate to another area of U.S. jurisdiction.

Workers and their families left Puerto Rico with hopes that life in the Pacific Islands would be less bleak and provide more opportunities for stability and success. Ismael García-Colón discussed the concept of *buscando ambiente*, or looking for opportunities, "a phrase used by both the landless and the parcel holders, [which] expresses the desire to improve one's living conditions by looking for a place that offers better economic and social opportunities."[5] This motivation to constantly seek better circumstances propelled Puerto Ricans to migrate to Hawai'i. Puerto Ricans numbering 5,023, including the Souzas, took advantage of their new colonial status and left poor conditions in Puerto Rico from November 1900 to September 1901 to work on Hawai'i sugar plantations.

The U.S. federal government and the HSPA also had high expectations for Puerto Rican colonial labor recruitment to Hawai'i. Officials in departments that managed colonial matters, such as the Bureau of Insular Affairs (BIA) and the Division of Territories and Possessions in the Department of Interior, encouraged intra-colonial movement to Hawai'i as a remedy for unemployment and poverty in the Puerto Rican colony, as well as a solution to the constant labor shortage in the Pacific. The booming Hawai'i sugar industry, established in 1835, always needed workers. From 1856 to 1940, labor-intensive sugar production in the islands grew from 547 tons per year to its peak of 9,170,279 tons annually in 1936.[6] The HSPA hoped the settlement of Puerto Rican workers would provide a permanent solution to the consistent labor scarcity in the islands. U.S. colonial status also made Puerto Ricans attractive recruits due to their assumed new loyalty and dependence on the United States.

Despite the abundance of job opportunities in Hawai'i, open colonial mobility within United States jurisdiction, and substandard living conditions in the Caribbean, Puerto Ricans stopped migrating to Hawai'i after less than one year of recruitment. This chapter examines the ground-level experiences of early Puerto Rican colonial migrants to Hawai'i, including the recruitment process and daily circumstances, as well as reactions to these policies. In the end, the desires of federal officials for such migration directly conflicted with the wishes of Territory of Hawai'i leaders and the Puerto Rican government and people. Such tensions demonstrate the discrepancies that can occur within a global colonial system. In the case of Puerto Rican migration to the Pacific, intra-colonial policies encouraged by the highest level of government administration were rejected by other levels of the U.S. empire.

The Puerto Rican Recruitment Process

Two years after Puerto Rico became a territorial possession of the United States, the region's inhabitants became the first U.S. colonial group recruited to Hawai'i. The HSPA hired third party agencies in the Caribbean to enlist Puerto Ricans as permanent settlers, preferably families, to work on Hawai'i sugar plantations starting in the summer of 1900. As independent companies, MacFie and Noble, as well as the New York and Porto Rico Steamship Company, advertised HSPA labor opportunities in local papers and obtained recruits from those who came to their offices in the port cities of Ponce, Mayagüez, Arecibo, Aguadilla, Adjuntas, and San Juan.

Recruiters received payment from the HSPA based on the number of people they recruited. These profit-oriented businessmen consequently shipped anyone they could convince to get on a boat. Little effort was made to examine Puerto Ricans during the boarding process. If you showed up at port on the day of a ship's departure, you would likely be able to leave. Health inspections occurred upon arrival in New Orleans and Honolulu. The recruitment process was quick and haphazard.

The range of recruits included entire families, young single men and women, and some underage boys who left for Hawai'i without their parents' permission.[7] The majority of workers came from the hurricane-ravaged southwest coffee growing region of Puerto Rico, a people described in one Spanish-language newspaper as "ruined by the lack of resources and poor credit.... [T]his month high winds of the storm have destroyed guavas, leveled guaragunos and destroyed large buds during the height of the flowering of the coffee crops."[8] Agriculture in this region was devastated, creating a large, desperate pool of potential laborers.

Map of Puerto Rico

In 1899, there was also an outbreak of thefts, cattle killing, and crop destruction by impoverished peasants throughout Puerto Rico.[9] In Yauco, an angry mob visited a local coffee estate, killing the owner and cutting off the ear of the field boss.[10] In 1900, more than two hundred out of eighteen thousand people in Adjuntas were reported to be dying every month due to starvation.[11] No longer able to survive in the countryside, people from this area went to cities to find other ways to make a living. This population was the main target of recruiters for the HSPA.

Many U.S. colonials were willing to leave Puerto Rico because labor agents encouraged the belief that Puerto Ricans could lead a better life in Hawai'i. Some migrants claimed that recruiters promised certain benefits that they never received. According to one recruit interviewed by the *San Francisco Examiner*,

> [Señor MacFie] said . . . that before leaving San Juan I should be presented with $23, and that on the voyage from San Juan to New Orleans there should be for the Porto Ricans a physician known to us and good clothing for all who were in need of it. But at San Juan he at first refused to pay me any money, and when all of us made protest and many refused to make the voyage he paid each of us $5 and promised that more should be paid later, which has

not been done. And the physician was not provided, nor the clothing, except that a few who were nearly naked were a very little helped."¹²

When promises of monetary compensation, material goods, and health services did not materialize, recruits tried to protest. Sometimes they succeeded in receiving better treatment. But once they embarked on the long journey to Hawai'i, these intra-colonials had little recourse if their demands were not met. Aurelie de Soto explained, "When I began to learn my situation I wished to quit, but I was told that it was dangerous to rebel in the United States, because I might be hanged on a telegraph pole."¹³ Rumors, uncertainties, and fears about their unknown futures were common on the trip to the Pacific.

Some recruits claimed they were told that Hawai'i had similar conditions to Puerto Rico. One recruit, named Santiago, was told "that Hawaii would be like Porto Rico to me, because there the Spanish language was everywhere."¹⁴ Conditions were actually quite different. Few people spoke Spanish, and Puerto Ricans were unaccustomed to the food available in the Pacific, as well as the higher costs of products. According to a Spanish-language article by Puerto Rican columnist Manuel Romero Haxthausen, "The food there is very different from our own and also very expensive."¹⁵ As scholar Norma Carr explained, women had to bring samples of the food they wanted to buy to communicate their grocery needs to non-Spanish-speaking plantation store clerks.¹⁶ Unfulfilled migrant expectations created during the recruitment process led to negative views of both enlistment procedures and life in Hawai'i among Puerto Rican U.S. colonials.

These views soon came to shape how the Puerto Rican migration process to Hawai'i was reported in both English- and Spanish-language newspapers printed in the continental United States and Puerto Rico. One report in the *San Francisco Chronicle* claimed that "they were loaded on a boat in Porto Rico with the understanding that they were going to the opposite side of the islands to work, but after six days they were landed in New Orleans and rushed on to a train. They learned in San Antonio where they were being taken to, and have since been trying to escape."¹⁷ This story of complete deception contrasts with another story about the happy ignorance of recruits printed just seven days later. An article in the *San Francisco Call* claimed that Puerto Ricans were "happy, well fed and ragged, joyously jingling small change . . . not a word of evidence that they were being mistreated."¹⁸ Such a range of reports obscures the details of what labor agents actually told U.S. colonials to convince them to board boats in Puerto Rico. Recruiters may have given individuals false information, or they may have been misunderstood by migrants, who may have had unrealistic expectations. Recruitment terms were likely misrepresented or misinterpreted by people on both sides.

Throughout this process, the Puerto Rican government chose not to get involved. Charles H. Allen, the U.S.-appointed civil governor general, distanced himself from recruitment activities, simply stating in his first annual report in 1901 that "it is the privilege of every person to emigrate if he chooses so to do."[19] With regard to the future of Puerto Rico's economy, Allen downplayed the effects of out-migrants, who he said totaled less than half of 1 percent of Puerto Rico's population. He did not see Puerto Rican intra-colonial movement to Hawai'i as significant or cause for concern.

With no local government involvement in this process, for-profit recruitment agencies hired by the HSPA were free to inundate the Puerto Rican public with unfettered advertisements and unchecked promises about a superior life in the Pacific. In light of the horrible economic conditions in Puerto Rico at the time, this strategy worked initially. However, once firsthand accounts about the poor conditions during the trip to Hawai'i and the reality of work and living circumstances in these Pacific Islands were sent back to Puerto Rico, support for this type of intra-colonial movement quickly dwindled.

The Long Journey

The intra-colonial journey to Hawai'i was long and arduous. The voyage lasted about twenty-one days. First, Puerto Ricans boarded boats in the Caribbean for the Port of New Orleans. From there they took cross-country trains to either Los Angeles or San Francisco, where they were transferred to ships bound for Hawai'i. In Honolulu, many were placed on smaller, inter-island boats to reach their final destination at an outlying Hawaiian island. Eleven groups of Puerto Ricans traveled to Hawai'i between 1900 and 1901, the first on November 22, 1900. Though this initial group of 114 survived the trip, complaints about food during transport and a handful of deaths were common in subsequent shipments of migrants.[20] With every group of approximately 522 recruits, there was an average of sixteen individuals who did not continue at some point during the migration. Some decided to stay at a transfer point, while others died en route.[21]

Conditions and treatment on the different segments of the voyage were poor. According to the *San Francisco Chronicle*, on trains from New Orleans to the West Coast, Puerto Ricans were "in a pitiable condition from a sanitary standpoint, having been in the same cars for ten days. Two of the women have given birth to children in the cars and are in bad condition."[22] These images might have reminded readers of horrific images from the African slave trade before abolition or of the general treatment of cattle at that time.

Circumstances on ships were just as bad. According to a Spanish-language newspaper in Puerto Rico, in January 1901 a group of about three hundred Puerto Ricans revolted on a ship from San Francisco to Honolulu because "they were almost starved to death. They compelled the vessel to be taken back to the Port for provisions."[23] Prior to this stage of the trip, U.S. colonial recruits had become frail and ill on the journey from Ponce to New Orleans. According to *La Correspondencia*, the recruits "arrived weak, many of them sick and all of them hungry and miserable . . . the company responsible for what has happened to these unfortunate natives of Puerto Rico deserves the strongest censure."[24] These vocal protests against ship conditions pressured the HSPA to provide clothing for future groups of migrants. According to a *New York Times* article on April 4, 1901, "The emigrants, most of whom were in rags when embarking, will be cheaply but substantially clothed at the expense of the Hawaiian Sugar Planters' Association, and the entire party will be vaccinated. Rations of codfish, beef, potatoes, rice, beans, bread, and coffee are served twice daily."[25] The HSPA only improved transport conditions after complaints from the recruits actually impeded valuable labor deliveries to the Pacific.

Despite reported access to clothing, vaccinations, and food rations, the intra-colonial voyage to the Pacific continued to result in great suffering.[26] In April 1901, two recruits bound for Hawai'i returned to Puerto Rico after a horrific trip to New Orleans. Policarpo Ulises Negrón and Ramón Oms stated in Spanish that "the treatment they received on board was terrible and resulted in the deaths of 6 children and 8 women from Guánica to New Orleans."[27] Even though the sugar industry spent about one hundred dollars for the passage of each individual, this intra-colonial journey remained long and difficult for most who left Puerto Rico.[28]

Seasickness and the rapid change in temperature during transport were major factors in the deterioration of the health of labor recruits. Puerto Ricans who arrived in May 1901, according to a *New York Times* article, "are in such state from the need of food that they must be held at the quarantine station and fed until they regain strength sufficient to enable them to bear the journey to the other islands and to the plantations on which they will work . . . all were more or less emaciated. This is attributed to lack of food in their old homes."[29] This article blamed the poor condition of Puerto Ricans on their previously inferior standard of living in their home region. Recruits were assumed to be feeble and fragile before embarking on the intra-colonial voyage. But if these migrants were unhealthy prior to departure, they would likely have died during the trip, as some did. Those who arrived in Honolulu survived because they were healthy enough to endure the challenging voyage. This long journey, however, was just the beginning of shocking experiences and sources for protest among this intra-colonial group.

Conditions in Hawai'i

Due to the great cost involved in the recruitment and transport of Puerto Ricans to Hawai'i, the HSPA developed many strategies to rehabilitate and maintain these intra-colonials for sugar plantation work after arrival. The sugar industry gave needed medical attention to the ill and provided free, nutritious food to strengthen and support Puerto Rican recruits. The HSPA also offered higher wages to Puerto Rican U.S. colonial workers than other plantation workers at the same time and place. According to a 1933 report on Puerto Ricans in Hawai'i, the 1901 recruits "were given every consideration to help them adjust, such as a bonus fifty cents a week if [they worked] steady, free lunches and extra food. Most of them had new quarters, better than the Asiatics and much better than their former homes in Porto Rico."[30] One plantation provided a dedicated doctor to care for Puerto Ricans. Another location offered food at wholesale prices just for these U.S. colonials. Yet another plantation gave a free sack of flour to each Puerto Rican family.[31] The Commissioner for the U.S. Department of Labor also found that the HSPA fulfilled all Puerto Rican labor agreement terms, such as free housing, fuel, and water.[32] Other labor groups at the same time and place did not receive similar types of amenities.

Girl with parents in front of a plantation house. *Blase Camacho Souza Papers*, Archives of the Puerto Rican Diaspora, Centro de Estudios Puertorriqueños, Hunter College, CUNY.

While the HSPA felt they went beyond labor agreement requirements to keep these intra-colonials happy, Puerto Ricans still found plantation life grueling and restrictive. In addition to backbreaking labor, Puerto Ricans were upset about the strict regulation of their workday. John Santana, a Puerto Rican born on the Kohala plantation in 1906, recalled how "people had to work about 10 hours a day. They would start at 6 o'clock in the morning, they had a coffee break about 8 o'clock in the morning, breakfast time, then 11:30 was lunch time; they had half an hour [for] lunch. Then at 4:30 it was quitting time."[33] On the plantation, there was little room for independent action or free time. Trinidad Marcella, born to a Spanish mother and Puerto Rican father on the island of Hawai'i in 1913, explained how the foremen "were very mean. They wouldn't let you talk, you see. Even with us, we couldn't talk in the fields. We had to continue working. If you would stand up for one or two minutes, that foreman would jump on you."[34] Marcella believed the personal ambitions of the foremen, or *lunas*, resulted in harsh conditions more than the general plantation policies.

Some Puerto Ricans complained about conditions in the Pacific because they were accustomed to a very different kind of work environment in their home region. Multiple labor relationships existed on coffee plantations in Puerto Rico. As scholar Laird Bergad explained, some workers were *agregados* (service tenants living on an estate), *arrendatarios* (renters), or *peones* (resident laborers on a hacienda).[35] These groups lived permanently on southwestern coffee estates, providing certain services or improvements to plantations in exchange for the use of a small parcel of land for their own purposes. While working for these Puerto Rican plantations, individuals retained a form of independence through these small plots. In Hawai'i, laborers could also tend to their own gardens in plantation camps. However, their main source of subsistence came from paid wages, not the food they produced on their own.

Labor agents in Puerto Rico also brought in day laborers, or *jornaleros*, to fill the increased labor demand during planting and harvest times. Jornaleros participated in a more flexible and seasonal work pattern than other coffee laborers. These temporary workers came from the coastal regions of Puerto Rico to engage in intensive labor for six months of the year. Some jornaleros worked only until they acquired a desired amount of money, and then they stopped showing up in the fields. Such inconsistent labor was common in the region. Puerto Rican employers understood the attitude of temporary workers and did not try to stop or change such absenteeism. In contrast, plantations in Hawai'i were intolerant of people who did not fulfill their labor agreements. People who left their assigned locations would lose access to accumulated benefits and privileges.

U.S. colonials who migrated to Hawai'i came from all of these labor groups in Puerto Rico. Such a diverse and accommodating work environment on coffee plantations in this Caribbean region was quite different from sugar plantation circumstances in the Pacific. Laborers from Puerto Rico were accustomed to engaging in independent pursuits and flexible labor agreements. The HSPA neither encouraged nor supported such job elasticity. Instead, the sugar industry prioritized stability and consistency.

During the cultivation and harvest seasons in Puerto Rico, individuals received additional wages for working the fields during peak season. Coffee plantation laborers in this Caribbean region were accustomed to an increase in pay commensurate with the greater demand for labor. Such a variation in the scale of earnings did not exist at Hawai'i sugar plantations, which set specific wages and bonus schedules from the outset. The HSPA never intended to increase rates over time.[36]

Puerto Rican laborers in Hawai'i were also isolated on rural plantations. With no public transportation system available, it usually required several hours on foot to reach the closest town. Laborers were often limited to purchasing their supplies from company-owned plantation stores. These locations set prices so high that workers barely made ends meet. Puerto Ricans earned about twenty-two dollars a month, or ninety-two cents a day, wages that did not cover the daily expenses for a family. In one letter home, Juan Draytom complained in Spanish: "[D]ear God, this is a horrible place.... We are very badly off, my friend . . . things are very expensive . . . rice costs 8 to 10 cents, codfish from 15 to 20 cents, and a cigar costs 5 cents."[37] This intra-colonial worker highlighted the high price of these staples of Puerto Rican consumption in Hawai'i. He went on to lament the poor medical care on plantations, the inability to purchase liquor, and the requirement to purchase food in larger, more expensive quantities. Draytom found little comfort in the islands. Difficult working conditions for subsistence-level wages made a damaging impression on the first groups of Puerto Ricans who migrated to Hawai'i.

Complaints about Conditions in Hawai'i

Unhappy with conditions in Hawai'i, Puerto Rican U.S. colonials openly and freely objected to their situation in the islands. Letters home became the mechanism through which depressing images of life in the Pacific deterred future recruitment to Hawai'i. In a letter of complaint printed in Spanish in the *San Juan News* on February 17, 1902, Vincente Armesquita and forty-two other Puerto Ricans claimed they were "deprived of all liberty and suffering the yoke of the despotic landowner . . . abused by the inhabitants of the Country . . . we cry for protection."[38] These workers referenced U.S. tenets of freedom and liberty in an attempt to convince the U.S. colonial government to intervene in their oppressive situation in the U.S. Territory of Hawai'i. By describing slave-like conditions, Puerto Rican intra-colonial laborers hoped their petition would garner sympathy from the public and governments in both the United States and Puerto Rico.

While labor migrants of all backgrounds experienced similar harsh conditions on Hawai'i plantations, Puerto Ricans, as well as Filipinos, assumed they possessed an additional claim to assistance from the U.S. colonial government because they were wards of the United States. According to scholar Mariano Negrón-Portillo, the urban working class in Puerto Rico at the turn of the twentieth century "viewed the North American government as a guarantor of fundamental civil rights in Puerto Rico. Workers had a high regard for the political and teaching institutions in the United States."[39] Santiago Iglesias, a major Puerto Rican labor leader at the time, also stated that the "American Republic in its womb and practices, performs equitable, fair and scientific administrative and governmental procedures, and . . . there is nothing in the country [Puerto Rico] that is more advantageous, even in theory."[40] Such proclaimed faith in the promises of the United States government also existed among some Puerto Rican intra-colonials in Hawai'i.

These U.S. colonials sent morally based complaints to Puerto Rican leaders such as resident commissioners, high-level elected government officials, and newspaper editors, as well as loved ones back home. Many intra-colonials demanded shorter working hours, longer breaks, better treatment from *lunas*, or field overseers, and free return transportation to their native land. According to one Spanish-language complaint in 1902, workers at the Paauilo plantation were "encountering a deplorable state of desperation. . . . We are treated like dogs . . . instead of working 8 hours we are working 11½ . . . rice is 10 cents a pound . . . we are denied all the freedoms we left to get higher wages."[41] All dissenters wanted improved plantation conditions, and many hoped for paid return passage to Puerto Rico. The numerous protests, however, failed to convince federal, Territory of Hawai'i, or HSPA officials to resolve the difficult circumstances facing Puerto Ricans in the Pacific Islands.

In reaction to worker complaints and growing anti-recruitment sentiments among this group of intra-colonials, the Territory of Hawai'i conducted investigations of Puerto Rican conditions on plantations. These investigations were often questionable because the process ultimately fell into the hands of the sugar industry itself. U.S. federal agencies usually asked the Territorial Government of Hawai'i to examine Puerto Rican grievances. Officials in the islands created reports from information provided by the HSPA. The central sugar office supplied self-supportive content that glorified their policies and disproved labor complaints.

Responding to Armesquita's 1902 complaint, the HSPA obtained a letter of retraction from Puerto Ricans, which stated, "We said things which we now believe were unfair and misleading . . . a number of our countrymen at first were disposed to be quarrelsome and . . . they were really the one to blame for our sending the former letter, and they wrote it and got us to sign it, without our knowing what they had written in it, until after we had signed the letter . . . we get all the wages we were promised before we came to Hawaii, and we are treated in all respects just as fairly as other laborers . . . no innocent man among our countrymen has been punished."[42] According to this statement, Puerto Ricans felt satisfied with their conditions in Hawai'i. Their expectations were being met and they were getting fair treatment. Just a handful of agitators were responsible for inducing others to sign the initial petition. However, these findings did not assuage Puerto Rican complainants because plantation managers, not independent and impartial investigators, acquired the retraction. The letter was also questionable because only one of the ten signatures on the follow-up statement matched names on the original petition.

This case exemplifies how plantation management in Hawai'i worked hard to positively portray life on plantations to maintain access to laborers. They quickly addressed worker complaints but rarely made serious changes or improvements. Even though the HSPA provided a larger amount of benefits to Puerto Rican U.S. colonials than to other plantation laborers in general, the sugar industry remained stalwart in their opposition to major modifications in the work process. Grievance inquiries conducted by the oligarchy in Hawai'i — the coalition of like-minded Anglo businessmen and territorial government officials — aimed to diffuse Puerto Rican anti-recruitment attitudes in the islands and Puerto Rico.[43] These problematic reports, however, did not fool Caribbean U.S. colonials into moving to Hawai'i en masse. Questionable investigations simply reinforced negative perceptions stemming from Puerto Rican letters home.

Protests in Puerto Rico

When complaints like Armesquita's did not result in any real change in plantation life, Puerto Ricans in Hawai'i and Puerto Rico focused their energy on preventing further movement to the Pacific. Stopping migration out of the Caribbean was the one part of the recruitment process that U.S. colonials could control. In Puerto Rico, newspapers used complaints like Armesquita's to fuel local anti-recruitment efforts. Regional media frequently published discouraging stories about movement to and life in Hawai'i. Using rhetoric of U.S. freedom ideology similar to Armesquita's complaint, an article in *La Correspondencia* lamented in Spanish how Puerto Ricans "had been taken to that country [Hawai'i] as slaves and that they were put on a plantation from where escape was impossible because of the heavy guard."[44] According to this and other news reports, both the journey to and life in Hawai'i involved horrible experiences of captivity and bondage. The prevalence of such atrocious images in local papers created a strong and clear understanding amongst the Puerto Rican public that life in Hawai'i was oppressive and should be avoided at all costs.

Puerto Rican print media also portrayed the Pacific Islands as a truly foreign place. From July 1900 to April 1901, Manuel Romero Haxthausen wrote regularly in Spanish for *La Correspondencia* against the recruitment of Puerto Ricans out of the region. In one article, he discussed how "there is a lot of suffering with leprosy . . . harsh climate and rough work in the field."[45] Haxthausen highlighted the inhospitable conditions in Hawai'i to prevent his compatriots from being lured to this far-away and repressive place. As a Puerto Rican English professor who got his degree in the United States, Haxthausen asserted, "I should share my meager observations with my countrymen."[46] As an educated member of Puerto Rican society, he consistently wrote against the outmigration of Puerto Ricans, as well as dreadful intra-colonial experiences in Hawai'i. Such appalling stories about life and treatment in Hawai'i pervaded regional newspapers. These accounts became infused into the general consciousness of Puerto Rican society and resulted in an unsupportive local environment for HSPA recruitment efforts throughout the first half of the twentieth century.

Business leaders in Puerto Rico also spoke out against the departure of workers for Hawai'i. On March 25, 1901, leading agriculturalists and tradesmen met in Ateneo "*para acordar el medio de impedir el mal que nos amenaza de muerte*" (to decide on measures that would put a stop to this disease which threatens our lives).[47] According to this group, movement to the Pacific was a terrible experience for the individual and a menace to the home country. In the early years of U.S. rule in the region, business elite in Puerto Rico believed the retention of a large population was essential for the growth of local commerce. These leaders worried that if too many people left Puerto Rico, there would not be enough laborers for economic development in their own region. Puerto Ricans needed to stay in the Caribbean to work on strengthening the homeland and its industries.

Agriculturalists in Puerto Rico also resisted the exit of workers who supplied seasonal labor for local crop production. One Spanish-language newspaper article stated, "Our working class is leaving for foreign lands never to return, thus depriving our agriculture of its principal asset."[48] Agrarians were concerned that the permanent departure of Puerto Ricans to other parts of the globe would result in labor shortages for farming pursuits in

Puerto Rico. While trade relations with the United States eventually resulted in a shift from agriculture production to "an export-oriented manufacturing platform with decaying agricultural activity" by the 1950s, such future conditions were unknown at the turn of the century.[49]

Besides the economic threats involved with outmigration, some leaders portrayed mobility away from the home region as a danger to Puerto Rican society as a whole. Carr found that politicians and the press in this Caribbean region were arguing "that increasing emigration would weaken the social and cultural fabric of the island."[50] The draining of native peoples from the home region was seen as a detriment to all Puerto Ricans. If people looked to other places for happiness and fulfillment, then cultural pride and nationalism would diminish in the home region. Puerto Ricans needed to stay in Puerto Rico to contribute to the growth, success, and vibrancy of their own people and region. People should work hard to support their homeland, or *patria*, not some other foreign place.

Many scholars have viewed cultural nationalism as a major reaction that Puerto Ricans had to U.S. colonialism. Raquel Rivera explained how "a basic tenet of all cultural nationalists is 'defending,' celebrating, or nourishing the national culture, a struggle that has most often been described as preserving and nurturing Puerto Rican customs and traditions—the 'roots' of Puerto Rican culture."[51] Juan Flores also described how "traditionally, it has been the national territory that has been thought of as the fount of cultural perspectives that are alternative and oppositional to hegemonic metropolitan cultures of domination, and that this contestatory culture of resistance then informs the cultural perspective of the nation's diaspora within the metropolis."[52] This territory-based focus for the development of cultural nationalism was also popular at the turn of the twentieth century. Elites during this period wanted to build a unique and strong group identity separate from the United States. Through such social unity Puerto Rican cultural nationalists hoped to work against U.S. dominance and rule in the region. As part of this effort, Puerto Rican leaders did not want anyone to leave the area, especially to work in another part of the colonizer's empire for the profit of the United States.

One's residency status was a major factor for membership in and claims to a Puerto Rican national identity during the first half of the twentieth century. Jorge Duany stated that before the 1940s, Puerto Rican nationalism was focused on those who stayed in Puerto Rico.[53] Due to this emphasis on location, migrants were not included in projects of cultural nationalism or government assistance until the influx of workers to the continental United States after World War II.[54]

The experience of intra-colonials in Hawai'i highlights the effect that land-based definitions of Puerto Rican national identity had on migrants before 1950. In the first few months of movement, people in Puerto Rico worried about the well-being of their compatriots in the Pacific. But soon after the first shipments of recruits left Puerto Rico, elites and the print media changed focus, speaking against outmigration to Hawai'i. Part of their argument involved a unified, territory-based cultural nationalism that was being developed to fight against U.S. rule in the region. Their focus centered on the protection of Puerto Ricans in Puerto Rico.

Strong anti-migration and nationalistic rhetoric from business leaders, anti-U.S. groups, and the print media expanded negative perceptions about going to Hawai'i. Those who left were assumed to lose contact with their Puerto Rican roots. Those in the homeland also felt they could no longer protect intra-colonials. These ideas added to the negative stories about intra-colonial movement to Hawai'i. In addition to the difficult journey to the Pacific and poor circumstances on sugar plantations, once these U.S. colonials left the Caribbean they became outsiders to residency-based Puerto Rican cultural and political nationalism. All of these factors greatly outweighed the promises of steady wage labor in Hawai'i.

Puerto Rican Requests for Return

By the time the last ship of Puerto Rican recruits arrived in the islands in October 1901, more than five thousand Puerto Ricans had migrated to the Pacific. The poor living and working conditions in Hawai'i continued, and many migrants wanted to go back to the Caribbean. For several years, intra-colonials contacted the Puerto Rican government for financial assistance to pay for transport home. However, as workers recruited for permanent settlement in Hawai'i, these U.S. colonials were seen as external to the Puerto Rican territory. Outside the financial and social responsibility of the Caribbean government, no Puerto Ricans in Hawai'i received money to return home.

From 1901 to 1904, Puerto Rican governor general Allen received at least twenty-six complaints in Spanish and English from mothers, fathers, brothers, sisters, ministers, grandmothers, attorneys, as well as the labor organization *Federación Libre de Trabajodores*.[55] These complainants requested investigations into the conditions of Puerto Rican in Hawai'i and free passage for dissatisfied migrants. In one 1904 case, Maria Torres explained how she was recently widowed at age fifty-eight and wanted government help to return to Puerto Rico with her four children.[56] In a handwritten, Spanish-language letter, Torres told the Puerto Rican governor of "the months of suffering of this family."[57] She made it clear that she was not asking for charity, offering twenty acres of land in Puerto Rico as a guarantee for their travel expenses back to their Caribbean homeland. Despite such collateral, which most requestors did not have, the Puerto Rican government denied this appeal.

In fact, a standard answer developed for these return requests: "There is no fund at the Governor's disposal for the purpose of transporting destitute emigrants."[58] The Puerto Rican government believed that workers had been brought to the islands as long-term residents. Once these migrants left the Caribbean, they were no longer the concern of the Puerto Rican government. Intra-colonial Puerto Ricans did not have a stipulation in their labor agreement for transportation back to the Caribbean, so they had no claims to return passage.

Ability to return to Puerto Rico was just as important to loved ones back home as those in Hawai'i. Many in Puerto Rico requested the repatriation of their relatives to help care for their families. Belen Fransinete y Rios submitted a Spanish-language request for the return of her son due to her inability to support herself. She explained, "[I am] completely poor, an elderly widow with chronic illnesses that prevent me from working and therefore needs the help of her child."[59] Her son, Felipe Cruz y Fransinete, had completed his three-year labor agreement and wanted to return home. In response, the Puerto Rican government stated that he was now a resident of Hawai'i and could not be repatriated. As a permanent settler to Hawai'i, he had no reason to expect or receive help to return to the Caribbean.

Without external financial support, most intra-colonial Puerto Ricans could not afford the high price of transport back home. They had no choice but to stay in Hawai'i. The inability of Puerto Rican intra-colonials to return only heightened the circulation of negative stories and ideas about experiences in Hawai'i that persisted in Puerto Rico throughout the first half of the twentieth century. Even though they could enter United States jurisdiction at any time due to their status as U.S. colonials, Puerto Ricans ended up resisting such movement after less than one year of HSPA recruitment. Whether motivated by García-Colón's concept of *buscando ambiente* or Sorensen and Olwig's idea of mobile livelihoods, Puerto Ricans stopped intra-colonial mobility to Hawai'i because they did not think they would have improved circumstances in the islands. While conditions at home were bad, individuals chose to remain in Puerto Rico to avoid the horrific circumstances reportedly facing migrants.

Conflicts among the U.S. Imperial Bureaucracy

Despite early negative and failed experiences with Puerto Rican migration to Hawai'i, the U.S. federal government continuously encouraged the recruitment of this U.S. colonial group for work in the Pacific. Theoretically, Puerto

Ricans should have been ideal workers for Hawai'i sugar plantations. These islands needed more laborers and citizens, while Puerto Rico suffered from overpopulation and unemployment. Puerto Ricans were also categorized as racially white by the U.S. government. Their recruitment could help alleviate the majority Asian population in this Pacific region. After Puerto Ricans became U.S. citizens in 1917, they were also expected to be more dedicated to U.S. interests than foreign labor groups were. Despite the romanticized characterizations of these U.S. colonials held by U.S. federal administrators, officials in the Territory of Hawai'i and Puerto Rico did not encourage the mobility of this group after 1901. Ignoring the wishes of federal officials, local governments resisted movement of workers from this Caribbean region to the Pacific.

With the government's categorization of Puerto Ricans as white for census purposes, federal bureaucrats hoped the recruitment of these U.S. colonials would infuse the Hawaiian Islands with more Anglo stock and thereby stem the need to recruit more Asians.[60] According to a 1931 War Department memorandum, the Bureau of Insular Affairs "has consistently advocated the emigration of Porto Ricans to relieve the problems arising from over-population . . . ; to Hawaii by removing the constant menace of a Japanese majority; to the United States, from a national defense standpoint, by having the garrison of Hawaii constituted of loyal American soldiers."[61] After the Japanese and Filipino labor strikes of 1920, as well as the Filipino labor strike of 1924, members of the Bureau of Insular Affairs and the U.S. military started to view Puerto Ricans as a positive racial counter to the political militancy of Asians in Hawai'i. A General Staff Study conducted by the Hawaiian Department of the Navy also claimed that "the Porto Rican is an American citizen and proud of it. Nothing insults him more than to be spoken of as though he were not an American."[62] Puerto Ricans were assumed to be white and loyal to the United States.

Another stereotype about Puerto Ricans that continued to persist in the U.S. federal bureaucracy, despite earlier failed recruitment to Hawai'i, was the idea that they would assimilate easily in the Pacific due to the geographic resemblance of their home region to their host region. Bureau of Insular Affairs chief McIntyre stated, "Personally, I have hoped that there would be established in some way quite a flow of Porto Ricans to Hawaii. The latter place offers a climate comparable to Porto Rico, but milder, and a far better opportunity for labor."[63] National officials who supported Puerto Rican intracolonial movement believed the similarities between Puerto Rico and Hawai'i would outweigh any differences. Federal bureaucrats such as McIntyre were often not aware of the social differences and the ethnic racializations that existed in Hawai'i and Puerto Rico regarding each other. Instead, government leaders in Washington, D.C., viewed Puerto Ricans from a typical imperial perspective: U.S. colonials were labor pawns that could be moved freely and easily within the U.S. empire. One tropical island was like any other tropical island. The people in these locations were interchangeable.

From their high-level positions, U.S. officials in the Bureau of Insular Affairs, the Department of Interior, and the military all had vested interests in the proper and effective management of U.S. colonials. If one region had population problems and another region had labor needs, the simple and practical solution would be to transplant those from the depressed region to the prospering location. According to Duany, "Since the beginning of the twentieth century, colonial officials embraced migration as a safety valve for the Island's [Puerto Rico's] overpopulation."[64] The constant insistence of U.S. officials to use Puerto Rican intra-colonials as a solution for labor scarcity in Hawai'i makes sense. But these D.C. bureaucrats ignored the reasons for the failed recruitment of these U.S. colonials at the turn of the century and did not facilitate better treatment for later intra-colonial workers in the Pacific.

In contrast to the high and generally unrealistic expectations of the federal government, the great resistance, numerous complaints, and negative stereotypes toward Puerto Ricans in Hawai'i ended up deterring leadership in the Pacific from pursuing this group as a long-term solution to their labor needs. Even though the federal government classified Puerto Ricans as white, such a categorization did not guarantee good treatment or positive views of Puerto Ricans in the islands. Territory of Hawai'i reports categorized early Puerto Rican intra-colonial recruits as sickly and unaccustomed to hard agricultural work. According to the Hawai'i commissioner of labor in 1902, "The [Puerto Rican] men had been carelessly recruited . . . a considerable number of petty criminals, wharf rats, and prostitutes . . . when they arrived, [they] gave the least promise, either as citizens or as laborers, of any immigrants that ever disembarked at Honolulu . . . they did not know how to care for themselves. They had to be taught."[65] Puerto Rican recruits were seen as people of bad character who did more harm than good in Hawai'i.

Due to negative stereotypes of Puerto Ricans in the Territory of Hawai'i, island officials consistently resisted further recruitment of this group. A 1905 report by the Hawai'i commissioner of labor stated that "the experiment of importing Porto Ricans, or any kindred labor from the West Indies, is not likely to be repeated; and those who are at present in Hawaii will doubtless continue to constitute a decreasing fraction of the plantation force, until they finally disappear as a separate nationality from the plantation pay rolls."[66] Regional government leaders expected no further movement from the Caribbean. They also hoped for the eventual dwindling of Puerto Rican intra-colonials in the islands. Even after wide-ranging immigration restrictions were put into place and these U.S. colonials became the best legal source of labor for the HSPA in the 1920s, Territory of Hawai'i officials consistently opposed the use of Puerto Rican laborers for the sugar industry.

Throughout the twentieth century in the Hawaiian Islands, these wards of the United States were portrayed as stupid, low class, and too lazy to create their own positive conditions and take advantage of their circumstances. Academic studies by the Romanzo Adams School of Sociology at the University of Hawai'i supported such negative views of Puerto Ricans in the Pacific. One common finding claimed that the Puerto Rican community had "social habits and attitudes unfavorable to order and organization."[67] At least four other research articles published in the journal *Social Process in Hawaii* between 1936 and 1948 reported that since their arrival, Puerto Ricans were a disorganized group with social values that fundamentally conflicted with American mores and folkways.[68] These scholars believed the innate cultural deficiencies of this group resulted in their high rates of convictions for murder, manslaughter, robbery, burglary, and sex crimes, as well as frequent desertion in marriage and extensive use of the welfare system. Such damaging images about Puerto Ricans pervaded Hawaiian society throughout the twentieth century and discouraged public support for any future enlistment of this group to work in the islands.

The Puerto Rican government also resisted later employment efforts to Hawai'i due to the stories of mistreatment and poor conditions reported by the first groups of intra-colonial recruits in the Pacific. Theodore Roosevelt Jr., the governor of Puerto Rico in 1930, exemplified the attitudes of officials in this Caribbean region toward migration to Hawai'i. He stated that "the government's only relations to it [HSPA labor inquiry] was that of the protector of the interests of the Porto Rican workers . . . it would receive his support and encouragement only to the extent that it benefited the people of this island."[69] Puerto Rican government officials would promote Puerto Rican mobility to the Pacific only if it helped U.S. colonials. If not, such movement would not be encouraged or authorized.

Leaders from both colonized areas did not believe additional Puerto Rican recruitment to Hawai'i benefited either region. U.S. colonials staying in the Caribbean seemed like the best choice for each location and the peoples of those islands. But the labor migration policy decisions of the federal bureaucracy did not always coincide with the desires of local and regional U.S. colonial governments. High-minded, big-picture, and out-of-touch U.S. federal administrators continued to believe that Puerto Rican recruitment to Hawai'i was positive and beneficial. As outsiders to the ground-level social realities in the Territory of Hawai'i and Puerto Rico, federal colonial bureaucrats merely tried to move imperial pawns around the chess board of U.S. empire.

Later Attempts at Puerto Rican Recruitment

Due to continuing and multiple negative perspectives toward Caribbean migration in the islands, the HSPA did not invest much effort into recruiting Puerto Ricans between 1901 and 1920.[70] The sugar industry did not want to waste its time attracting Puerto Ricans if there was no support at local and regional levels in Hawai'i and Puerto Rico. However, in the 1920s, circumstances changed. Agricultural industries in the Pacific faced a massive labor shortage, starting in 1919. The HSPA worked with the Territory of Hawai'i government to proclaim a state of labor emergency. In 1921, both entities requested a temporary exception to the Chinese Exclusion Acts from the U.S. federal government to alleviate this crisis.[71] The HSPA was also recruiting as many Filipinos as possible.[72] Western European and Anglo U.S. citizens could come to Hawai'i, but they chose to avoid difficult plantation work. Since the Chinese exemption appeal did not succeed, the HSPA had no other choice but to attempt to bring Puerto Rican U.S. colonials to the islands once again.

After the wave of complaints and appalling images from turn-of-the-century migrations to the Pacific, the Puerto Rican government decided it could not take a back seat as it did during the last recruitment effort. This time around, Puerto Rican officials played an active role in developing an intra-colonial migration program to Hawai'i. For the 1921 labor agreement, the Puerto Rican government negotiated set wages, a three-year bonus schedule, and funds for any necessary legal investigations. The HSPA agreed "to pay all expenses, attorney fees inclusive, incurred by the Department of Agriculture and Labor in case that judicial intervention is necessary of violation of this contract."[73] Recruiters were required to read all of these terms to recruits before they departed Puerto Rico. If the HSPA violated any of these conditions, the Puerto Rican Bureau of Labor reserved the right to stop intra-colonial worker movement to Hawai'i immediately.

Even though the HSPA negotiated protracted labor agreement terms with the Puerto Rican government between 1921 and 1931, only 683 Puerto Ricans migrated in 1921. Why did recruitment efforts fail throughout this decade? Soon after the arrival of the first ship of 683 Puerto Ricans in 1921, these U.S. colonial recruits wrote the Puerto Rican government about violations in work agreement conditions. According to Manuel Soto Rivera, "Work here is very hard and . . . the employers are very bad."[74] In general, this group claimed no opportunities to work for maximum pay, lack of free medical treatment, high food prices, no local representative, and poor treatment.[75] According to these complaints, Hawai'i sugar plantations did not meet any of the promises made to Puerto Ricans laborers. These intra-colonial workers submitted complaints and requested aid to return home. Whether grievances were true or not, such quick protests led Puerto Rican government officials to suspend immediately any further movement to Hawai'i.

The HSPA tried to recruit more Puerto Rican U.S. colonials in 1923, 1924, 1925, and 1931, with continued support from the U.S. military and the Bureau of Insular Affairs.[76] In 1924, BIA chief McIntyre still encouraged Puerto Rican migration to Hawai'i "for two reasons—that it would relieve congestion in Porto Rico, and bring to Hawaii the class of residents that are most desired there."[77]

However, after the failed recruitment of 1921, the Puerto Rican government developed an oppositional stance to U.S. federal bureaucratic recruitment of intra-colonial labor to Hawai'i. Officials in the Caribbean region started to demand even more stringent and detailed labor agreement conditions from the HSPA. These terms included the guarantee of permanent work and the commitment to pay $2,000 a year for any potential investigations.[78] Puerto Rican officials prioritized the well-being and personal prosperity of U.S. colonials over the economic needs in or policy recommendations from other regions or levels of the U.S. empire. In 1924, Governor Horace Towner of Puerto Rico stated that "the only part the Insular Government may properly take in the matter is to see that its citizens are not deceived by false inducements and that the welfare of the laborer and his family shall be carefully guarded."[79] Since the sugar industry functioned for maximal profit, the HSPA did not concede to costly requests such as guaranteed wages and bonuses, a one-hour lunch break instead of the standard half hour, or payment for a Puerto Rican labor representative in Hawai'i. When the cane growers would not agree to these terms, the Puerto Rican government responded by not supporting Puerto Rican migration to the Pacific.

While part of the global U.S. imperial system, leaders in Puerto Rico and the Territory of Hawai'i did not always follow the preferences of the federal government. Different levels of the colonial bureaucracy could clash and conflict, resulting in the inconsistent application of administrative directives. United States business and government policy makers in Washington, D.C., were not all powerful. Instead, local government officials, as well as Puerto Rican U.S. colonials themselves, could choose to not support or engage in mobile livelihoods or intra-colonial mobility to Hawai'i. Without the collaboration of these groups, efforts to bring Puerto Rican U.S. colonial migrants to the Pacific throughout the first half of the twentieth century failed miserably.

Conclusion

The sugar industry always prioritized access to labor. HSPA recruitment and retention efforts focused on supplying enough workers for cane cultivation.

Unlike the Anglo-American elite in Hawai'i, Puerto Rican government leaders, and federal bureaucracy officials in Washington, D.C., plantation leadership did not care where laborers came from, what their personal needs were, or what color their skin was. The sugar industry just needed diligent, long-term workers.

HSPA employment policies always tried to control the mobility of workers. When options were limited, Puerto Rican U.S. colonials resisted movement to Hawai'i. If these intra-colonials were dissatisfied with work and living conditions, they vocally protested. They also stopped migrating if their concerns were not addressed satisfactorily. Puerto Rican and Filipino recruitment to Hawai'i thrived only when it represented the free will of these groups and supported their personal needs and desires. Recruitment and retention programs had to benefit workers as much as, if not more than, employers. If U.S. colonials had choices, they came willingly, as seen in the next chapter. With the failure of Puerto Rican recruitment at the turn of the century, Filipinos became the last legal and willing source of labor for Hawai'i sugar plantations.

2. *Flexible and Accommodating*

SUCCESSFUL RECRUITMENT
AND RETENTION OF FILIPINOS

On January 8, 1921, Matias Miguel arrived at the Port of Honolulu as a sugar plantation labor recruit from San Nicolas, Ilocos Norte, Philippines. In 1926, he returned to the Philippines to get married, then traveled back to the Hawaiian Islands with his wife Lorraine that same year. In 1930, Lorraine got sick and the Miguels returned to the Philippines. After she recovered, they went back to Hawai'i again, in 1930. In 1950, the Miguels moved to San Nicolas with hopes to stay permanently. But Lorraine and the children had become accustomed to life in the U.S. territory and did not want to stay in the Philippines long term, so they went back to the islands three months later. Matias followed nine months after.[1] Such frequent and easy movement back and forth to Hawai'i was unique among all sugar plantation labor groups in Hawai'i.

As with Puerto Ricans, Filipino recruitment to Hawai'i stemmed from their political-legal relationship with the United States. Administrators in Washington, D.C., actively encouraged the movement of these legally mobile imperial wards to fill labor needs throughout the U.S. empire. As seen in chapter 1, the federal government had earlier advocated for Puerto Rican migration to Hawai'i without much success. In contrast, Filipinos willingly took advantage of HSPA recruitment and retention programs—policies that often catered directly to Filipinos' open colonial mobility. These programs, especially free return passage and family reunification programs unique to

Filipino laborers, were developed in light of earlier failed efforts to recruit Puerto Ricans. As R. Gerard Ward explained, "Every contract labor system is a product of a particular time and place and is itself part of wider political, economic and social systems."[2] In this case, accommodating HSPA employment policies, open U.S. colonial mobility, and individual and group choices to engage in mobile livelihoods resulted in Filipino intra-colonials becoming the largest and most stable source of labor for Hawai'i sugar plantations throughout the first half of the twentieth century. Almost 126,000 Filipinos moved intra-colonially to Hawai'i between 1906 and 1946.[3] In 1922, Filipinos comprised the majority of the sugar plantation workforce, numbering 19,419 out of 40,213, or over 48 percent of the unskilled laborers throughout the islands. Japanese came in second with 14,533, or a little over 36 percent of the unskilled laborers.[4]

The HSPA first tried to recruit Filipinos after they became U.S. colonials at the turn of the twentieth century. But sugar industry inquiries about the possibility of recruiting Filipino labor in 1901 got lost in the new military and civil colonial bureaucracies in the Philippines. It took six months for HSPA requests for workers to be answered by Anglo-American officials in the archipelago. On October 25, 1901, William Haywood, an HSPA representative in Washington, D.C., sent a letter to the Bureau of Insular Affairs stating "After four months loss of valuable time to the plantations . . . I have therefore to earnestly request that you inform me at your earliest convenience, whether the Government will make any objections to our bringing labor from the Philippines."[5] Since the mere establishment of basic communication with the Philippine government took an extremely long time, the HSPA abandoned early efforts to recruit laborers from the Philippines. The sugar industry did not have the patience to deal with the inefficient, fledgling, colonial government bureaucracy in the Philippines. Instead, the HSPA focused on other available workers at the turn of the century, such as Japanese, Koreans, and Portuguese.

After the 1907 Gentlemen's Agreement, Japanese and Korean laborers could no longer enter Hawai'i. The Japanese strike of 1909 also motivated the HSPA to look for another source of workers to balance out this large and contentious group of Asian laborers in the islands. Legally mobile Western Europeans and Anglo U.S. citizens stayed away from difficult plantation work. With Puerto Rican U.S. colonials resisting further movement to Hawai'i, Filipinos became one of the last legal and untried labor groups for the sugar industry. The HSPA consequently renewed its efforts to recruit Filipinos in 1906. By this time, colonial bureaucracies in the Philippines were solidified, and the U.S.-controlled Philippine government cooperated more quickly and easily with the HSPA.

The sugar industry worked hard to develop new and appealing recruitment and retention policies for legally mobile Filipino U.S. colonials. The HSPA learned from the unsuccessful movement of Puerto Ricans to Hawai'i and adjusted their tactics to acknowledge the needs and expectations of Filipino laborers. While Puerto Rican recruitment was impersonal and rigid, Filipino recruitment became creative and flexible, involving a range of choices. Instead of haphazard hiring, negative letters home, and lack of financial support for return passage, the HSPA standardized employment processes, encouraged the circulation of positive stories about life in Hawai'i, and provided free transport back to the archipelago after three years of work. This chapter examines the range of recruitment and retention efforts applied to Filipinos. The HSPA willingly modified labor conditions to encourage future intra-colonial migration. Since Filipinos valued, used, and enjoyed their ability to move freely between the Philippines and Hawai'i, the sugar industry created a wide assortment of mobility programs to cater to such preferences. These employment strategies motivated this U.S. colonial group to become the best source of constant labor for Hawai'i sugar throughout the first half of the twentieth century.

Personal and social circumstances also contributed to the successful migration of Filipinos to Hawai'i. While the HSPA created and paid for unique Filipino recruitment and retention benefits to maintain a steady flow of these U.S. colonials to Hawai'i, the sugar industry also gave Filipinos much control over their individual, family, and community mobility experiences to the islands. Therefore, this chapter also demonstrates individual stories and motivations behind U.S. colonial participation in both common employment efforts and unique recruitment and retention processes. Filipinos actively chose to move to Hawai'i, return to the Philippines, re-migrate to the islands, and bring family and friends to the Pacific in large numbers. Ultimately, the combination of personal and group support for migration, accommodating sugar industry mobility policies, and intra-colonial open movement allowed Filipinos to fulfill personal desires, family needs, and community expectations through mobile livelihoods in Hawai'i.

Common Recruitment and Retention Practices

HSPA efforts to bring Filipinos to Hawai'i and keep them in the islands involved extensive bureaucratic policies and administrative structures. The sugar industry dedicated substantial personnel and monetary resources to encourage letter-writing campaigns, step up recruitment in the Philippines, and provide letters of recommendation for re-employment. The central sugar office also distributed many memos and created numerous application forms to ensure the smooth function of these programs. While other labor groups could access similar kinds of strategies, only Filipino processes became thoroughly institutionalized. Since Filipinos could move easily within U.S. jurisdiction, they could take full advantage of common recruitment and retention programs. HSPA policies also reflected lessons learned from failed Puerto Rican recruitment.

Letters Home

The HSPA always encouraged laborers to send positive messages about life in Hawai'i to family and friends back home. While the sugar industry hoped letters from the islands would result in steady labor flows from all areas of the world, anti-immigration legislation made such continuous mobility difficult for most groups. Legally barred foreigners faced strict migration rules that impeded the movement of their family and friends to Hawai'i. Filipino U.S. colonials, on the other hand, could and did motivate loved ones to follow them to the islands through encouraging letters home. Voluntarily engaging in this typical recruitment tactic, intra-colonial Filipinos fostered translocal chain migration, or the progressively increasing movement of family and friends from one specific location in the Philippines to one specific plantation in Hawai'i.[6]

In 1907, the HSPA encouraged Filipino intra-colonial laborers in Hawai'i to send optimistic letters about conditions in the islands to the home region. George Wagner, an HSPA recruiter in the Philippines, telegrammed the central HSPA office in Honolulu to urge laborers to write more messages to family and friends in the archipelago. In response, Ola'a plantation manager John Watt stated, "I have seen the Filippino [sic] interpreter, and requested him to tell his people to write letters home more frequently than they have been doing in the past. He says that he has written three times himself but he promises that he will have these people write immediately and keep up a regular correspondence."[7] By developing a pleasant and advantageous image of plantation life in Hawai'i, the HSPA hoped to attract and maintain a continuous stream of Filipino U.S. colonials for sugar plantation work.

Filipino letter-writing campaigns proved effective, with many oral histories citing a message from a relative or friend in Hawai'i as one reason—if not the main reason—for movement to the islands. Stories of abundance in the Pacific contrasted with poor conditions in the Philippines. Difficult economic circumstances typified life in the Ilocos and Visayas regions of the Philippines during the first half of the twentieth century. In these locations, land had become overcultivated and barren by the 1920s. Baldomera Pervera Labrador discussed how in Cebu, Visayas, there was "no more nothing

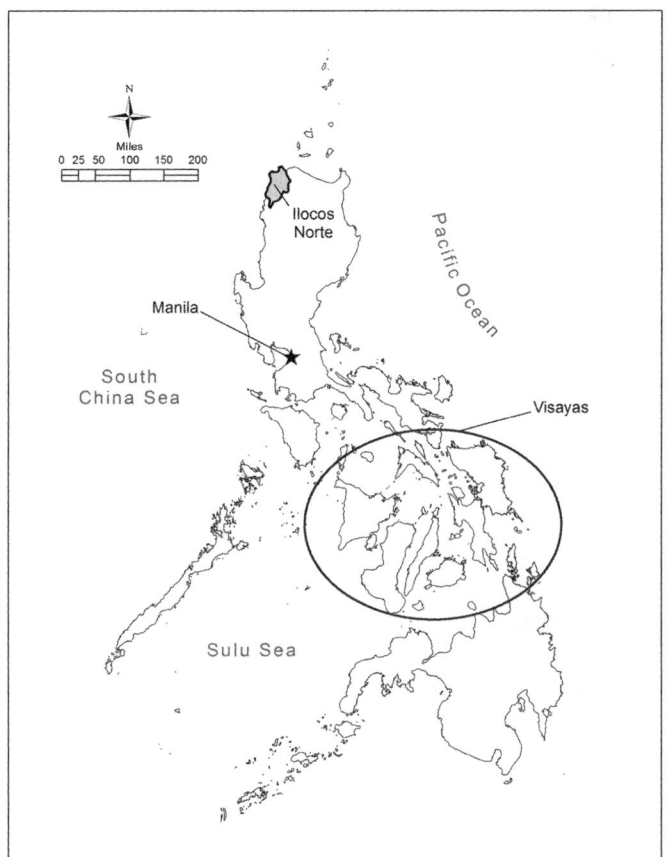

Map of the Philippines

[rice]. No can alive. No can grow."[8] Bernabella Abril also spoke of the arduous lifestyle in Laoag, Ilocos Norte. She explained, "We had a very pitiful house . . . we had a very hard life . . . we did not own property."[9] Compared to declining subsistence-based lives in these rural areas of the Philippines, intra-colonial movement to and wage labor in Hawai'i became attractive.

Filipinos believed sugar plantation work in the islands offered better alternatives to rice cultivation or homesteading in the archipelago.[10] While they could barely cultivate enough food to feed their own families at home, Filipinos in Hawai'i could earn a consistent wage every day of the year. Abril explained, "We heard from people going to Hawaii about the good life here, so my parents decided to come to Hawaii. My parents thought, perhaps, we find a better life here."¹¹ Since conditions and opportunities in Ilocos Norte and the Visayas were poor and limited, many people from these regions, like Labrador and Abril, found hope in the stories from the Pacific and decided to move intra-colonially to Hawai'i. Filipino migrants to Hawai'i initially came from the Ilocos region in large numbers and in later years from the Visayas in smaller numbers. In general, people in the Philippines received many more optimistic reports about movement to Hawai'i than individuals in Puerto Rico. In contrast to the anti-recruitment and negative employment attitudes prevalent in Puerto Rican letters home, Filipino messages to loved ones became an effective HSPA recruitment tool.

However, not all messages were optimistic. According to Alex Ruiz, "My brother was here [Hawai'i] already. He was here. And he writes back that plantation life is very hard, he cannot take it. So my mother said, 'Your brother cannot take it. I don't think you can take it.' I said, 'No, my brother is a silk.'"¹² Despite his brother's complaints and his mother's discouragement, Ruiz still wanted to go to Hawai'i for adventure. Ruiz also believed he was a physically and mentally stronger person who could survive better in the islands than his brother. While not all letters were positive, many still migrated despite discouragement of their relatives or friends already in the islands. Underlying both negative and positive stories was the consistent message that wage labor was abundant in Hawai'i. Such economic opportunities often outweighed negative work and living conditions.

Visayan migrants to Hawai'i were likely familiar with the sugar cultivation process, as well as the hierarchical and often exploitative nature of the industry. According to historian Filomeno Aguilar, those involved in the sugar industry in Negros, Visayas, accepted the idea of "wealth obtained by whatever means."¹³ In this context, some Filipino migrants to Hawai'i could have been very aware that they occupied the lowest rung of the sugar plantation hierarchy. With this understanding, these intra-colonials might have been willing to endure grueling plantation life in exchange for steady wage labor.¹⁴

Even though Filipinos could not be forced to write positive letters, many did so because they truly believed movement to Hawai'i could benefit their family and friends. Marcella Queypo Amoroso explained how "people always talk about Hawai'i's good. So long you work, you got money. Everybody said that, so when my sister wanted to come, I did follow them, too. Husband and wife."¹⁵ Through the spread of optimistic economic accounts of life in Hawai'i, relatives, friends, and friends of friends in the Philippines willingly followed the path established by laborers already in the islands.

Over time, those in the home region had "more knowledge about the conditions on plantations and other places of employment.... Even recruits who had not been . . . heard which plantations had good or bad reputations . . . developed preferences for work in particular coastal regions. A form of chain migration developed with recruits seeking to go to those places where they knew they would find others from their own language group."[16] Through letters home, Filipinos knew exactly what kind of environment they would encounter, which specific island they wanted to move to, which plantation manager they wanted to work for, and which Filipinos they wanted to live with.

Messages to the Philippines thus resulted in translocal chain migration, creating a continuous flow of intra-colonials between specific hometowns and certain plantations in the islands. Scholar Alberto Palloni explained how "social networks connections create conditions that facilitate the migration of others (decreasing costs, augmenting potential streams of future income, reducing risks, transmitting information). As a result, individuals who are related to migrants will . . . be more likely to migrate themselves."[17] The level of migration from a particular place usually increased when others from the region already lived abroad. Such a phenomenon was also the case with Filipinos moving to Hawai'i. The experience and knowledge of earlier migrants helped their loved ones also decide to move to Hawai'i.

In addition to letters, many laborers in Hawai'i sent money home to support the families they left behind. Unlike the lack of money sent home by Puerto Rican intra-colonials, large Filipino remittances evoked images of unlimited possibilities to gain wealth in the islands. Lope Ancheta explained, "I send [money] all the time as soon as I get some. I have to send them because they need it. All these years I been here, I send little by little as soon as I get enough to send."[18] In 1930, the HSPA estimated that Filipino laborers in Hawai'i sent more than $4 million dollars in remittances to the Philippines annually. The sugar industry also reported that "nearly 15,000 Filipino depositors had accounts totaling $3,111,000 in the savings banks of the Territory."[19] Compared to the hand-to-mouth lifestyle in the Ilocos and Visayan countryside during this period, such demonstrations of wealth and success in Hawai'i further bolstered the desire of Filipinos to go to the islands.

While Puerto Ricans at the turn of the century had no easy way to send money back home, the HSPA set up its own process to facilitate an efficient and reliable way to transfer money from Hawai'i to the Philippines. Filipino laborers could deposit their earnings with their plantation office, which would send the funds by mail to the HSPA central administration in Honolulu. Those leaders then notified the Manila HSPA office of the transferred amount. With a simple visit to the plantation manager, Filipino workers could quickly initiate the transfer process. Loved ones in the home region could pick up remittances from Hawai'i sugar agents in Manila, Cebu, and Ilocos within a few days.[20] Through the establishment of their own remittance procedure, the HSPA strongly contributed to positive perceptions in the Philippines about the large amounts of money to be made through plantation work in Hawai'i.

Letters and remittances home also effectively recruited more Filipinos than other foreign laborers because of the group's open colonial mobility. The family and friends of U.S. colonials had the actual legal means to go to Hawai'i if so enticed. Foreign laborers could keep in touch with their home regions and send money home, but their ability to foster chain migration to Hawai'i became much more limited throughout the twentieth century. Loved ones of foreign laborers had to deal with strict U.S. immigration restrictions while Filipinos could go to Hawai'i at any time. Unrestricted mobility, social encouragement, and economic enticements influenced Filipino decisions to move intra-colonially.

Recruitment Agents

The HSPA usually set up recruitment offices in the regions where they wanted to employ laborers. Independent nations often closely regulated the movement of their citizens to other countries. In the Philippines, the HSPA worked directly with the Philippine Bureau of Labor. This agency, established in 1916, oversaw the practices of HSPA agents in the archipelago. While Bureau of Labor administrators were appointed by elected Philippine politicians, all of these leaders were subject to the approval of U.S. Anglo-American officials supervising the Philippine colony. As a ward of the United States, the Philippine government rarely developed guidelines that interfered with hiring for U.S. business interests.

The Philippine Bureau of Labor created a specific process and set of regulations to govern Filipino recruitment to Hawai'i. HSPA recruiters had to obtain government licenses to open offices and hire workers in designated provinces. Once the proper permits were acquired, the HSPA could freely travel to "barrios carrying promotional literature, stereopticon slides, postcard pictures, or movies."[21] As long as an individual signed a labor agreement in a region approved for hiring, he could be legally recruited to Hawai'i. This process gave both the fledgling Philippine Bureau of Labor and the HSPA legitimacy and authority to handle Philippine labor employment outside the supervision of colonial administrators in Washington, D.C.

HSPA cooperation with Filipino Bureau of Labor policies fostered a supportive political environment to develop and sustain intra-colonial mobility to Hawai'i. During Puerto Rican hiring, in contrast, the HSPA used third-party companies to enlist any willing individual who showed up at their offices. Since recruiters received payment per person, these businessmen transported anyone they could convince to board a ship. The haphazard nature of migrant selection became an issue for the Anglo-American elite in Hawai'i. The Puerto Rican government also had no role in the recruitment process. With no regulations placed on recruiters and lack of government oversight, Puerto Rican employment to Hawai'i failed miserably. About fifteen years later, the HSPA worked closely with the Philippine colonial government to create hiring standards and systematize employment procedures. With the establishment of such policies, leaders in both Hawai'i and the Philippines supported and encouraged the movement of Filipinos to the islands.

The experience of one Filipino, Tito Nicolas, highlights the ground-level recruitment process in the Philippines. The arrival of HSPA agents in rural Philippine villages created much commotion, and crowds often gathered when recruiters entered town. This environment of curiosity immersed individuals like Nicolas in the HSPA employment process. While waiting for a bus in his hometown of Badoc, Ilocos Norte, Nicolas's friend encouraged him to line up for HSPA health inspections. Nicolas's friend wanted to check out the events surrounding the sugar industry agents. Perhaps he had heard enticing stories about opportunities in Hawai'i from relatives and town mates. Nicolas's friend ultimately convinced Nicolas to join him in entering the building where the inspections were taking place. Nicolas explained:

> My friend pulled me inside too. I said, "Eh, I don't want to" . . . [he said] "No no, come come and look what's going on" . . . everybody start taking off clothes. But I didn't, I didn't take my clothes off because I didn't know what goes-ing on. And then when he [the doctor's secretary] called . . . your name you go take your paper and go by the doctor and the doctor . . . put his stamp, "Pass. Next." See, that's how fast those [inspections were] . . . then I ask him, "Hey, what's going on?" Then my friend told me that this sign for this [labor agreement] . . . [the doctor] told the driver to make me sign. So I did sign the paper. He tell me, "Well, you pass, go to Hawaii." I say, "But I . . ." He say, "No, never mind, you're one of the *sakadas* [Filipino labor recruits to Hawai'i] now."[22]

Even though Nicolas entered the building due to the urging of his friend, and he did not comply with all the directions given by the inspection team, he still gained approval to go to Hawai'i. In the field, the head doctor's main goal was to obtain as many healthy labor recruits as possible. He viewed anyone he came across as a potential sugar plantation laborer. When he identified strong recruits, like Nicolas, he did not want to lose them. The doctor and his staff compelled hesitant men to leave through a speedy recruitment process and emphasis on the finality of inspections.

Unsure recruits had little time to reconsider going to Hawai'i. After approval at the local level, recruits were quickly sent to Manila, where they underwent another round of medical inspections and boarded the next available ship.[23] While different steps of the recruitment process established by the Philippine Bureau of Labor might not have been followed stringently, the existence of standardized procedures provided enough legitimacy, stability, and credibility to the overall hiring process in the Philippines to satisfy government officials in both the Pacific and the archipelago.

Even though Nicolas originally had no interest in going to Hawai'i, two weeks after his first health examination he was on a ship bound for the Pacific Islands. Unlike later Visayan migrants to Hawai'i, the majority of earlier Filipino migrants from the Ilocos region, like Nicolas, were not previously exposed to sugar cultivation and had less familiarity with both the basic process and resulting socio-economic environment of plantation life. But in the short period between his initial inspection and his departure for Manila, Nicolas eventually decided it was in his family's best interest to go to Hawai'i.

In 1914, Nicolas's family lost their home during a storm that hit the Ilocos region. Six months later, his father passed away, leaving his mother alone to care for three children. Nicolas's mother allowed him to leave for Hawai'i since their life in Badoc was difficult. Nicolas also believed he could better support his family through wage labor in Hawai'i. As a sugar plantation worker, he could earn and save U.S. dollars to send home. When facing poor circumstances at home, some migrants "decisively abandoned their birthplaces for better wages."[24] Many people, like Nicolas, would have preferred to stay in their home region. But unexpected economic and social circumstances motivated some to leave for the benefit of an entire family. While most people migrated to escape desperate conditions, not all were excited to move intra-colonially. Nicolas's journey to Hawai'i was just as much a group decision as an individual choice. His eventual departure to the Pacific involved the multiple hopes, needs, and pressures of his family, friends, and recruiters. Such personal contexts coincided with HSPA employment programs and U.S. colonial status to result in large numbers of Filipinos entering Hawai'i during the first half of the twentieth century.

Letters of Recommendation

Letters of recommendation became one form of retention for all laborers in Hawai'i. When a good worker decided to leave for his home region, a local plantation manager could write a letter stating his willingness to employ the individual upon return to the islands. Managers hoped this document would facilitate the reentry of loyal laborers to their specific plantation. This informal system, created at the local level, represented a basic attempt by sugar managers to encourage departing workers to re-migrate to Hawai'i. Since Filipinos, like Matias Miguel, could and often did move around within U.S. jurisdiction, Filipino U.S. colonials were better equipped to take advantage of this unofficial reference system than foreign labor groups.

Plantation managers understood the constant desire of Filipinos to return home. Lope Ancheta stated, "As soon as I can earn some money, I have to return. But I did not return until after the war [World War II] (*chuckles*). That's about twenty years after that."[25] Filipinos went to Hawai'i for temporary work, and many expected to return to the Philippines after completing their three-year labor agreement. They usually wanted to make enough money to provide for their families back home. Most did not move with the intent to permanently settle in the islands. But desire to return did not always result in actual journeys home.

Scholars such as Jon Goss and Bruce Lindquist have shown how temporary labor often becomes permanent because families at home become dependent on remittances from abroad while settler countries continue to use and pay for migrant labor to support their economies.[26] Several Filipino intra-colonial workers realized the best way to support their families involved long-term work for the labor-needy sugar industry in Hawai'i. Many signed additional labor agreements, with some taking trips back to the Philippines between each labor stint. These workers became used to arduous plantation life and willingly renewed their labor agreements because they knew good money was guaranteed if they continued to work diligently.

Letters of recommendation maintained a personal and supportive connection between local plantation managers and mobile laborers. In one 1921 letter, Ola'a manager A. J. Watt explained, "Policarpio Antaran, who formerly worked on this plantation, has for the past two years resided in SN Nicolas, Manila, P.I. He wishes to return to the Hawaiian Islands and as he was a good and faithful worker while here, any assistance that can be rendered him to facilitate his return with his wife and family to this country will be greatly appreciated."[27] These documents motivated many Filipinos to resume work at their original plantations upon return.

Filipinos' active use of letters of recommendation became a long-term problem for the HSPA bureaucracy. In 1933, the labor supply in Hawai'i stabilized and the HSPA did not need to recruit as many workers. That same year, numerous Filipinos showed up at HSPA offices in the Philippines with letters of recommendation from their previous plantation managers. These U.S. colonial laborers requested transport back to Hawai'i and expected an immediate departure. In 1939, Domingo Ombon wanted to go back to the

Ola'a plantation after returning to the Philippines. He explained, "Now I wish to return to Hawaii by the validity of this certificate."[28] Since he had stayed out of the islands for more than the five-year stipulation for reentry in his letter of recommendation, he was not allowed to return.

By the 1930s, HSPA leaders in Hawai'i and the Philippines were applying employment standards more stringently than before. Not desperate to ship as many Filipinos to the Pacific, HSPA Bureau of Labor and Statistics director W. Pflueger stated in 1933, "In view of present labor conditions, with so many citizens and Filipinos still unemployed in this Territory, this man [a Filipino worker] should not be allowed to return to Hawaii."[29] Officials at HSPA headquarters in Honolulu also asked local plantation managers to stop talking about the ease with which Filipinos could return to the islands. HSPA director J. K. Butler mandated that "in the future care be taken about making promises to laborers returning to the Philippines as to the re-employment on their coming back to Hawaii."[30] But even during this period of labor abundance, the HSPA leader still offered a caveat regarding good workers: "In the case of good men whose return is desired . . . it is requested that the management provide the laborer with a letter stating the conditions and promising re-employment."[31] The HSPA always wanted to maintain a connection with loyal and hard workers.

Despite the central HSPA office's desire to manage the ballooning recruitment process in the Philippines, local plantation leaders continued to provide letters of recommendation to most Filipinos who left for the archipelago. These ground-level sugar managers understood many Filipinos engaged in intra-colonial mobility and would likely return in a few months. Even though the number of workers in Hawai'i was sufficient at that time, plantation managers always worried about upcoming labor needs. Workers had been scarce in the past and would likely be scarce in the future. These local plantation leaders consequently ignored high-level HSPA directives to stop issuing references to departing laborers. Individual managers did not follow the administrative policy of the central sugar office because they believed letters of recommendation were important to the maintenance of a long-term supply of good workers at the local level. Like the different levels of the U.S. imperial system discussed in chapter 1, HSPA leadership did not always act uniformly. Different areas of management could and did disagree with each other about best practices for laborers and the industry.

Plantation leaders also defied central HSPA rules by employing older returning workers. Upon departure from the Port of Honolulu, the central HSPA office often marked the work records of mature laborers as "not to be returned."[32] Sugar industry policymakers in Honolulu viewed the hiring of people over age forty-five as a financial risk. However, local plantation managers, in contrast, cared less about the age of a laborer than individual loyalty, experience, and diligence. For example, Candido Mariano wrote the Ola'a plantation in 1926 requesting permission to return for work in Hawai'i. The plantation manager contacted the central HSPA office, noting that he "remembers this Filipino very well and knows him to be a very good worker and one he would rather like to see back on the job. This man is a valuable one, certainly a very much better worker than the majority of the younger men who are arriving, and would like to see him back in his old position with this company. If you can see your way to let him pass we would be very glad to receive him here."[33] For ground-level plantation leadership, a dedicated and hard-working U.S. colonial laborer was useful at any age.

Sugar managers also preferred older, proven employees over younger recruits. Elder individuals might complete their tasks at a slower rate, but new laborers were inexperienced, unpredictable, and flighty. With an increasing number of labor strikes on Hawai'i sugar plantations throughout the first half of the century, a trustworthy U.S. colonial worker became even more important and advantageous. Eventually HSPA leadership acknowledged these circumstances. Since the local plantation deemed Mariano a desirable laborer with a good work history, the central HSPA office made an exception to the age-limit policy and allowed him to return. Again, local plantation leaders were willing to work against general HSPA rules to maintain labor flows.

After failed Puerto Rican recruitment at the turn of the twentieth century, the HSPA always had their own recruitment agents abroad, encouraged positive letters home, and provided documentation to maintain a continual supply of labor from all areas of the globe. But these general policies applied to and attracted Filipino U.S. colonials in particularly effective ways because of their ability to move intra-colonially. Foreigners could not take advantage of these programs to the same extent as legally mobile Filipinos because they could not easily flow back and forth between Hawai'i and their home regions. Common HSPA recruitment and retention programs, consequently, became more successful for Filipinos than foreign laborers. Filipinos also participated in these programs to improve their personal, familial, and community economic lives. A combination of industry, individual, and group influences resulted in large numbers of Filipino workers going to Hawai'i.

Unique Recruitment Programs

Filipinos also gained access to new and unique programs established to encourage and maintain their intra-colonial presence in Hawai'i. The HSPA, in a policy move counter to that which they maintained for other labor groups, permitted legally mobile and willing Filipinos to come as men without their families, funded their return home after the completion of their temporary labor agreements, paid for their wives and children to join them in the islands at a later date, and created formal systems that facilitated the recruitment of family and friends for work in Hawai'i. The HSPA also made special attempts to place Filipino laborers at the same plantations as their family and friends. As the best source of labor for sugar plantations during this period, the HSPA developed strategies to accommodate Filipino desires for back-and-forth mobility. Such efforts combined with lessons learned from failed Puerto Rican recruitment to create flexible and accommodating HSPA policies for Filipinos. No other labor group in Hawai'i could access such programs.

Going Solo

Besides Chinese laborers, all other sugar labor recruits to Hawai'i were recruited as permanent residents and were encouraged to relocate with their families. The HSPA believed this requirement would result in a steady workforce in the islands. If a laborer came with his loved ones, he would be more likely to work hard to provide a stable environment for his wife and children. The recruitment of settler families became such a high priority that the HSPA gave bonus commissions to agents who convinced laborers to bring their wives and children to the islands.[34]

Since the beginning of Filipino recruitment in 1906, the HSPA and the Territory of Hawai'i encouraged the settlement of entire Filipino families in the islands. However, early Filipino male laborers did not want to bring their loved ones to Hawai'i. According to Ola'a plantation manager John Watt in 1911, "We have interviewed all of the Filipinos in regard to those who wish to have their wives or prospective wives come to Hawaii . . . [and] we have failed to get any definite answer from any of them. They seem to be very suspicious of the arrangement, but we will interview them again to see if anything can possibly be done."[35] Early Filipino laborers did not want to uproot their families in the Philippines. These men also wanted to protect their wives and children from potentially undesirable circumstances in Hawai'i. U.S. colonial laborers preferred to separate temporarily from their loved ones than to subject them to unknown working and living conditions in the islands. To maintain this valuable and rare willing source of labor, the sugar industry allowed Filipino male laborers to migrate with short-term labor agreements without their families.

Anglo-Americans living in Hawai'i and the continental United States expressed extreme anger and anxiety over the creation of a predominantly male Filipino community in U.S. jurisdiction. Negative stereotypes have always existed about single-male labor communities.[36] Anti-bachelor society rhetoric began in the continental United States with Chinese indentured workers in the mid-1800s. During the first half of the twentieth century, such social stigmas transferred to Filipino migrant laborers who formed predominantly male agricultural labor communities in Hawai'i and the West Coast. Scholars Linda España-Maram, Dawn Mabalon, Rhacel Parreñas, and others have shown how taxi-dance halls, where Filipino men could pay ten cents to dance for the length of one song with a white woman, spurred much controversy.[37] These men became racialized as sexual predators who threatened the virtue of white womanhood through activities such as interracial dancing. Throughout the West Coast, anti-Filipino sentiment spiraled into race riots and violence, which forced this group of U.S. colonials out of many towns.

Desperate for workers and running out of areas to recruit from, the HSPA ignored continental U.S. social fears and pressures against the recruitment of Filipino men in order to gain and maintain access to this crucial labor supply for Hawai'i sugar. Since fewer and fewer groups were able or willing to migrate to the islands in the twentieth century, the HSPA permitted legally mobile and eager Filipino U.S. colonial males to come to Hawai'i alone. The HSPA also permitted these intra-colonial laborers to enter without their families on a temporary basis because long-term settlement did not succeed with Puerto Rican U.S. colonials. Likely recognizing the failures in the permanent recruitment of this other U.S. colonial group, the HSPA was more willing to accommodate Filipino preferences for short-term labor agreements. Filipinos became the only twentieth-century labor group to go to Hawai'i predominantly as impermanent male migrants.

Many Happy Returns

The sugar industry also knew how important the ability to return home became for Puerto Rican laborers in Hawai'i. Learning from past intra-colonial requests for passage back to the Caribbean, the HSPA allowed Filipinos to become the only group of plantation workers to obtain free transport home. Since many laborers rarely considered movement to Hawai'i as permanent, free return passage could motivate Filipinos to leave for the islands. The possibility of open flow back and forth from Hawai'i to the Philippines also made it easier for married labor recruits to leave without feeling like they were abandoning their families. At the very least, they had a guaranteed way to return home in three years. Other Filipinos liked the free-return-passage provision because it helped them engage in continuous intra-colonial mobility. Workers like Matias Miguel could temporarily visit the Philippines for free, then return a few months later to resume work in Hawai'i. Regardless of their ultimate goals, 55,396, or almost 44 percent, of the total Filipino migrant population returned to the archipelago through this program.[38] The HSPA paid for Filipinos to go back home because they understood that some might not come to Hawai'i without such a benefit. Return passage became an important component of Filipino intra-colonial mobility, as well as a unique and successful HSPA recruitment strategy for these U.S. colonials.

Starting in 1915, all HSPA labor agreements included free transport back to the Philippines after three years of service. In 1921, this amenity became retroactive for any Filipino who fulfilled an HSPA labor agreement. The sugar industry willingly risked losing diligent U.S. colonial workers who returned home and endured the financial burden of paying for expensive transport fares because the availability of free return passage not only motivated many Filipinos to migrate but also encouraged them stay on their assigned plantations and work hard to qualify for the benefit. This strategy created a valuable in-flow of stable laborers who completed their labor agreements.

This program also attracted more recruits from the Philippines who witnessed the material success of returning laborers. As Roman Cariaga and Miriam Sharma have shown, those who went back to the archipelago built extravagant homes, wore fancy clothes, and gave impressive gifts to their families and friends in the villages.[39] According to Severo Dinson, "You get $1,000 over here, [it's worth] $7,000 in the Philippines. You see? Big shot, already."[40] The flashy spending and big-talk of pioneering migrants encouraged more people to leave for Hawai'i. In this way, demonstrations of wealth by returning intra-colonials also supported HSPA recruitment efforts.

Qualifications for free return passage detailed the ideal characteristics of a plantation worker: He came to Hawai'i through an HSPA recruitment program and signed an official labor agreement. He provided loyal service on his assigned plantation and never went on strike. He worked six days a week for at least three consecutive years. If a laborer did not follow these guidelines, he would not receive free transportation back to the Philippines.

Since return passage involved losses of both labor and capital for the HSPA, plantation leadership wanted to make sure each returnee truly earned this benefit. Those whose work records could not be found or fully recreated did not receive free transport back to the Philippines. In 1928, the HSPA would not provide free transportation to Ambrocio Aducayan because "the man has no contract whatever with the Association, therefore he is not entitled to this privilege."[41] Wives and children who could not provide legal documents proving their relationship with the qualifying returnee also did not get paid return passage. At one point, Pflueger stated, "We have been unable to find the record of this woman in our office. The man is entitled to free transportation, but before we can return his wife, we must have her record and be sure that she has been divorced from a previous husband, if she came to the islands as a married woman."[42] Without official marriage or birth certificates, the HSPA automatically assumed intra-colonial laborers and their families did not meet requirements for free passage back to the Philippines.

The return-passage approval process was neither simple nor straightforward. Applications for free transport home involved numerous steps. First, plantation managers sent return requests to the central HSPA office in Honolulu with the work records and original labor agreement of each individual. If either could not be located, the association needed to know what steamer the laborer arrived on and the name of the plantation where he first worked. With access to all of this information, the HSPA central office could respond to return-passage requests within a day.

If a worker had moved among various plantations, the HSPA had to get work records from each location to calculate if the individual worked the required number of days to complete his labor agreement. Fewer than 270 workdays days per year, or 810 workdays total, resulted in disqualification. Sometimes records became difficult to piece together because individuals had multiple *bangos*, or work identification numbers. Filemon Jose had two bangos, one for his job as a day laborer and another for his independent contract cultivation work.[43] Claudio Danlag had five bangos.[44] Some individuals also used different versions of their first and/or last names. As one HSPA communication noted, "As in the case of all Filipino names there may be some differences in spelling."[45] And sometimes an individual with the same last name showed up for someone else. In 1926, the HSPA granted free passage to Licario Labrador.[46] But Sixto Labrador showed up at the port on departure day. HSPA officials would not allow this individual to return to the Philippines until they figured out his true identity and clarified his work record. Filipino intra-colonials' actual usage of the return-passage program created a variety of unexpected issues for the HSPA administration in the implementation of this benefit.

The sugar industry consequently developed a detailed evaluation and approval process for return passage. Four classes of return transport emerged. Sick and elderly laborers qualified for Class 1 return passage. These individuals returned at the expense of plantations. Since they needed special accommodations and care on boats, only a limited number of invalids could depart on each ship. Class 2 passage went to ideal laborers who fulfilled all labor agreement requirements. Class 3 passage, known as long-service passage, went to faithful and hardworking laborers who arrived before 1915 and who never had return passage as part of their labor agreement. Class 3 passage also applied to men who came to Hawai'i during the transition from HSPA-funded transport to Hawai'i to self-payment of passage to the islands in 1927. No labor agreements were available during this short period. The HSPA consequently provided free passage to any of the several hundred Filipinos who entered Hawai'i on Dollar steamships at the beginning of unpaid recruitment, did not have HSPA labor agreements, and had exceptional work records. Class 4 passage went to individuals who did not qualify for free return passage but paid for their own return home.

Those who qualified for one of these four classes of return passage received a transport number and a specific date of return to the Philippines on a particular ship. The process generally took about one month between submitting a return request and actually boarding a ship for Manila. Depending on the number of applicants during a given period, the wait between receiving a transport number and sailing for Manila sometimes took up to two months. More people usually returned for the second half of the year (August to December) during the slow season for sugar cultivation and the holidays.

Some return-passage applicants were extremely excited to journey home. Instead of waiting for a ship assignment, they left for the Port of Honolulu as soon as they received approval. Unfortunately, with the large number of applicants in the 1920s and 1930s, ships filled up fast. Intra-colonial laborers could not always get a spot on a boat right after they qualified. The HSPA encouraged workers to remain on plantations until they were officially notified to go to port. In an effort to keep returning Filipinos from becoming loiterers in Honolulu, Philippine Resident Commissioner Francisco Varona encouraged Filipinos to continue working at their assigned plantations until space on a specific transport became available. He stated, "We must show now that the Filipino laborers realize and know how to respond to all that is right and just . . . while waiting for your passage and the time of your departure, don't leave the plantation on which you are working. Thus you can earn more money while waiting."[47] According to Varona, staying at plantations until one was assigned a ship was an ideal situation. Good Filipino laborers would receive free transport home as soon as possible. Until then, they had the opportunity to earn more money. Field workers likely viewed the situation much differently from this colonial official. Laborers probably did not care about demonstrating their moral restraint to Anglo-American society. They likely wanted to leave back-breaking plantation work as soon as possible. Relaxing in Honolulu and enjoying the entertainments of the city seemed more attractive than additional labor on a rural plantation.

Even when intra-colonial workers received return-passage approval and a departure date, not all of them left right away. According to Ola'a plantation manager A. J. Watt, "In some cases Filipinos who apply or pay their passages, after advising them of the sailing date, come to us later telling their intention of postponing their trip for some reason or another."[48] Some workers applied for free transport simply to see if they qualified. Others changed their minds about leaving Hawai'i. The lack of daily mail and isolated worker camps on outer islands also resulted in some Filipinos receiving notice too late to reach their assigned boat in Honolulu. Others had extenuating circumstances that kept them in the islands, such as personal illness or the need to look after a sick or troubled loved one. Some did not leave because they needed to settle their financial accounts or wanted to wait until they received their year-end bonuses.[49] Others wanted to return on the same ships as relatives or friends. Such was the case with Pedro Pantorilla and Milicio Bacarisas, who were able to return home together because they submitted their applications at the same time.[50] But others did not get assigned to the same ship and chose to wait until they could leave with their compadres or family.

U.S. colonials who did not leave after getting a transport number became such a problem that in 1934 the central HSPA office asked plantations to clarify if applications were merely inquiries or actual requests to return.[51] If a manager found out certain workers were postponing their departure and others wanted to return right away, or with specific people, he would write the central HSPA office to suggest substitutions for the open spots.[52] With many people wanting to return to the Philippines and some deciding not to go on their assigned ship, local plantation management tried to juggle berth assignments to please all parties.

No amount of detailed forms, instructions, or procedures could force Filipino laborers to return on a particular ship at a specific time. As Goss and Lindquist have noted, "Migrant networks seem to have a life of their own."[53] When using the return transport system, Filipinos submitted many requests, engaged in some deception, and created much confusion over multiple names, identification numbers, and changes in departure dates. Qualifying Filipino workers traveled as they pleased, using their transport benefit when convenient and desirable for them.

Free return passage ultimately involved an enormous amount of HSPA manpower, time, and resources. Each plantation generated multiple cubic feet of documentation regarding return-passage requests and responses. But the HSPA endured such drains on their labor force and monetary coffers to develop and maintain this valuable and rare willing and legal source of workers. The sugar industry did not provide this benefit or create such an extensive bureaucratic and administrative machine for any other labor group in Hawai'i.

Family Reunions

While free return passage motivated many Filipinos to temporarily move to Hawai'i, the HSPA also created programs to keep these U.S. colonial workers in the islands. One way the sugar industry tried to retain Filipino laborers involved the payment of transport for workers' wives and children to join them in Hawai'i. While the first groups of Filipino migrants did not want to bring their families to the islands, by the 1920s some laborers had saved enough money to live comfortably in the Philippines. To avoid losing good workers who wanted to rejoin their loved ones in the archipelago, the HSPA created a family reunification program centered on the Recruit Transport Application (RTA). If a loyal laborer agreed to sign another three-year work agreement, the HSPA paid for his family to come to Hawai'i. As long as Filipinos renewed their temporary labor relationship with an HSPA plantation, trusted workers could send for their wives and children whenever they wanted. Filipino U.S. colonials were the only migrant group in Hawai'i to have a formalized process to bring their wives and children to the islands. Their position as legally mobile and willing workers resulted in such a unique benefit.

Later Filipino migration to Hawai'i often involved calculated, measured, and rational decision making, especially when family reunification was involved. Filipinos who used the RTA system likely believed the islands offered better opportunities for their whole family than life in the Philippines. From 1928 to 1934, fifty-two Filipino male laborers at the Ola'a plantation took advantage of the HSPA's willingness to pay for the transport of their wives and children to the islands.[54] Even though these applications represented only about 2 percent of the entire Filipino population at this plantation, the RTA program still allowed Filipino laborers to make their own decisions about intra-colonial mobility and the reuniting of their families.

But the RTA program did not provide ideal benefits. The HSPA would only pay for up to two offspring to join their father, claiming the cost of transporting more children to be too expensive for the HSPA. In December 1923, HSPA assistant secretary H. A. Walker stated, "We do not bring to Hawaii the families of men who have more than two children. If a man is a very good worker, we have at times brought his family when it consists of a wife and not more than two children. This is our policy when we recruit in the Philippines of bringing not more than two children, and therefore we do not care to increase the size of the family which makes the cost too great."[55] Such restrictions outlined HSPA and Anglo-American standards of the ideal nuclear family. This requirement clashed with the tendency of Filipino families to be large and showed one indirect way HSPA policies coincided with U.S. imperial desires to mold U.S. colonials according to U.S. social standards.[56] Transporting limitless numbers of kids could have become a huge financial burden for the HSPA. If Filipinos applied for RTAs in even just a fraction of the numbers as they did for return passage, the sugar industry would have spent a significant amount of their profits to pay for this benefit. Instead, the HSPA only supported intra-colonial family mobility to a certain extent.

Such limitations on the number of minors who received free transport to Hawai'i likely deterred many Filipino intra-colonial laborers from using this program. If they did not want to uproot their loved ones and expose their families to harsh conditions in Hawai'i in the years after 1906, they likely would also not be willing to desert some of their children in the Philippines. The set number of children allowed through the reunification program might also explain the refusal of some wives to use RTA funds to join their husbands in Hawai'i. In 1928, for example, Epifanio Gaba's wife refused to go to Hawai'i.[57] While there are no available details about why Mrs. Gaba did not want to join her husband, women in the Philippines might have chosen to continue their long-distance marriages, which usually included regular monetary remittances, than reunite with their husbands and leave some of their kids parentless in the Philippines. C. C. Cortezan, a Filipino minister for the Hawaiian Evangelical Association, reported on worker conditions in Hawai'i in 1930. When he spoke with wives still in the Philippines, he found that these women "were holding the land and taking care of the pig and the chickens and the rice field, and they expected their husbands to return, because they had only expected to stay three years . . . money had been sent home by those who had been away long enough to save anything."[58] The continued belief that workers would return, as well as domestic obligations, encouraged some women to stay in the Philippines separate from their husbands in the islands.

Filipinos tried to maneuver around RTA restrictions. Bernabella Abril stated, "Because only two [children] were allowed to accompany a couple, my sister was paired with my uncle because she wanted also to come to Hawaii . . . my other two siblings were left with my aunt because the agent did not allow all the children to accompany their parents . . . we did not pay our fare and we can go back to the Philippines free after completing the three-years contract."[59] While Abril and another sibling came to Hawai'i through their parents' two-child quota, Abril's sister traveled as the fake daughter or wife of their uncle.[60] The rest of her siblings had to remain in the Philippines.

Despite efforts to adjust the RTA system to their own needs, the families of Filipino sugar plantation workers could become disjointed by the RTA limit of paid transport for only two children.[61] Since the RTA program offered family mobility in only a limited sense, few Filipinos chose to participate in this process. Even though Filipinos used RTAs less often than other HSPA strategies, this program still demonstrated the unique administration, assistance, and choice this group experienced due to their status as U.S. colonials.

Come One, Come All

In addition to the RTA program, Filipino U.S. colonial laborers in Hawai'i had the ability to bring male relatives or friends to the islands, as long as the new migrants were willing to work on sugar plantations. When the HSPA stopped paying for Filipino transport to Hawai'i in 1927, the sugar industry simultaneously created a Paid Transport Application (PTA). The PTA program allowed Filipino laborers to pay for the transport of a prospective laborer from the Philippines to the islands. This policy ended up benefiting both the HSPA and Filipino U.S. colonials. The sugar industry received a continued flow of laborers for cane cultivation without paying for their transport. Filipino intra-colonials were able to augment their social communities in the islands and provide economic opportunities for their family and friends.

To take advantage of the PTA program, Filipino workers in Hawai'i simply had to submit the money and names of individuals whose passage they wanted to pay for to their plantation manager, and then the HSPA took care of the rest of the process. Once notified by local sugar managers, bureaucrats at HSPA headquarters in Honolulu transmitted the names and locations of identified recruits to their regional offices in the Philippines. Agents in the archipelago searched for and informed the funded individuals of the opportunity to leave. HSPA officials also helped potential laborers through each step of the process to migrate to Hawai'i successfully. The HSPA handled the paperwork, managed the bank deposits, contacted the possible recruits, as well as scheduled and arranged the transports to Hawai'i. As long as current workers were willing to provide the money, the sugar industry was willing to invest the time and effort needed to actualize the migration of more Filipino male laborers to the islands.

During the first fourteen months of the PTA program, the HSPA received and accepted 346 applications.[62] According to one HSPA memo, Ola'a became one of the three most successful plantations utilizing the PTA program. J. K. Butler explained, "Some plantations are conspicuously represented in the numbers of their laborers who deposit money in this fashion to bring their relatives or friends. Ewa, Honokaa, Hawaiian Commercial and Olaa."[63] From 1927 to 1928, thirty-five workers from Ola'a wrote family and friends back home to join them in Hawai'i. All of these laborers provided money to pay for the transport of their brothers, uncles, brothers-in-law, and cousins.

The PTA program became a method for Filipino workers already in Hawai'i to strengthen family connections and develop social networks in the islands through translocal chain migration. Extensive HSPA recruitment programs meant that Filipino migrants did not need community connections to obtain work or housing, as was the case in other global migrant situations. However, these intra-colonials were strongly motivated to move to the islands through the encouragement of loved ones already in Hawai'i. According to historian Yukari Takai, "[The] family was both a unit of migration and a source of information about U.S. destinations for immigrants."[64] In addition to letters from earlier migrants and stories from those who returned, the PTA program provided later recruits with the financial funds and social network support to persuade them that work in Hawai'i was a safe and profitable venture. Newer migrants consequently wanted to work on the same plantations as their experienced family and friends.

The PTA process often resulted in ever-widening circles of affiliation and kinship. For example, many members of the Dagdag family arrived through the PTA program in 1929. That year, Leon and Bernandino Dagdag received money to go to Ola'a while Victoriano Dagdag gave PTA money to Gaspar Dagdag and Munico Cabalo. Melecio Guzman also paid for Silvestre Dagdag's passage that same year.[65] The Dagdag clan used the PTA program to become a large and well-established family and social network at the Ola'a plantation.

Many new recruits also sent PTA funds within a year of their own arrival. In early 1928, Juan Dagdag paid for Federico de Fiesta to come to the Ola'a plantation. By mid-1929, de Fiesta could afford to send money for Severino de Fiesta to come to Hawai'i. The continuous use of the PTA program by the Dagdag clan clearly demonstrates how "newcomers who relied on chain migration networks to make their transition a smooth one later returned the favor by aiding both recent . . . migrants and established residents."[66] One-way passage from the Philippines to Hawai'i cost about sixty-six dollars. If workers made at least twenty dollars a month for twenty-six days' work and spent their money carefully or shared daily expenses with other family members or friends, they could send money for another loved one to join them relatively quickly.

Like positive letters home, the PTA process helped Filipinos in Hawai'i develop translocal chain migration networks between specific Philippine clans and villages in the Ilocos and Visayan regions and certain plantation sites in Hawai'i. Many laborers at the Ola'a plantation, like the Dagdag family, came from the same town in Ilocos Sur. As scholar Dorothy Fujita-Rony has found, recruitment by friends and relatives gave individuals confidence to leave home and eased the minds of those remaining in the Philippines.[67] Not occurring at a nation-state or even regional level, the PTA program was a highly translocal process, directly connecting one exact rural location in the Philippines to one particular sugar camp in Hawai'i.

The PTA process succeeded due to the active participation of both those in the islands and those in the archipelago. Filipinos in the Pacific willingly provided their own money for the PTA program to expand their personal and social network in the islands. The constant and intense recruitment of family and friends, as seen with the Dagdag clan, demonstrated the strong desire of Filipinos already in the islands to have more compatriots surrounding them who could keep them company and also benefit from stable wage labor in Hawai'i. Those in the Philippines who took advantage of the PTA program followed the encouragement of their loved ones already in the islands. They expected earlier migrants to look after them. Newer migrants likely also wanted to make money and be as successful as their family and friends already in Hawai'i.

Both chain migration and family reunification relied on and benefited from the pioneering experiences of earlier migrants. While early Filipino intra-colonials exercised a degree of faith and risk in the unknown economic and social situation in the islands, subsequent migrants could rely on established workers to teach them how best to survive daily plantation life, provide them with a close-knit social and cultural community, and, after 1927, pay for their transport to the islands. Such a supportive environment made the difficulties of life in Hawai'i more bearable. Filipinos moved intra-colonially not only because of their political-legal status and labor industry inducements but also due to their trusted social networks and the development of translocal chain migration.

Pick Your Place

Filipinos, like other laborers, frequently moved among Hawai'i sugar plantations. Butler explained how "large numbers desert the plantations and go to other employment or in fact even leave the territory after earning enough money to follow their own inclinations."[68] Instead of blacklisting mobile Filipino workers, which failed to stop the movement of Puerto Rican laborers at the turn of the century, the HSPA allowed Filipino U.S. colonials to request transfers to other locations. In November 1928, the Filipino labor agreement included the ability to transfer to other plantations after one year of service. The HSPA hoped the formalization of a transfer process would reduce the constant movement of these intra-colonial workers around plantations. The central sugar office also started asking new recruits which plantations their relatives worked at so they could immediately assign laborers to the locations they might naturally gravitate toward. Keeping legally mobile and willing Filipino laborers in general cane cultivation was more important to the HSPA than forcing workers to remain on randomly assigned plantations.

Once again, tensions between central sugar industry officials and local plantation managers surfaced. Seven months after the implementation of this new policy, some local plantation leaders still did not support the transfer system. Local managers did not want to lose workers and preferred to avoid the entire situation by ignoring requests to move. On June 17, 1929, Butler sent a memo to encourage all plantation heads to embrace the new policy. The letter discussed how Filipinos would likely move even without approval. The sugar industry believed "the provision for transfer is a control measure rather than a prohibition one and it is most likely that the general stability of work on plantations will be finally better by reasonable and tolerant attitude."[69] While the transfer policy might seem inconvenient to plantation managers in the short term, once Filipinos were placed with family and friends, they would likely work at that location as long-term, stable labor. HSPA headquarters advised local sugar managers to have a more positive attitude about this program.

The central office's prioritization of keeping the Filipino labor supply within the sugar industry over the stability of these workers at one particular location overruled local managers' desires for laborers to stay at their specific plantations. While ground-level leaders exercised significant influence over re-hiring decisions, as in the case of Candido Mariano, the HSPA main headquarters had more control over the general movement of workers in the islands. After the creation of the transfer request process, a plantation manager's personal connection with a specific laborer did not guarantee that the Filipino would be expected to or would want to stay at his particular site.

HSPA leadership in Honolulu understood that they could not force U.S. colonials to stay and work at one location. But bureaucrats wanted to manage their movement by institutionalizing a transfer policy. If the sugar industry could get Filipinos to file the correct paperwork, the HSPA could track and monitor the movement of each labor recruit. While the implementation of this program was not embraced by every local plantation manager, the attempt to systematize Filipino movement among plantations ultimately allowed these U.S. colonial workers to express, acknowledge, and act upon their internal mobility preferences with the approval of the central sugar industry.

Filipino U.S. colonials became so accustomed to mobility flexibility that 18,689 individuals, or almost 15 percent of Filipinos who migrated to Hawai'i, moved on to the continental United States between 1906 and 1946. They often migrated to the West Coast to work in other agricultural industries. According to scholar Rick Baldoz, Alaskan canneries tried to recruit Filipino sugar plantation workers away from Hawai'i to this other U.S. territory after 1910. In the 1920s, Baldoz notes, "the majority (56%) of Filipino arrivals during the 1920s migrated from Hawaii to the West Coast. The exodus from Hawaii to the U.S. mainland was the product of both economic and political factors."[70] Both harsh plantation conditions and the blackballing of workers who went on strike during that period motivated Filipinos to leave the islands. Baldoz also explains how "the number of arrivals in the Golden State [California] swelled from an average of 618 per year from 1920 to 5,408 per year from 1926 to 1929. The majority of these newcomers (82.3%) arrived at the port of San Francisco, with the other 17.7% entering through Los Angeles. Seattle was another key port of entry because of its proximity to the Alaskan canneries."[71] Despite the numerous flexible and accommodating HSPA recruitment and retention programs that Filipinos had at their disposal, these intra-colonials, like Puerto Ricans, could not be forced to stay in Hawai'i long term. If they believed there were better prospects at another location, or if they were convinced to relocate by other industries or loved ones, Filipinos willingly used their open colonial mobility to move to other areas of U.S. jurisdiction.

Conclusion

Local plantations could have faced grave labor shortages without Filipino intra-colonial workers. The HSPA consequently had to be innovative with Filipino recruitment and retention programs. When Filipinos became aliens subject to immigration quotas after the Philippines became a U.S. Commonwealth in 1935, the Tydings-McDuffie Act, which outlined the region's independence process, included a legal loophole for Filipinos to continue to enter the Territory of Hawai'i. Section 8A1 of the Philippine Independence Act allowed the Department of Interior to grant Filipino laborers entry to Hawai'i "on the basis of the needs of industries in the Territory of Hawaii."[72] Business and government leaders in Hawai'i vigorously lobbied the U.S. Congress for this provision that created an exception to the new limit of fifty Filipinos entering the entire U.S. empire per year. These men argued that despite negative attitudes and events toward these U.S. colonials in the continental United States, Filipinos played a crucial role in the daily function and survival of the economy in Hawai'i.[73] The barrage of telegrams from high-level Hawai'i leaders resulted in a congressional guarantee for the continued mobility of Filipinos to the islands, despite changes to their political-legal status within United States jurisdiction.

Unique programs created specifically for Filipinos gave this group of workers a range of mobility choices that Puerto Rican intra-colonials did not have, such as predominantly male migration, free return passage, and family-and-friends reunification programs. Filipinos also took full advantage of existing hiring strategies for all labor groups, like letter-writing campaigns, recruitment agents in their home regions, and letters of recommendation. Ultimately, HSPA recruitment and retention policies acknowledged and accommodated Filipino desires for choice in migration. Filipinos came to the islands because they believed such mobile livelihoods or intra-colonial movement was in their best interests. Filipino employment in the islands was consequently more successful than recruitment from any other region in the world.

However, only obedient workers could take full advantage of the HSPA recruitment and retention policies. If an individual went on strike or protested poor conditions, he would not be able to participate in these programs. Just like industrial welfare policies created during the Progressive Era in the continental United States, employer-funded benefits came with the expectation to work hard and remain dedicated regardless of work conditions. Any minor infraction or act of noncompliance could result in the removal of benefits. These policies became a subtle way for companies to exercise control over the behavior of their workers.[74] Filipinos had to follow HSPA expectations and guidelines closely to gain access to recruitment and retention programs. Plantation work still remained difficult and wages stayed low. The next two chapters will discuss how many Filipinos and Puerto Ricans in the islands filed complaints and engaged in different forms of labor protest.

3. *Indefinite Dependence*

U.S. CONTROL OVER PUERTO RICAN
LABOR COMPLAINTS

In 1919, after eighteen years of difficult sugar plantation field work, Pedro Guzman signed a labor complaint with twenty-five other Puerto Ricans at the Honoka'a plantation about twenty-eight miles up the coast from Hakalau on the island of Hawai'i. During this era of growing immigration restrictions, the HSPA had an increased need for laborers and refocused their recruitment efforts on Puerto Rico. To prevent other Puerto Ricans from experiencing the same negative social and economic circumstances they faced as permanent settlers, these intra-colonial complainants protested in English: "Porto Ricans live in the worst houses . . . we live like goats in a corral . . . all the other races have better houses, and their conditions are better than ours."[1] In addition to their protest over inhumane living conditions, Guzman and the others detailed dreadful working conditions. They worked six days a week, ten hours a day, with half an hour for lunch, for about twenty-two dollars a month, or ninety-two cents a day. The Honoka'a complainants did not realize that the recipient of their grievance, Puerto Rican senator Mariano Abril, was just the first person in a formal and complex chain of bureaucrats who would handle their petition.

Unlike other labor groups in Hawai'i, including Filipino U.S. colonials after 1923, Puerto Rican intra-colonials did not have local government representatives. This leadership vacuum had both negative and positive effects on this group. When Puerto Ricans had complaints about life in the islands, they had to submit their grievances to a slow, cumbersome, and apathetic bureaucratic communication hierarchy that spanned their home region, Washington, D.C., and the Territory of Hawai'i. Without a designated official in the region empowered to look after their affairs, Puerto Rican intra-colonials saw their issues take many months to be discussed and often received pro-plantation investigative results that discredited and dismissed their complaints. In contrast, other labor groups had government officials specifically assigned to deal with their concerns quickly and locally. The absence of a regional representative in Hawai'i meant the needs of Puerto Rican intra-colonials were often ignored or disregarded.

However, the lack of an official leader in the islands also gave Puerto Rican migrants a degree of independence in their daily lives. Without a government representative in the area to oversee them, these intra-colonials often chose to move among plantations, out of the sugar industry, and eventually on to the continental United States as methods to cope with the harsh economic and social conditions they faced in the islands. Through open colonial mobility within U.S. jurisdiction, Puerto Ricans did not have to stay on plantations or remain in Hawai'i. Many ignored HSPA directives to make them stable and long-term workers at one specific plantation. Without the same supervision or advocacy from local leaders as other labor groups, Puerto Ricans could both benefit and suffer from the absence of regional government representation.

Puerto Ricans never gained access to a dedicated official in the islands due to their status as impermanent wards of the United States. Historically, the U.S. government always maintained a degree of supervision over Puerto Ricans and their home region. While Puerto Rico was a valuable gateway for U.S. trade and influence in the Caribbean and Latin America, Congress was unsure if this set of Caribbean islands should become a full-fledged member of the union. The federal government wanted to take advantage of Puerto Rico's strategic location and useful resources without committing to the region's inclusion into the nation-state.

A hierarchical and bureaucratic communications process became one way the U.S. government perpetuated the subjugation of this group to U.S. control. All Puerto Rican issues, including those of intra-colonials in the Pacific, had to be funneled through the Bureau of Insular Affairs. Under the supervision of this federal agency in Washington, D.C., Puerto Ricans were limited, managed, and regulated by this referral process. The Puerto Rican Honoka'a complaint consequently had to travel from Hawai'i to the Caribbean to Washington, D.C., then back to the Territory of Hawai'i government and the HSPA. This first leg of the process usually spanned about four months. After the HSPA received the grievance and developed a response,

Indefinite Dependence 77

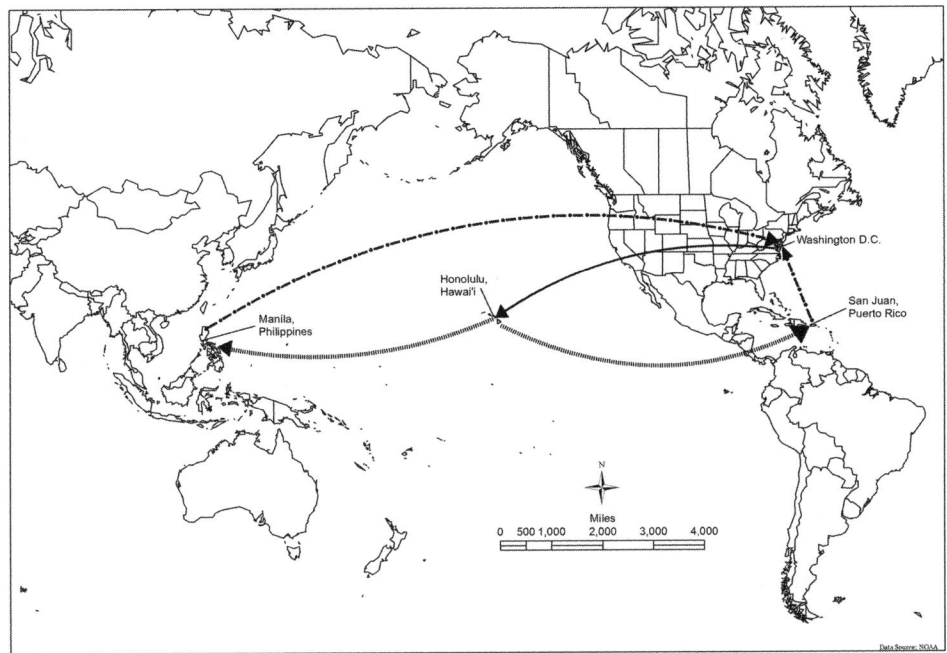

Map of U.S. colonial communications circuits

their answer was sent back through the same channels in reverse. This circuitous global complaint procedure enforced Puerto Rican dependence on the United States administration for the resolution of both common and major issues. Even after becoming U.S. citizens in 1917, resistance and ignorance to this change in status led this group nevertheless to contact Puerto Rico for assistance for several years. Such a unique migrant-labor communication process stemmed from Puerto Ricans' in-between political-legal status as intra-colonials with no strong local community leadership in Hawai'i.

This chapter also discusses some of the social situations Puerto Ricans faced after recruitment and settlement in the Pacific. The lack of an official local representative to advocate for their affairs made these intra-colonials more vulnerable to territorial government and sugar industry abuses than other labor groups. Puerto Ricans faced much discrimination, mistreatment, and harassment in the islands. While their concerns were often overlooked or mishandled, these U.S. colonials did not passively accept this poor economic and social environment. They filed complaints, fought for their rights as citizens after 1917, and used their legal mobility as U.S. colonials to create a better life for themselves and their loved ones. Despite difficult living and working circumstances, Puerto Rican U.S. colonials were able to shape and control some aspects of their daily experiences in Hawai'i.

Conditions Facing Puerto Rican Settlers in Hawai'i

As discussed in chapter 1, more than five thousand Puerto Ricans, including a young Pedro Guzman, decided to leave desperate circumstances at home to pursue work opportunities in Hawai'i at the turn of the twentieth century. These individuals had high hopes for their intra-colonial move to the islands. But working and living conditions in the Pacific did not meet Puerto Rican expectations. Several intra-colonials submitted petitions and complaints about conditions in Hawai'i to loved ones, newspapers, and government officials in their home region in the first years of settlement, resulting in the failed recruitment of this U.S. colonial group to the Pacific Islands.

Migrants already in Hawai'i had to stay in the region due to the lack of funding for return transport. These permanent settlers and their descendants had difficulty gaining social acceptance in the islands throughout the twentieth century. Tanilau Dias, born in 1908 in Hilo, Hawai'i, explained how during World War II he worked on radios and transmitters for the military. One day a Chinese military clerk told him, "Puerto Ricans, as far as technician and educational class, we dumb. You not Puerto Rican. I tell him, I'm Puerto Rican. He tell me, You're not supposed to be doing what you're doing; Puerto Ricans are stupid."[2] The view of Puerto Ricans in Hawai'i as incompetent and uneducated pervaded multiple social groups and industries in the islands.

Other adverse conceptions existed about this group in Hawai'i. Ramona Ramos, born on O'ahu in 1902, remembered being called a "Puerto Rican black nigger" in school.[3] She wanted to hit the kid who insulted her but instead reported the incident to her teacher. George Flores, born on Maui in 1925, discussed how his first wife's family held negative stereotypes about Puerto Ricans. They thought Puerto Ricans were "low class people . . . cause they had no one in office, no one holding good jobs and what not."[4] Even though these individuals were U.S.-born citizens, deleterious perceptions about their ethnic background prevailed over their status as members of the United States. Such hostile experiences dominated their memories of social interactions in the islands.

The constant othering of Puerto Ricans in the islands was also exemplified by the fight for voting rights. The Jones Act, passed on March 2, 1917, made Puerto Ricans U.S. citizens. Puerto Ricans in Hawai'i, like Daniel Maldonado, worked hard to get their ethnic group to register to vote.[5] Manuel Olivieri Sanchez was another Puerto Rican activist who went to the Honolulu city hall on April 11, 1917, to register to vote. City Clerk David Kalauokalani refused to accept Sanchez's voter registration form. This Native Hawaiian administrator did not believe Puerto Ricans new status as U.S. citizens applied to migrants in the Territory of Hawai'i. Kalauokalani did not think Sanchez was "a citizen of the United States and therefore not entitled to register as a voter."[6] Even though there was no local Puerto Rican official to assist him in this matter, Sanchez refused to accept the clerk's decision. He hired lawyers to help him file a writ of mandamus, or court order, to force Kalauokalani to process his voter registration request. Serving as a Puerto Rican interpreter for both the HSPA Bureau of Labor and Statistics and the Territory of Hawai'i court, Sanchez knew how the legal system worked in the islands.[7] As a well-informed, newly minted U.S. citizen, he willingly fought for his basic constitutional right to vote.

On May 2, 1917, the Territory of Hawai'i Circuit Court "denied the peremptory writ of mandamus demanded, dismissed the alternative writ and discharged the respondent with costs."[8] Despite the prosecution's argument that Puerto Ricans in Hawai'i became U.S. citizens through the Jones Act, the local court agreed with Kalauokalani that upon migration to Hawai'i, Puerto Ricans lost their affiliation with their home region. These settlers in Hawai'i could not become U.S. citizens because they were not Puerto Rican.[9]

Sanchez appealed this ruling and his case went to the Territory of Hawai'i Supreme Court. In a quick and unanimous decision, the highest court in Honolulu confirmed Puerto Ricans' status as U.S. citizens and their right to vote in the islands. On October 22, 1917, just five days after hearing case arguments, Justice J. Quarles stated that through "the act of Congress of March 2, 1917, the petitioner became a full-fledged citizen of the United States . . . and as he has resided in the Territory of Hawaii and in the city and county of Honolulu for more than one year prior to his application to be registered he was entitled to have his name enrolled upon the great register of the city and county of Honolulu as a voter, and that it was and is the duty of the respondent to so enroll and register the petitioner."[10] Puerto Ricans who came to Hawai'i after the Treaty of Paris of 1898, who did not declare Spanish citizenship, and who continuously claimed to be a subject of the United States were U.S. citizens. As long as a Puerto Rican resided in a particular city and county in Hawai'i for more than one year, he or she had the right to register to vote in the islands.

Justice Quarles also denied Kalauokalani's request to dismiss the case based on the fact that the election Sanchez wanted to participate in had passed, making the issue obsolete. Quarles stated that the court "cannot accept this view. The election laws of Hawaii provide for permanent registration and the application of the petitioner was for such registration and his right to the remedy herein sought is a continuing one and did not expire with the holding of the primary election mentioned."[11] While Sanchez succeeded in obtaining his basic right as a new citizen to register to vote, the city clerk's attempt to terminate the entire case because that year's election was finished demonstrated the strong and continued resistance among leaders in Hawai'i to treating Puerto Ricans as full-fledged members of the United States.

Despite the territorial supreme court's ruling in *Sanchez*, Puerto Ricans continued to be mistreated in the islands.[12] Raymond Pagan explained how his mother-in-law tried to get "some kind of government aide and they [the government] claimed that she wasn't a citizen. So then we started to make a lot of phone calls, calling immigration and the governor's office. And we stirred up quite a bit of controversy on that. But I know for a fact that we became citizens in 1917 . . . a lot of people that are working for the federal government, our state government, do not have the knowledge that the people in Puerto Rico are actually American citizens."[13] Much misinformation and miscategorization persisted over Puerto Ricans' legal status throughout the twentieth century. Some Puerto Ricans in Hawai'i were also not aware of their own status as U.S. citizens. When interviewed in 1978, Hawai'i-born Puerto Rican John Santana did not know Puerto Ricans received citizenship in 1917.[14] Without a local government representative willing to publicize their rights, ignorance over the political-legal status of Puerto Ricans remained prevalent in the islands.

When local attorney Antonio G. Correa, who served as one of the legal counsels for the Sanchez case, was being considered for the position of deputy county attorney in 1919, Republican senator Stephen L. Desha Sr. discouraged his appointment, stating, "Correa filled the 'Great Register of Electors' with names of people not able to vote, as they are Porto Ricans."[15] Regardless of confirmed U.S. citizenship through the Sanchez case, anti–Puerto Rican officials in the islands still did not believe these U.S. colonials could or should have the right to vote. Such a perspective was a clear statement that these U.S. wards and their allies did not deserve the same access to constitutional provisions and fair treatment as other members of the United States.

Such negative attitudes toward Puerto Ricans in Hawai'i continued through the twentieth century. In the 1930s, some members of the American Legion wanted half-Puerto Rican, half-Portuguese Alfred Santiago to join their organization. When he went to the office to apply, the clerk said his name did not appear on the list of approved members. A Legion member pulled him aside; he remembered the conversation later: "[The member said,] 'You know why they don't want . . . [to] put you in the American Legion? Because your name is Santiago. But if you change your name to Ferreira,' he say, 'you can join.' I said, 'No way.' I said, 'My name is Santiago and I die with that name.'"[16] The organization would not allow Santiago to become a member due to his Puerto Rican last name. Other Puerto Ricans were able to join because they did not appear to be overtly Puerto Rican. Santiago refused to deny his last name or Puerto Rican heritage. He would not submit to such de-racialization.

Another negative social experience for Puerto Rican intra-colonials involved their levels of arrest and incarceration in Hawai'i. These U.S. colonials were disproportionately accused and jailed for crimes in the islands compared with other ethnic groups. According to scholar Norma Carr, "The highest rate of Puerto Ricans [arrested] was on the island of Kauai where they had already been labeled troublemakers—14% were Puerto Ricans (171 of 1,209)."[17] This stereotype of Puerto Ricans as criminal continued through 1960.[18] The presence of a local official willing to investigate and address these circumstances could have helped to develop a more positive social environment for Puerto Ricans in Hawai'i. Without such a leader, Puerto Ricans in Hawai'i were frequently susceptible to political and social abuses in the Pacific. Such overall poor social circumstances provided the context from which Pedro Guzman and twenty-five other Puerto Ricans filed their complaint in 1919.

Pedro Guzman's Complaint

When Pedro Guzman and twenty-five other intra-colonial workers in Hawai'i wrote their complaint petition, they claimed, "[In] Hawaii, we Porto Ricans are abused and despised more than any race."[19] These workers were fed up with substandard treatment and conditions. They hated backbreaking field labor for pittance wages which barely paid for basic family necessities. They did not trust their unsympathetic field supervisors. They also felt uncomfortable approaching plantation police with their grievances. In addition to the hardships of plantation life, these workers lamented the negative stereotyping and consistently inferior social treatment of Puerto Ricans in Hawai'i.

Despite gaining theoretical citizenship in 1917, Puerto Ricans did not have a local government representative in the islands who was willing to advocate for their issues. Instead, Guzman and his fellow laborers looked to Senator Abril to champion their grievance and use his position as a Puerto Rican government official to take action. They also knew about Abril's Spanish-language anti-migration articles printed in the Puerto Rican newspaper *La Democracia*.[20] On March 5, 1919, these workers sent their complaint to this ethnic leader. Guzman and the others hoped once those in Puerto Rico learned about their continued horrible conditions in the Pacific, they would support their cause, reprimand the HSPA, and rectify the situation. Similar to turn-of-the-century Puerto Rican protesters from Hawai'i detailed in chapter 1, Guzman and the other complainants wanted to prevent future recruitment from Puerto Rico. They also wanted funds to pay for their return transportation home. The protesters stated, "We wish and beg to be repatriated at once. We wish to advise our brothers in Porto Rico not to emigrate to Hawaii, for a Porto Rican in Hawaii is of less importance than a criminal in Porto Rico."[21] The complaint provided many details as to why life for Puerto Ricans in the islands was so poor, and the protesters believed any inquiries into their situation would support their claims.

The investigation of this grievance failed to meet such expectations. Since Puerto Rican leaders were subject to the oversight of Anglo American officials in Washington, D.C., any issues these Caribbean officials wanted addressed had to be shuttled through their superiors in the nation's capital. Guzman's petition, as well as all other Puerto Rican intra-colonial grievances, had to travel through cumbersome, long-distance bureaucratic hierarchies in three different regions of U.S. jurisdiction: Puerto Rico, Washington, D.C., and the Territory of Hawai'i. Communications about this particular case took a total of seven and a half months.

After Senator Abril received Guzman and the others' complaint, he brought their concerns to the Puerto Rican legislature. Both the Puerto Rican Senate and House passed resolutions that requested investigations of conditions in Hawai'i.[22] The declarations claimed, "[Puerto Rican] laborers are victims of unjust treatment, contrary to the American laws."[23] These Caribbean leaders, however, were not able to handle intra-colonial issues on their own. Local politicians could demand the creation of inquiries, but the real power to launch inspections lay with the Bureau of Insular Affairs.

Without the ability to require or enforce any concrete actions, leaders in Puerto Rico remained indefinitely dependent on BIA officials to resolve their common and major political, economic, and social concerns. Since this federal agency oversaw all matters related to Puerto Rican affairs, the most Puerto Rican legislators could do for the Guzman and other cases was forward resolutions to the Puerto Rican resident commissioner in Washington, D.C., Felix Cordova Davila. Davila then sent declarations to BIA chief Charles C. Walcutt Jr., who contacted Secretary of War Newton D. Baker. Baker's assistant, John W. Hallowell, forwarded the appeals to Secretary of Interior Franklin Knight Lane. Assistant Secretary of the Interior S. G. Hopkins then contacted C. J. McCarthy, the territorial governor of Hawai'i. For the Honoka'a case, Governor McCarthy contacted Hawai'i's attorney general's office to request an investigation. Attorney General Harry Irwin then contacted the HSPA about the grievance. Labor Bureau Director Royal D.

Mead of the HSPA contacted the Pacific Sugar Mill in Kukuihaele, Hawai'i. On July 11, 1919, more than four months after Guzman and the others wrote their letter, the complaint finally reached the plantation manager in question, W. P. Naquin. After two and a half months of investigations, the attorney general's report about this complaint was shuttled back through the cross-regional, colonial hierarchies of communication, taking another month and a half to travel across the U.S. empire. This convoluted and large-scale complaint process ultimately did not help Guzman and his fellow workers. Instead, such an elaborate complaint-resolution system sustained overall Puerto Rican dependence on the United States government to solve their daily problems.

This chain of bureaucratic command, mandated by federal officials, allowed D.C. leaders to maintain close supervision and control over these wards of the United States. When Anglo-Americans established civil rule in Puerto Rico, they sent numerous memos and messages explaining, reminding, and demanding that Puerto Ricans follow the correct, designated hierarchy of colonial communication. According to a 1909 Puerto Rican government administrative bulletin, "All official communications from departments, offices, officers, and employees of the Government of Porto Rico, to any official, bureau or department in the United States, or to any person, firm or corporation outside the territory under the jurisdiction of this government, shall be sent through the office of the Governor of Porto Rico for transmittal to their destination through the Bureau of Insular Affairs of the War Department."[24] No one in the Puerto Rican government could engage in any correspondence with anyone in the U.S. government until the BIA approved the message and the recipients. Puerto Rican U.S. colonials were not expected or trusted to handle their own issues. This strictly regulated communications path supported the colonial administration's desire to keep Puerto Rico and Puerto Ricans reliant on the United States for the governance of their political, social, and economic policies.

While this process involved extensive oversight, such procedures also provided a way for Puerto Ricans to submit complaints to high-level federal agencies in the capital. Foreign laborers did not have access to the same kind of a high-level resolution for their grievances. Instead, they had consul generals living and working in Hawai'i. During the first half of the twentieth century, there were always at least sixteen foreign governments with consular offices in Honolulu.[25] These representatives had the authority to contact and negotiate with territory officials and the HSPA, independent from their home government and continental U.S. leaders. A Spanish, Portuguese, or Japanese worker could contact his or her assigned mediator in Honolulu, who would then notify either the territorial government or interact directly with the sugar industry to address the concerns. These grievances remained local and regional leaders could deal with issues quickly, sometimes within a week of development.

In 1915, a Spanish laborer named Jose Marques Gonzalez wrote a letter of complaint to Luis Gil, consul for Spain residing in Honolulu.[26] He claimed that the Ola'a manager laid him off for being sick and refused to pay him his bonus. The same day he received the grievance, Gil wrote to C. F. Eckart, the plantation manager in question. Eckart responded three days later, stating that the plantation "sent him to Honolulu to consult with the best specialist in that city, all his expenses including that incurred medically being defrayed by this Company."[27] The doctor found that Gonzalez's eyes were weakened by smoking, not by any work-related activity. When the laborer returned to Ola'a, Eckart stated that Gonzalez refused to resume work and started to cause trouble in the area. Even if Gonzalez had returned to work, the bonus payout would not occur until the following month. Irrespective of the verity of the plantation manager's statement, foreign affairs were rapidly dealt with among leaders in Hawai'i without much communication with national government officials. Instead, consul generals worked closely with the HSPA and the Territory of Hawai'i administration to deal with these problems swiftly and quietly in the islands.

While foreign-worker concerns were often handled within a week or two, their grievances rarely came to the attention of leaders in Washington, D.C. Foreign laborers usually did not get high-level or large-scale investigations into their conditions as U.S. colonials did. Such an absence of federal government involvement could have resulted in regional leaders' collaborating with each other, as opposed to working in the interests of their constituents. For the most part, communications were businesslike and cordial.[28] Regardless of the personal motivations or tendencies of consul generals, these foreign officials would likely not fully submit to U.S. interests over those of their own sovereign people and government. Their ground-level presence was a form of leadership that Puerto Rican intra-colonials in Hawai'i were never able to access.

Generally accepted U.S. citizens in the islands, such as Anglo-Americans and Native Hawaiians, also had multiple sources of support for their labor issues. They had elected representatives, complete judicial rights, and full constitutional protections to guard and defend their interests at local, regional, and federal levels.[29] Anglo citizens were the most protected group of those working on the plantations. They received priority in hiring, as well as the highest salaries and positions of power in and out of the plantation system. However, this group did not participate in HSPA cultivation in significant numbers. Of the 2,247 skilled men on plantations in 1922, only 369 were classified as American.³⁰ Of the 40,213 unskilled laborers, only 43 were American. Most Anglo U.S. citizens in sugar production worked in mid- to high-level management. They were typically the subject of complaints, not the filers of grievances.

While all forms of conflict resolution rarely changed HSPA work conditions, Puerto Rican intra-colonials faced a more tedious and time-consuming complaint process than foreigners and other citizens in Hawai'i. Anglo-American administrators in the Bureau of Insular Affairs and Department of Interior also had little vested interest in Puerto Rican matters and did not become advocates for intra-colonial laborers in Hawai'i. These officials seldom followed up on issues with genuine concern, and they generally did not care about protracted delays to responses. They also rarely conducted their own investigations. Mid-level D.C. bureaucrats usually just complied with their administrative obligation to funnel colonial grievances through the complex and slow-moving communication system. Basic endorsements such as "inclose herewith for such action as may seem appropriate" often represented the extent of involvement that U.S. officials had with Puerto Rican affairs.³¹ Some complaints could travel through five different government agencies with all of their input fitting on one $8\frac{1}{2}$" × 11" piece of paper. These civil servants fundamentally had no intention or motivation to modify government policies or business practices. They followed up on grievances only when the complainants continually contacted them.

On April 9, 1902, the secretary of Puerto Rico wrote to the Department of Interior about Puerto Rican complaints regarding treatment in Hawai'i. The Department of Interior asked the governor of Hawai'i to investigate the situation on April 29. When no report developed, the secretary of the interior sent an additional letter on July 26 asking for a response to this complaint. The Territory of Hawai'i government sent a report about another set of complaints on September 4, which the Department of Interior forwarded to the governor of Puerto Rico on September 20. The governor wanted a more specific response to the April grievance, so the Department of Interior once again requested the Territory of Hawai'i look into the situation facing these other complainants. Finally, on November 25, the governor of Hawai'i provided a response to the April complaint that "reaches the conclusion that the discontent among the Porto Ricans in that country has no substance in fact, but is due in a great measure to home-sickness."³² While the grievance was on the radar of the Department of Interior every two to three months, the ultimate report from Hawai'i summarily dismissed the grievance that had been written and submitted seven months earlier. The federal agency accepted the statement at face value and removed the administrative task of regularly following-up on the complaint from its quarterly to-do list.

Even though the bureaucratic hierarchy of governance gave U.S. colonials a method to express their concerns at the national level, their grievances became neutralized by the indifference of administrative paper-pushers who handled daily imperial communications.

Such a detached process of colonial communication also represented one way the long-distance authority and control wielded over Puerto Rican intra-colonials differentiated their experiences from U.S. colonials in Puerto Rico. Without trusted local leadership, intra-colonial issues could fall through the cracks of imperial bureaucracy. If they had a supportive regional official in the Pacific, Puerto Ricans would know whom to share their grievances with. But these intra-colonials were isolated from leaders in Hawai'i and Puerto Rico. Not everyone in the islands knew how to file complaints or with whom to address them. Many migrants were also illiterate, so they could not write down their concerns. Without the ability or knowledge to start the colonial process of complaint, many Puerto Rican intra-colonial issues were likely not addressed.

The remote and diffuse system of bureaucratic referral was also ineffective in handling intra-colonial affairs because the HSPA was usually in charge of investigating plantation conditions. While the Guzman complaint generated a sixty-seven-page description of Puerto Rican experiences in the islands, Attorney General Irwin based his report on data provided by the sugar industry. Irwin acquired positive statements from all eighteen plantations that employed these U.S. colonials in Hawai'i.

When gathering information for this report, the central sugar office asked local plantation management to approach only those workers likely to provide optimistic responses. Secretary Mead of the HSPA requested plantation managers to "talk with your responsible Porto Ricans and if they are satisfied with conditions to get statements from them in writing, showing that the Porto Ricans on the plantations are well treated; that they are satisfied with their condition. . . . any statement either from the Porto Ricans or by yourselves, which will show the Porto Ricans are not abused and that their living conditions and earnings are good, will be appreciated."[33] The majority of those surveyed worked in skilled, high-level, or high-paying positions, such as *lunas* (field overseers), blacksmiths, and teamsters. These Puerto Ricans had few complaints because they already occupied positions of privilege on the plantation. According to Eufemio de la Rosa, Pedro Gonzales, and Jose Gavino, they "never received bad treatment from the employees or their superiors."[34] These men worked as blacksmiths and earned good pay for their skilled labor. The HSPA used letters from these workers, not the unskilled field laborers who originally signed the petition, to counter the

1919 grievance. In total, the HSPA sent Irwin fifty-two positive statements from Puerto Ricans at six different plantations.

From this skewed sample of this ethnic group in the islands, the attorney general decided that the situation described in the Guzman complaint typified industry experiences and affected all residents equally. Irwin stated, "[Puerto Rican] conditions are normal and satisfactory to the large majority of agricultural laborers in this Territory."[35] All workers received comparable pay, housing, medical treatment, work hours, and type of work on plantations. These findings implied that Guzman and his fellow laborers just complained more, expected too much, or did not work hard enough to earn a comfortable lifestyle. Irwin constantly referred to Puerto Ricans as "this class of laborers," describing them as having "less pride in keeping their immediate surroundings planted with trees and flowers than some of the other nationalities."[36] Any issue Puerto Ricans had could be attributed to their own shortcomings.

Since Irwin's data came from the very plantation managers who were being investigated, report conclusions were clearly subjective. But at no point did Territory of Hawai'i or federal bureaucrats question the content of materials generated by the HSPA. They accepted accounts as factually accurate and merely forwarded the results back through the colonial communication hierarchy. The apathy of far-off, mid-level BIA officials toward the well-being of Puerto Ricans in Hawai'i only facilitated the distribution and use of these questionable studies about the situation facing this group in the islands.

Seven and a half months after Pedro Guzman and the others sent their petition, a report reached the Puerto Rican resident commissioner in Washington, D.C., that completely dismissed the 1919 complaint. Irwin stated that he had "found no evidence of discrimination against Porto Rican laborers in this Territory."[37] The attorney general also claimed that the grievances were unsubstantiated and that protests were just led by a small group of hooligans. The Guzman letter failed to modify plantation conditions or result in free return passage to Puerto Rico.

Even though investigative reports did not result in massive change in Puerto Rican work or living experiences, these complaints did get acknowledged and addressed. Despite the pro-HSPA findings of investigations that completely dismissed these grievances, biased reports still required plantation management to examine the situation and justify their actions toward Puerto Ricans. Complaints sent through the far-flung bureaucratic hierarchy of communication also became opportunities for Puerto Ricans to inform high levels of the U.S. government about their troubles in Hawai'i. These letters allowed Puerto Ricans to express their anger about the poor quality of ground-level conditions on plantations.

While Guzman and the other petitioners did not gain passage back to Puerto Rico, their complaint alerted the Puerto Rican government to continuing labor and social problems in the islands. This grievance warned Puerto Ricans in Puerto Rico about the dangers of migrating to the Pacific that still existed in the 1920s.[38] The Guzman complaint contributed to the prevention of additional intra-colonial movement to the Pacific.

Puerto Rican Actions on Plantations

While the 1919 investigations of the Guzman complaint ended up presenting the HSPA perspective on plantation conditions, Attorney General Irwin's report also revealed ways Puerto Ricans historically exerted a degree of control and independence over their labor experiences in Hawai'i. These workers often disregarded the expectations or demands of the sugar industry. One main way they exercised personal choice in their daily lives involved their frequent movement from plantation to plantation. Managers who contributed information to the Irwin report blamed this ethnic group's lack of dedication to one place as the reason for such mobility. According to Irwin, "The dissatisfied ones are confined to the class that prefers to wander around from place to place, and are thus unable to obtain the higher consideration which follows long employment in one place, or the maximum wage which is the reward of steady labor."[39] This statement portrayed Puerto Ricans as more inconsistent and itinerant than other labor groups. From a worker's perspective, however, constant movement among sugar locations became one strategy to deal with harsh economic and social circumstances.

Without an official local representative dedicated to their issues, Puerto Ricans often used internal mobility to obtain better living and work conditions. Since the beginning of their settlement in Hawai'i, these U.S. colonials were generally willing to move to another site. Blase Camacho Souza believed her paternal grandparents regularly moved from plantation to plantation because they were always "looking for something a little more, a little better."[40] They relocated with the belief that better opportunities existed elsewhere.

These intra-colonials also switched locations to escape unjust conduct by their bosses. Many Puerto Ricans refused to stay and work at a job where they received poor treatment. If these U.S. colonial workers did not like the leadership at a particular place, they willingly gathered up their belongings and left for another plantation. Some men were willing to transfer their entire families if they felt insulted or abused by their *lunas*. Souza recounted one time when her father came home after working in the fields and told the family to start packing. They left that very day. While it is unclear what happened to her father, Souza implied that some type of exploitation motivated him to uproot the family to another site.[41] Several families changed locations frequently.

Tana Rios also stated how Puerto Rican clans often transferred from plantation to plantation together. She explained, "They all follow each other, yeah? From Kohala, they all follow there. The Cravalhos, the Rodrigues. All, most relatives. So they stick to each other. When one would leave one camp, the other follow."[42] The lack of a devoted government official in the region to control Puerto Rican internal mobility gave this group a modicum of autonomy in their decisions to move where they wanted, when they wanted.

Puerto Ricans in Hawai'i also prioritized being with family members over maintaining their labor agreements at a particular location. Charles Fraticelli believed Puerto Ricans went to other plantations because kinship networks were split up. He stated,

> Maybe you came with, you know, your husband and your children, then your sister or your brother came and maybe somebody else you knew. And then, all of a sudden they send you to Kauai and they send him over there. So you felt real lonely, you know. . . . But they used to manage some way to make a trip and maybe go back to where their family is. And I think that's why they moved a lot. . . . it didn't take much to move, you know. We didn't have no furniture, nothing. Just a few little clothes and pots and pans and off you go.[43]

Living in an unfamiliar social and cultural environment, Puerto Ricans usually wanted to stay as close to their relatives as possible. With few personal belongings and no attachment to assigned plantations, Puerto Rican families readily shifted around. As long as they could save enough money for local transport, these intra-colonials often tried to reunite with loved ones scattered throughout Hawai'i. Like Filipino intra-colonial laborers in chapter 2, Puerto Rican migrants prioritized working and living with their family and friends over loyalty to and stability at one plantation.

Since 1901 the HSPA was frustrated with Puerto Rican mobility. That year the board of trustees passed a resolution to blacklist anyone from this ethnic group who left their assigned plantation without an honorable discharge. HSPA board member C. C. Kennedy spearheaded the proposal that "no employment be given to Porto Ricans after this date [November 19, 1901] except such as reach the plantations directly through the Hawaiian Sugar Planters Association, or except through the [presentation of] an honorable discharge, or except also those who are required by the police authorities to find work."[44] The sugar industry did not support internal job mobility.

Plantations were also supposed to refuse work to labor-agreement breakers. But such sanctions did not scare Puerto Ricans into staying at one location. They continued to move to different plantations. If they could not find cane work, they were willing to leave the sugar industry and look for a different job. The vice president of Olaʻa's financial agency in Honolulu, Elmer E. Paxton, explained how there were a number of "Porto Ricans who are loafing around Honolulu, the alternative of going out on the plantations to work or being arrested as vagrants."[45] If they could not obtain employment in other trades, some Puerto Ricans chose to stop work completely instead of suffering the mistreatment and disrespect of HSPA supervisors or forced separation from their families.

Since the blacklisting policy did not stop Puerto Ricans from leaving plantations, this directive soon became ineffective, as well as impractical and detrimental to the HSPA labor supply. According to Paxton, many Puerto Ricans who "left the plantations with the idea of doing better in Honolulu . . . would now go back to work if an opportunity was given them . . . sending these Porto Ricans back to the plantations will be good."[46] Puerto Ricans seemed willing to return to work in the fields, and the sugar industry needed their labor. The HSPA consequently rescinded the blacklist rule less than two months after it was established. Plantations resumed hiring internally mobile Puerto Ricans, regardless of their discharge status from their former positions. In this case, as with other examples of Puerto Rican mobility to multiple areas, the existence of a local official willing to convince, coerce, or reprimand intra-colonial workers into compliance with HSPA expectations or policies could have benefited the sugar industry and limited Puerto Rican movement to different plantations and out of the vocation.

Puerto Ricans were also accustomed to job mobility from past work experiences in their home region. According to historian Laird Bergad, the coffee industry in Puerto Rico transformed many people from the mountain interior into "a mobile labor force dependent on these wages (cash, chits, or consumer goods)."[47] The expansion of coffee production in Puerto Rico between 1850 and 1897 created a class of laborers who frequently switched locations. Most Puerto Ricans who migrated to Hawaiʻi had participated in this system of coffee labor, so they were used to a significant degree of movement in wage labor.

In addition to shifting among plantations and filing labor complaints, Puerto Ricans protested work conditions by destroying plantation property. The 1919 Irwin report stated that "some of these [Puerto Ricans] are very destructive and careless about their houses . . . using these [home furnishings] up for firewood about the time they intend to leave."[48] From the HSPA perspective, Puerto Ricans were savages who created their own state of deprivation through dreadful behavior. From a U.S. colonial worker's point of view, the same actions could be seen as ways to express their displeasure and anger over unacceptable plantation conditions. According to Miguel Rodrigues, Puerto Ricans "were more like slaves, in the plantation. That's why they got mad. And they had to fight back."[49] Sociologist Kelvin Santiago-Valles also found that the working-class in Puerto Rico often resorted to violence in response to grave economic conditions.[50] Unruly social practices functioned as methods for Puerto Rican survival during periods of despair and desperation.

Irwin's report also stated, "It is a well recognized fact in this community that the less thrifty of the Porto Rican laborers, as the time when they receive their bonus, usually take a vacation from work, which continues until the bonus money is exhausted."[51] The bonus was supposed to be an incentive for continued steady labor. Instead, Puerto Ricans used the additional money as a way to take a break from the severe and constant demands of sugar plantation work. While Irwin believed such choices demonstrated Puerto Rican laziness or lack of practical financial skills, the tactic of taking a vacation during periods of high cash inflow could also be seen as a smart and resourceful way to deal with oppressive labor conditions.[52] Some of these intra-colonial migrants chose to take a temporary hiatus from arduous plantation labor when they could afford to not earn a wage. By taking vacations instead of leaving employment altogether, Puerto Ricans could get periods of relief from demanding manual labor while retaining their jobs. As discussed in chapter 1, *jornaleros*, or day laborers in Puerto Rico, also stopped work after they made enough money for their personal needs. Puerto Rican decisions to engage in variable work attendance, internal labor mobility, and property destruction had roots in previous work experiences in Puerto Rico.

Many Puerto Ricans also chose to move off plantations into other vocations as soon as financially possible. Since labor agreements in the islands were nonbinding to employees after 1900, discontented workers always had the ability to leave the sugar industry. According to HSPA secretary W. C. Smith, 37 percent (1,079 out of 2,930) male Puerto Rican laborers deserted cane cultivation by February 28, 1902.[53] Intra-colonial Puerto Ricans viewed plantation fieldwork as the most undesirable job in the islands. Many believed that if they could gain employment outside this particular business, they could improve their social and economic conditions.

Some looked for jobs in Hawai'i cities, becoming construction workers and small-business owners. In the 1920s and 1930s, Andalecio Trochez's brothers worked for the telephone and electric companies, John Santana was a security guard and construction worker, and Danny Ongais was an electrician and piano tuner.[54] After Puerto Ricans became citizens in 1917, they could also be employed in higher-paying civil-service jobs with extensive benefits. Many, like John Vegas, got jobs in the navy shipyards.[55] Moving into other trades in the islands, Puerto Ricans could blend more easily into mainstream society in Hawai'i.

Leaving Hawai'i became another way Puerto Ricans could escape poor conditions in the islands. Their access to legal, open colonial mobility before 1917, and freedom of movement as U.S. citizens after 1917, gave Puerto Ricans the opportunity to migrate at will to other parts of the United States throughout the twentieth century. While return transport to Puerto Rico was often too expensive for the average worker, some eventually saved adequate funds to travel to the U.S. West Coast. If they became recruits for jobs in the continental United States, the hiring company might also pay for their transport.[56] According to scholar Edwin Maldonado, Puerto Rican migrants from Hawai'i to California became the second-largest population of this ethnic group in the United States from 1910 to 1950.[57] These U.S. colonials concentrated in San Francisco, Oakland, and Los Angeles.[58] All of these locations had ports with direct connections to Hawai'i.

Military-based flow out of the islands, particularly to the San Francisco Bay Area, increased as a result of the World Wars. During this period, Puerto Rican movement from the Pacific to California was fostered by the recruitment of this group into the armed forces after they became U.S. citizens. According to scholar Victor Rodriguez, "Puerto Ricans came as employees of military federal installations in the state, enlisted personnel (including many who retired from service and stayed in California)."[59] Many were stationed in California and chose to settle there after completing their terms of service. A significant population of Puerto Ricans from Hawai'i eventually developed near Hayward, California, due partially to the military base in the area. Fermin Pagan "moved to California after World War II. He had been working in Pearl Harbor Navy Yard. When war veterans returned, he was demoted. So he went to California," he said, "'for better opportunities for myself and my children . . . the schools are better, it doesn't cost as much to live and investment opportunities are better.'"[60] Rodriguez also explained how "California Puerto Ricans have higher median household income, are older, have a higher educational background and lower levels of segregation than Puerto Ricans in the Midwest and Northeast."[61] Puerto Ricans in California generally had more positive economic and social experiences than those in other regions of the United States.

All nine of Andalecio Trochez's children moved out of Hawai'i and most settled in California. He explained how "some was in the Army—when they came out from the Army they came to California and right there they let them go. And they stayed there . . . they went to get better jobs . . . I don't think they could get a job over here [in Hawai'i] . . . I think they did better by going down there [to California]."[62] In general, Puerto Ricans in Hawai'i who left for the continental United States were hoping for better work and living opportunities.

In the Pagan family, "four out of seven boys and five out of eleven girls" moved to California.[63] Once one family member became established in the continental United States, their family and friends had a support network to help them start chain migration in a new area of U.S. empire. Early migrants to particular locations in California often provided their loved ones in Hawai'i with crucial insight on work and living conditions in the West Coast, detailed information about job possibilities, and a comforting place to stay until they got settled. Puerto Ricans moving from Hawai'i to the West Coast engaged in similar translocal chain migration as Filipino intra-colonials discussed in chapter 2.

Going to the continental United States also brought these individuals one step closer to Puerto Rico. Trochez stated how those who left Hawai'i "didn't go straight to Puerto Rico but they went to the mainland, a few of them, went to the mainland. Yeah. And from there, they went Puerto Rico. Few, not very many."[64] While return to Puerto Rico by migrants from Hawai'i rarely occurred, living in the contiguous forty-eight states fostered hope in the possibility of cheaper and more accessible future travel to Puerto Rico.

Despite the inability of most intra-colonials to travel to their home region, Puerto Rican migrants found multiple ways to escape the severe conditions and treatment they faced in Hawai'i. Whether they relocated to the continental United States, a different industry in the islands, or a different plantation, many of these U.S. colonials used their status as legally mobile workers to protest negative conditions and mistreatment on plantations. Just as Puerto Ricans in the Caribbean could not be forced to migrate to Hawai'i, intra-colonials in the Pacific could not be forced to stay in one area long term. Without a local government representative dedicated to monitor their actions, Puerto Rican intra-colonials actively and freely chose to move around and out of Hawai'i.

Conclusion

Puerto Rican laborers in the Pacific faced a unique complaint-communication hierarchy that other workers did not encounter when submitting grievances. This process reflected both Puerto Rico's specific colonial relationship with the United States government and the imperial policies of the U.S. federal bureaucracy, even after gaining U.S. citizenship in 1917. Such long-distance supervision meant complaints, like the Guzman petition, reached high levels of U.S. colonial government. However, investigations failed to produce meaningful change because the Bureau of Insular Affairs usually deferred issues to the Territory of Hawai'i government, which relied on the HSPA to conduct their own research on grievances.

Between and among dominant labor policies and ineffective colonial communication systems, Puerto Ricans in Hawai'i tried to create better working conditions and a more supportive living environment on their own terms, especially through relocation, unpermitted vacations, and property destruction. The absence of official representatives willing to advocate for this community in Hawai'i also meant that Puerto Ricans had to deal with many negative stereotypes, much poor treatment, and strong discrimination in the islands on their own. Sometimes Puerto Ricans succeeded in combatting injustices, as in the Sanchez case. But more often than not, this ethnic group was treated as second-class citizens with little respect in the islands. Such problematic social conditions further motivated them to abandon sugar work, pursue jobs in other fields, and head to the continental United States.

While Filipino migrants faced similar harsh working conditions and unique U.S. colonial situations as Puerto Rican laborers in Hawai'i, these two intra-colonial groups generally did not interact with each other. Puerto Ricans were usually assigned to plantation camps separate from Asians.[65] When they did intermingle with Filipinos or Japanese, it was because their children attended the local school together. However, schoolchildren of different backgrounds often did not choose to interact with each other.[66] Puerto Ricans also served as lunas for Filipino work gangs, which further reinforced a sense of difference. Such racial divisions were established and encouraged by the HSPA and were difficult to breach until after World War II, as explained by sociologist Moon-Kie Jung. The difference in period of migration also prevented Puerto Rican and Filipino intra-colonials in Hawai'i from forming horizontal connections with each other. Their political and cultural commonalities did not result in many partnerships or much cooperation between these two groups in the islands.[67]

This lack of intra-colonial cross-group interaction was reinforced by the U.S. government, which did not treat the colonies identically. Puerto Ricans were seen and handled as long-term dependents of the United States, while Filipinos were on the path to eventual self-governance. This divergence in approach led to the varied intra-colonial complaint processes that developed for Puerto Rican versus Filipino U.S. colonials in Hawai'i. U.S. colonials had unique experiences from each other, as well as from foreigners and citizens.

4. *Tensions of Colonial Cooperation*

PHILIPPINE AUTHORITY OVER LABOR COMPLAINTS

When boiling tar accidentally fell on Victorino Laino's leg while he worked at the Ola'a plantation, Laino sent a complaint about his treatment to Cayetano Ligot. As the new Philippine resident labor commissioner living and working in Honolulu, Ligot read Laino's letter in his Honolulu office in September 1923. Laino claimed that he received extremely poor-quality food during his recovery in the hospital. The worker also stated that he did not receive any salary for the days of work he missed. This Filipino intracolonial felt such treatment for a work-related incident was unjust. Laino hoped Ligot would help him get fair compensation. Even though Ligot was a Philippine government official responsible for looking after Filipino labor issues in Hawai'i, he was also an elite U.S. colonial trained to prioritize U.S. interests over those of the Philippines. Ligot often supported the needs of the Hawai'i sugar industry over Filipino workers in the islands.

On September 26, 1923, Ligot forwarded Laino's grievance to Ola'a plantation manager, A. J. Watt.[1] Watt dismissed the accident as minor and accused Laino of lying about hospital conditions and trying to secure unneeded benefits.[2] In response, Ligot apologized for bothering the sugar manager with the supposedly warrantless claim.[3] Six months after starting his job, Ligot was more willing to believe the perspectives of plantation managers over the U.S. colonial workers he was paid to represent. He did not have a good opinion of working-class Filipinos in the islands and rarely supported them against plantation management.

Before 1915, Filipino complaints followed a circuitous path similar to that of Puerto Rican intra-colonials in Hawai'i: they sent letters to leaders in their home region or resident commissioners in Washington, D.C., who then informed the Bureau of Insular Affairs, who communicated with the Department of Interior, who contacted the Territory of Hawai'i government. When the complaint landed, at last, on the desk of the HSPA central office, they alerted the sugar company, which informed the plantation manager in question. The creation of the Philippine Bureau of Labor in 1915 vastly simplified the process. This chapter discusses the resulting shift, which placed all Filipino complaints in the hands of the Philippine elite.

All wards of the United States were subject to some form of U.S. authority when filing grievances. But each region was managed in a way that reflected its specific relationship with the U.S. federal government. As a result of Filipinization, or slow transition of government authority from appointed Anglo-American officials to appointed Philippine leaders, Filipino labor petitions after 1915 were dealt with by ethnic managers in their home region.[4] As indefinite dependents of the United States, Puerto Rican U.S. colonials did not experience a similar transfer of control over their work issues until their home region became a U.S. commonwealth in 1952.[5]

The transition of labor-issue control from the U.S. federal government to Philippine leaders made the Filipino intra-colonial complaint process more similar to that of foreign laborers than to that of Puerto Rican U.S. colonials, whose grievances passed through the Bureau of Insular Affairs. After 1915, both Filipinos and foreign laborers in Hawai'i communicated directly with ethnic government officials who were empowered to resolve daily living and work issues. However, Philippine officials, like Bureau of Insular Affairs leaders in Washington, D.C., often emphasized U.S. business and government interests over those of Filipino laborers because the Filipino elite benefited from U.S. rule.

As several Philippine scholars have shown, United States political, economic, and social policies solidified upper-class structures of power in the archipelago.[6] The Filipino upper class became dependent on the U.S. government for preferential trade status, domestic defense forces, and the rhetoric of eventual independence for their own legitimacy, development, and security in the early twentieth century. These ethnic leaders, such as Ligot, constantly weighed the needs of U.S. institutions against those of the general Filipino population. Since U.S. pursuits usually received priority, Philippine government efforts to assist intra-colonial Filipino laborers in Hawai'i resulted in a mix of minor successes and major failures to improve plantation conditions in the islands. Even though Filipino and Puerto Rican worker complaints traveled through varied communication mechanisms and different levels of ethnic leadership, each process ended up generally disregarding the basic needs of these U.S. colonials. Despite such collaboration among Philippine and Anglo-American leaders, Filipino intra-colonials in Hawai'i found ways to express their own desires and free will.

Filipinization: Slow Shifts in Colonial Authority

Filipinos eventually gained authority over labor complaints in Hawai'i while Puerto Ricans never did. This difference in control occurred because the United States government had different colonial expectations for the Philippines than for Puerto Rico. While U.S. officials wanted to maintain indefinite control in Puerto Rico, Congress never wanted to make the Philippines a full-fledged member of the United States. The Philippines provided a useful military and trade base for the Asian region; however, federal leaders had no intention of incorporating more than 7.6 million Filipinos and seven thousand Philippine islands into the nation. Amy Kaplan has shown how anti-imperialists and nativists worried that the United States would become a "distended body that could be hacked apart, that could implode internally from its ingestion of foreign bodies."[7] Many in the United States feared that the incorporation of non–Anglo-Saxon groups into the United States would weaken and ultimately destroy the country and its morals.

To address such anxieties, the U.S. government claimed that they would only guide Filipinos for a finite period. U.S. presence in the Philippines was just a temporary but necessary step to train Filipinos in Western standards and principles, such as the development of import-export industries and the protection of male property owners.[8] Once these U.S. colonials proved they could follow such practices to the satisfaction of U.S. officials, the federal government would give Filipinos sovereignty. By doling out responsibilities and autonomy over a long period, the U.S. government could take advantage of economic and military benefits in the Philippines while avoiding accusations of being a tyrannical colonizer.

To implement this phased self-rule, the U.S. government started a Filipinization policy in 1913.[9] As part of the gradual transition of Philippine administrative responsibilities from Anglo-American leaders to Filipino representatives, labor issues became the responsibility of the newly formed Philippine Bureau of Labor in 1915. The transfer of power to this Filipino-run agency was so complete that in 1925, the Bureau of Insular Affairs in Washington, D.C., "had practically no information referring to present labor troubles in Hawaii. The Philippine government keeps in touch with the

Hawaiian situation through its representative there and not through this Bureau. Similarly, the labor people in Hawaii seem to correspond directly with the Philippine government and not with the Bureau."[10] By the mid-1920s, the U.S. government had no involvement with Filipino intra-colonial labor issues in the Territory of Hawai'i.

At one level, Filipinization incorporated ethnic elites into the local administration system. Filipinos were in charge of and responsible for dealing with Filipino issues. On another level, Filipinization coached Philippine officials to perpetuate Anglo-American ideals. Ligot is a prime example of both the upper-class empowerment and the collusion fostered by the Filipinization process. Throughout his life, he worked hard to climb social, political, and economic hierarchies in the Philippines. Born in 1877, Ligot and his family were not part of the elite class. In his twenties, Ligot attended the Philippine Normal School, the first institution of higher learning in the archipelago that followed U.S. educational standards. After obtaining his bachelor's degree in U.S.-style pharmacology, he worked as a teacher, school principal, and professor. In his late thirties, he became the owner and publisher of *Ti Bagno*, a weekly regional newspaper. During this period he served also as a provincial census inspector and established 121 rural credit banks in the Ilocos region. Both roles of gathering surveillance information about the Filipino population through census data and providing local farmers with credit to develop U.S. export agriculture supported United States business and government activities. At age forty-three, Ligot had accumulated enough political, economic, and social influence and support to be elected the provincial governor of Ilocos Norte in 1920. Abiding by U.S. institutional structures and following U.S. policies throughout his career, Ligot obtained high-level government positions, cemented his status as a member of the Philippine elite, and earned a substantial amount of money.

In 1923, Ligot was appointed as the Philippine resident labor commissioner for Hawai'i. In this position, he continued to follow U.S. standards and structures. As a self-created member of the Philippine elite, Ligot was accustomed to cooperating with U.S. officials in the archipelago. He also embraced U.S. paternalistic ideas about benevolent assimilation and racial hierarchy that assumed U.S. colonials did not have the proper upbringing or maturity to govern themselves. According to U.S. president William McKinley, "We could not leave them [Filipinos] to themselves—they were unfit for self-government—and they would soon have anarchy and misrule over there worse than Spain's was . . . there was nothing left for us to do but to take them all, and to educate the Filipinos, and uplift and civilize and Christianize them, and, by God's grace, do the very best we could."[11] With this outlook, the U.S. government believed it had the God-given burden and duty to help Filipinos improve themselves. Countless political cartoons, editorials, and speeches at the turn of the century also portrayed U.S. colonials as little brown brothers of the United States who needed civilization, development, and tutelage.[12]

In a similar way, Ligot also believed part of his job as labor commissioner involved the uplift of Filipino intra-colonial workers in Hawai'i. As a well-trained U.S. colonial official, he claimed "to seek the truth of all facts" so that he could "save the poor and ignorant laborers."[13] Much of Ligot's rhetoric echoed colonial concepts of benevolent assimilation and the whiteman's burden. His upper-class position combined with his imperial training to influence his attitudes and actions in Hawai'i. Despite his daily knowledge of labor complaints and his ethnic similarity with working-class Filipinos in the islands, Ligot usually prioritized the desires and directives of Territory of Hawai'i economic interests over those of U.S. colonials in the Pacific Islands.

Individuals who filled government positions through Filipinization were almost always members of the upper class. Scholar Vicente Rafael analyzed the ways Philippine elite historically collaborated with invaders to maintain their class position.[14] As Philippine resident labor commissioner in Hawai'i, Ligot also worked with U.S. institutions to maintain or increase his own power and influence within Philippine and Territory of Hawai'i societies. To support his political and social position, Ligot acted according to the expectations and needs of the U.S. imperial administration and elite leaders in Hawai'i. He also interacted closely with the HSPA to develop pro-plantation policies and programs for Filipinos. Such co-optation, or self-interested cooperation with foreign endeavors, resulted in Ligot's often siding with the sugar industry and doubting the validity of Filipino labor claims, such as that of Victorino Laino. Patricio Abinales discussed how "'Gilded Age,' party-driven patronage politics and the use of official positions for spoils and expanding political influence were widespread" in the Philippines.[15] Ligot worked with and took advantage of this system for the benefit of both himself and his U.S. allies.

While having a dedicated local government leader was a different situation from that facing Puerto Rican U.S. colonials in the islands, Ligot's presence did not dramatically improve Philippine intra-colonial living and working conditions in the Pacific. Instead, the Filipinization process made Ligot just as ineffective for Filipino workers in Hawai'i as the Anglo-American federal bureaucrats in Washington, D.C., who handled Puerto Rican labor grievances. Both groups catered to U.S. business interests over the daily well-being of U.S. colonials.

Early Philippine Labor Mediators

Before Ligot arrived as the permanent Philippine resident labor commissioner in 1923, other leaders tried to manage the issues facing Filipino intra-colonial workers in Hawai'i. These mediators fell into two categories: temporary Philippine government labor commissioners and local labor organizers. Both groups had a difficult time effecting changes in Filipino living and working conditions in Hawai'i. But at least Filipinos had access to multiple ethnic labor advocates throughout their time in the islands. Puerto Rican labor leaders in Hawai'i were rare.

Like other labor groups on Hawai'i sugar plantations, Filipino U.S. colonials had many grievances about life in the Pacific. Complaints from the Ola'a plantation in 1923 represented common problems found throughout Filipino camps in the islands.[16] Intra-colonial Filipino workers claimed that the Japanese camp boss discriminated against them and ignored their requests for camp improvements. Compared to Japanese housing, older Filipino homes typically had leaky pipes and no kitchens.[17] Filipinos had to resort to cooking under their houses. Antonio Evangelista, who migrated to Hawai'i in 1927, explained the cramped conditions: "[Houses] were small. It was like a garage. It wasn't only you living there. We were many living there in one room. . . . we were five."[18] Their bathing facilities were small, run-down, and lacked separate areas for men and women. Filipino dormitories were also overcrowded. Alex Ruiz, who came to Hawai'i in 1930, described the barracks-style housing for single men. He stated that the lodging "was just like one warehouse. . . . When you first see that, you don't feel like coming to Hawai'i . . . you got to room with somebody else . . . you live on the army cot."[19] Without a permanent local government representative to help them negotiate for better conditions, Filipino field hands took it upon themselves to hold major strikes in 1920 and 1924. Protesters stopped work to demand concessions beyond labor agreement terms. They wanted higher wages, a reduction in the amount of work required for bonuses, and overtime benefits, as well as the development and maintenance of better living, recreational, and health facilities.[20]

To address complaints from the islands, the Philippine government appointed short-term labor commissioners to travel to Hawai'i in 1912, 1919, and 1920.[21] The first commissioner, Joaquin Balmori, was a labor leader, journalist, and delegate to the Philippine Assembly. Between March and April 1911, he visited Hawai'i for thirty-nine days and went to twenty-eight plantations on O'ahu, Maui, Kaua'i, and the island of Hawai'i. Since the sugar industry paid for his travel expenses, the HSPA was able to dictate where the labor commissioner traveled and with whom he spoke, ensuring a generally positive account of Filipino intra-colonial experiences. The labor commissioner stated, "I have always been told that they [Filipino laborers] are contented on account of the good wages and good treatment they receive."[22] He believed medical treatment and housing were satisfactory. He also found that laborers had complaints at only two plantations. HSPA control over Balmori's trip skewed the results of his investigation in favor of the sugar industry. Anyone fully funded and shuttled around by the HSPA was likely to produce supportive yet questionable testimonies about Filipino conditions on Pacific sugar plantations.

The second and third temporary commissioners, Prudencio A. Remigio and Francisco Varona, were not financed by leaders in Hawai'i. However, the HSPA still allowed them to visit plantations because the sugar industry needed Philippine government support to continue their recruitment of valuable U.S. colonial laborers to the islands. HSPA officials might have also assumed that as members of the Philippine government who obtained their positions through the Filipinization process, official labor commissioners were likely to support U.S. business interests.

Both Remigio and Varona found Filipino conditions in the islands to be less satisfactory than Balmori had. Remigio was a Manila labor leader and member of the Philippine Assembly. For eighteen days in May 1919, he visited twenty-two of the forty-five plantations and mills on O'ahu, Maui, and the island of Hawai'i. He observed that Filipino housing was older than and inferior to those of other migrant groups. He also found medical treatment to be insufficient. Additionally, he believed it was almost impossible to meet the twenty-six days of work required for the monthly bonus. The work was just too hard to do without taking a few days off to recover. The food available in plantation stores also cost the equivalent of a day's worth of work. Remigio noted that "the situation becomes odious for some, forced for others, and desperate for all."[23] Filipino intra-colonials in Hawai'i faced many problems, and Remigio did not provide a supportive report about the sugar industry as Balmori had done.

After his visit to the islands, Remigio sent specific, individual Filipino grievances to the HSPA. These included complaints about married couples living in the same housing as single men, sick laborers not getting proper treatment, the lack of bathing facilities in some camps, harsh treatment by *lunas*, and fees for fuel, housing, and hospital visits.[24] The last set of complaints about monetary charges for basic services directly violated labor agreement terms, which stipulated that such items would be free.

In response to Remigio's findings, HSPA leadership urged local plantation managers to closely follow the terms outlined in Filipino labor agreements. As discussed in chapter 2, the sugar industry was willing to address

Filipino complaints to maintain this valuable source of openly mobile U.S. colonial labor. R. C. Walker, the treasurer of the Ola'a sugar agency, expressed "the vital importance of paying strict regard to the contract made with the Filipinos when they are brought to the islands; also the fact that the Philippine Islands is the only place in the world that we can look to for a supply of laborers; that this emigration is under constant attack by Filipino politicos and it has at times required great effort to prevent it bring stopped and that it surely will be stopped unless the plantations carefully live up to the contracts."[25] Since a consistent source of labor was the highest priority for the sugar industry, HSPA leadership pressured local plantation managers to avoid labor-agreement violations or situations that could cause leaders in the Philippines to restrict intra-colonial movement. Even when some complaints were not part of the labor agreement, HSPA labor bureau director Mead encouraged local managers to supply benefits like bathhouses, recreation, and amusement.[26] In addition to filing individual complaints, Remigio was able to obtain free return passage for Filipino laborers who worked steadily for all three years of their labor agreement, even if they switched plantations.

Remigio's report alarmed HSPA leadership because the commissioner advocated for stricter government regulation of recruitment out of the Philippines as the best way to improve the situation facing Filipinos in Hawai'i. Remigio stated that being "more restrictive of emigration is essential for the solution of this problem."[27] He felt that imposing taxes on recruitment agents would reduce the number of people they sent to the islands. The money collected could also become a pool of money to fund future investigations of Filipino conditions in Hawai'i. While this legislation did not go into effect, such recommendations worried HSPA leadership.

Despite the pro-Filipino labor agreement rhetoric of sugar industry leadership after Remigio's visit, poor treatment and agreement violations continued at local plantations, as found by the next labor commissioner, Francisco Varona. A year after Remigio's visit, temporary commissioner Varona lived in Hawai'i for six months between 1920 and 1921. During that time, this young editor and co-owner of the Philippine newspaper, *El Debate*, investigated Filipino conditions on thirty-six plantations. In November 1920, Varona filed eighty-seven individual complaints about poor treatment by managers, inferior housing, mediocre medical care, and insufficient supplies of water and fuel. At Ola'a he received complaints about inadequate housing and water, as well as the claim that "plantation policeman very cruel to laborers."[28] Varona tried hard to get the HSPA to improve the situations of these U.S. colonials in the islands.

This commissioner was able to obtain a wage raise from eighteen dollars to twenty dollars for men and from twelve dollars to fourteen dollars for women.[29] Workers who left their originally assigned plantation could also return within three months and still receive full benefits. His largest accomplishment was the procurement of free transport home for any laborer who worked at least twenty days a month for three consecutive years. Laborers had to work at one location consistently for just one year. While Remigio got return passage for laborers who fulfilled HSPA work agreements at various plantations, Varona secured paid transport home for any Filipino who worked in the sugar industry for three years, even those without a labor agreement. Varona also got the HSPA to provide transportation "not only to Manila but to the point from which he [the worker] was recruited."[30] This set of return-passage policies, known as the Varona Agreements, was implemented in January 1921.

The negative reports filed by Remigio and Varona resulted in greater work-agreement compliance. They also achieved some improvements in labor terms, such as the payment of return-passage transport for a wider range of workers. Even though Remigio and Varona were vocal and productive labor advocates in the islands, their temporary presence in the territory meant they could only accomplish so much. The HSPA also limited the kinds of changes they were willing to make. While the sugar industry adjusted their mobility policies and engaged in more labor agreement compliance, as discussed in previous chapters, this institution refused to make drastic modifications to the bonus system or camp layout. Filipino laborers still had many complaints about work and life in Hawai'i. But at least these U.S. colonials had local access to government officials with some degree of success in lobbying for improvements. Without a phased self-rule policy, like Filipinization, Puerto Rican intra-colonials did not have any government advocates to help them in the islands.

During the same time as the visits of short-term Philippine labor commissioners, local Filipino labor leader Pablo Manlapit started to organize workers in Hawai'i. Born in 1891 into a large working-class family in Lipa, Philippines, Manlapit was only financially able to obtain a middle school education. In 1910, against his father's wishes, he migrated to Hawai'i to become a sugar plantation worker at age nineteen. After being fired from plantation work for heading up a strike in 1913, he became a leader in the local Filipino community, particularly among the Visayan migrant population. He served as an interpreter in Territory of Hawai'i courts, managed a local pool hall, and published a weekly Filipino newspaper in the region, *Ang Sandata* in 1914.[31] In 1919, he also started the Filipino Labor Union and became a self-taught, practicing lawyer in the islands that same year.[32] An active leader in the strikes of 1920 and 1924, the HSPA identified Manlapit as one of the most threatening labor agitators in the islands.[33] They consistently refused any communication with him and encouraged the territorial police to watch his actions closely.

Unlike official Philippine government representatives who were accommodated by Territory of Hawai'i and the HSPA leaders, local labor organizers like Manlapit did not have much leverage with institutions of power in Hawai'i.[34] These ethnic mediators did not become leaders in the Filipino intra-colonial community through work within U.S.-created structures, like the Philippine Bureau of Labor or the Philippine legislature. Nongovernmental labor leaders were outside the direct influence of the U.S. imperial system. While these worker advocates could and did organize several strikes among Filipinos in the islands, they could not stop HSPA recruitment of more laborers from the archipelago. There was consequently no reason for the sugar industry to cooperate with these community organizers. Unofficial local labor advocates never received the same kind of positive welcome, treatment, or response from Territory of Hawai'i leaders as Philippine government representatives.[35] Instead, they experienced constant suspicion and much harassment.

During the 1920 strike, Anglo-American leadership in Hawai'i portrayed Manlapit as a corrupt and selfish leader. Frank E. Thompson, an established Anglo-American lawyer in Honolulu, "alleged that Manlapit had asked him for money in exchange for him (Manlapit) calling off the strike."[36] While those accusations were never substantiated, Manlapit was once again targeted after the 1924 strike. HSPA officials tried to smear Manlapit's reputation by spreading rumors that he was only interested in using worker donations for self-profit.[37] Without the same institutional connections and influence as official Philippine government representatives, local labor leaders like Manlapit had difficulty obtaining widespread changes or improvements for Filipino workers in Hawai'i. They diligently tried to organize workers, but their efforts rarely resulted in any major changes to labor or living conditions.[38] They also did not achieve strong unionization until after World War II.[39]

Short-term Philippine labor commissioners, on the other hand, had HSPA approval to visit plantations and submit complaints about Filipino conditions. They gained access to plantations due to their official government status and their ability to regulate worker recruitment to the islands. However, temporary labor commissioners rarely succeeded in improving the fundamental environment of intra-colonials because the sugar industry always wanted to maintain a wide range of control and influence over the work process. The HSPA provided some compromises in mobility policies to develop and maintain the open movement of Philippine laborers to Hawai'i. But the sugar industry would not make drastic changes to work patterns or wages. Short-term labor commissioners were consequently limited in the kinds of change they could achieve. These appointed leaders had a mixture of achievements and failures in resolving Filipino complaints. In the end, both temporary labor commissioners and local labor organizers were not wildly successful in resolving the major problems facing Filipino laborers in Hawai'i. Despite their inability to effectively address all U.S. colonial work issues, early Filipino labor advocates at least provided another source of leadership for this group of intra-colonials. Puerto Ricans in Hawai'i had little access to similar kinds of ethnic mediation.

Making the Resident Labor Commissioner

Though Manlapit could not persuade the sugar industry to improve working conditions on plantations, in 1921 he led a petition drive among Filipinos to request the creation of a permanent worker representative in the islands through the Philippine legislature. By 1922, three letters requesting a resident labor commissioner for Hawai'i had been sent to the president of the Philippine senate, Manuel Quezon. The first letter was sent on May 29, with subsequent messages on September 19 and October 25.[40] In their statement, Filipino laborers in Hawai'i complained that "friction and frequent misunderstandings resulted between them and their employers. . . . [I]t is our desire to avoid the possibility of any such occurrences [strikes] in the future. . . . [we] formally petition the Senate and House of Representatives of the Philippines to enact . . . the creation of an office to be known as RESIDENT LABOR COMMISSIONER for Hawaii."[41] Intra-colonial workers wanted a local official with the power to deal directly with the sugar industry and enact change, similar to that of foreign consul generals. These petitioners believed the complaint process would be more effective and responsive to their needs with a local and permanent government leader who could communicate face to face with the HSPA. They wanted the same kind of representation that foreign laborers received.

On October 27, 1922, Quezon forwarded the requests for a permanent labor commissioner to the Philippine senate. Soon after, the Philippine legislature approved Act 2486 to create the Office of Resident Labor Commissioner to Hawai'i. The law empowered the new official "to receive and hear all complaints for Filipino laborers, to settle their conflicts with their employers, to see that the contracts are fulfilled, and to look after the general interest of the Filipino Laborers in Hawaii."[42] The Philippine government took the appeals of Filipino U.S. colonials in Hawai'i seriously and acted on their request.

Through formal petitions, Filipino intra-colonials successfully changed one aspect of the colonial system that shaped their daily lives. Their ability to alter the complaint process shows how U.S. colonials were not completely powerless in the face of U.S imperialism. Just as Puerto Rican U.S. colonials in Hawai'i left plantation work when the HSPA failed to improve their conditions, Filipino intra-colonials took action in the face of negative circumstances to petition for a resident labor commissioner. Pressures for Filipinization did not occur simply as a high-level directive from the U.S. federal government. Philippine workers in Hawai'i also agitated for more ethnic government leadership. However, these laborers did not realize how Filipinization also involved the prioritization of U.S. interests. Such an emphasis ended up influencing the type of actions that Resident Commissioner Ligot engaged in.

The 1920 labor strike in Hawai'i became another major motivation for the Philippine government to create a resident labor commissioner in 1923. Despite slight wage and bonus improvements, as well as the development of a few social programs after the 165-day strike led by Manlapit, Filipinos remained extremely unhappy with living and working conditions in the islands. Without an empowered representative in Hawai'i to work on their issues, the threat of future strikes remained eminent. The Philippine legislature consequently created a permanent labor commissioner position to appease agitated Filipino U.S. colonial workers in the islands. Anglo-American Philippine governor general Leonard Wood even cabled Manlapit directly to tell him that a government leader would be coming soon. Wood wanted the labor advocate to "abstain from taking steps to further labor strike [and to] wait [for the] arrival [of the] commissioner to secure easier and satisfactory settlement conflict with [the] association."[43] Officials in the Philippines hoped the creation of a long-term and local work representative would prevent future strikes in the Pacific.

The Philippine government, sugar industry in Hawai'i, and Filipino intra-colonial workers in the islands all believed the presence of a permanent labor leader would solve work tensions in the region. Unfortunately, this did not occur. The creation of the resident labor commissioner position did not guarantee that the appointed official would support Filipino U.S. colonial laborers in Hawai'i, as had consul generals from independent nations. Sometimes foreign government representatives accommodated or compromised with U.S. goals.[44] However, these officials usually prioritized the interests of their own citizens over those of the United States, as discussed in chapter 3.

Philippine officials, on the other hand, were not independent from U.S. authority. As U.S. colonials, Filipino government leaders remained under the ultimate supervision and control of the United States. Even though Filipinos were being trained for self-governance, through Filipinization they were nevertheless expected to act according to U.S. interests. These officials were supposed to follow the guidelines and goals set by United States business and politics. Ethnic government leaders, like Ligot, were often deeply entrenched in imperial ideals and practices.

Cayetano Ligot's World

The Philippine government selected Cayetano Ligot to serve as the first, and consequently only, Philippine resident labor commissioner in Hawai'i. As governor of Ilocos, Ligot was well-qualified for the job. He already served as the elected representative for the region whence the majority of workers in the Pacific migrated. He spoke their local dialect, Ilocano. He was also an educated individual with proven leadership skills in rural settings.

In this newly created position, Ligot tried to fulfill many responsibilities in Hawai'i. He wanted to help Filipino laborers have the best experience possible in the islands. He also worked closely with sugar plantation leadership to get information and address the issues facing his constituency. As a Philippine official, Ligot tried to foster positive diplomatic relationships with both the HSPA and the Territory of Hawai'i government. As a member of the upper class, he enjoyed accessing elite circles in Hawai'i. He also made several personal negative judgments about the character of the Filipino working-class during his time in the islands. As a high-level U.S. colonial leader who gained government positions through Filipinization, Ligot was inclined to follow United States standards and expectations to maintain his position of power and influence. All of these concerns resulted in Ligot's combination of minor successes and major failures in addressing Filipino labor complaints in Hawai'i.

Upon disembarking at the Port of Honolulu on April 27, 1923, to start his position as resident labor commissioner, Ligot had two conflicting welcome reception invitations: one for an outdoor rally with Filipino workers and another for a formal soiree hosted by the HSPA. Ligot stated, "I pleased first the planters' party.... After I have done the official visit and courtesy to Governor Farrington, I was then conducted to Aala Park where thousand Filipinos were anxious to see me and hear my speech."[45] Ligot understood the potential political uproar that could develop in choosing one event over the other, so he attended both. But he went to the sugar industry event first, which included a variety of high-powered Territory of Hawai'i leaders, such as Territorial Governor of Hawai'i Wallace Farrington. Ligot's attendance of the fancy *haole* (Anglo-American) party prior to the gathering of Filipino laborers in a local park became an early example of his conflicting official responsibilities, as well as the apparent order of his personal priorities and interests.

When he first came to the islands, Ligot seemed to be the true advocate that Filipino workers in Hawai'i desired. He traveled to the islands on the *President Pierce*, the same ship as newly recruited Filipino laborers. On the five-day journey, he spent time talking to workers, offering advice on how to make their trip more comfortable. He encouraged Philippine passengers to practice good sanitary habits and remain aware of climate changes. Ligot also disapproved of the treatment Filipinos received on board. He did not believe these passengers received appropriate food. They were also located near the rear of the boat, while Chinese passengers stayed in the ship's more stable middle section. Upon arrival in Honolulu, Ligot immediately filed numerous requests to improve conditions on the transports for Filipino labor recruits. Writing to the Pacific Mail Steamship Company in Honolulu in late April 1923, Ligot requested that the crew "give Filipino food to any Filipino who embarked in their ships, and be prepared by Filipino cook, than a Filipino Steward be also appointed to take care of any Filipino in the ship. . . . Filipinos, being not well accostumed [sic] to make long voyage on the sea, should be located in a place of the boat where the least movement can be felt."[46] Stanley W. Good, the navigation company's Honolulu manager, promised to implement the commissioner's requests. His quick actions and ability to elicit response suggested Ligot was a powerful new leader for Filipino labor interests in the islands.

As resident labor commissioner, Ligot was responsible for gathering complaints and taking necessary action to resolve these grievances. Living on O'ahu, this official could conduct his own investigations at any time, generating full-scale reports similar to Irwin's 1919 investigation of Puerto Rican conditions in Hawai'i (discussed in chapter 3). Ligot could also secure employment for Filipinos and labor-agreement compliance from the HSPA. In his first year, he received 2,104 letters in various languages from Filipinos in Hawai'i.

At first, Ligot was warmly welcomed by Filipino labor organizers in Hawai'i, including Manlapit. These community leaders pledged support to the ethnic official if he gave "his best efforts towards a settlement of the existing controversy between the laborers and the planters."[47] Ligot asked Filipino workers to hold off on striking until he could conduct a full investigation. The laborers and their leaders complied. Since they successfully petitioned for a resident labor commissioner, the Filipino intra-colonial working class in Hawai'i hoped the permanent mediator position they created would foster equally significant changes in their living and working conditions. At minimum, they expected this new local ethnic official to be more effective than the temporary labor commissioners and nongovernmental labor organizers of the past.

On May 5, 1923, Ligot started to visit plantations on each island to get acquainted with the Filipino labor community. On a typical day, he would start by meeting with the plantation manager. Then he would tour plantation facilities, like hospitals, sources of water, and housing camps. He also ate and slept with intra-colonial laborers in their own homes. This initial investigative tour of about two weeks resulted in the identification of seven general needs among Filipino U.S. colonials in Hawai'i. These requirements involved getting more paternal advice from plantation managers, the construction of additional improved housing and recreational buildings, repairs to existing facilities, more Filipino store clerks who could speak Philippine dialects, the development of a Filipino bank, the improvement of hospital treatment when necessary, and the promotion of experienced and skilled workers.[48] When Ligot brought these and other issues to the attention of sugar industry leadership, he always received a response from the plantation or central HSPA office. These replies resulted in either concrete action or firm denial of claims.

Ligot succeeded in obtaining improved water quality at some plantations, re-accommodation for laborers in crowded living quarters, and more appropriate food for hospital patients.[49] As Filipino intra-colonials expected, this ethnic leader could achieve positive action on their behalf due to his physical presence in Hawai'i. Plantation management responded quickly to communications from this local mediator with whom they interacted on a regular basis.

Ligot also had the full backing of the HSPA because he was supportive of U.S. business interests. Through Filipinization, Ligot knew how to interact with Anglo-American leaders and demonstrate his loyalty and dedication to U.S. endeavors. In one memo to all plantation managers, HSPA Director Butler stated, "You will find that he [Ligot] is very reasonable, will understand things thoroughly when explained and is inclined to very much favor the same ideas that we do concerning the advisability of Filipinos working conscientiously. . . . [C]ooperate fully and help these arrangements [Ligot's visits] succeed."[50] Butler believed that Ligot was sympathetic to sugar industry needs and was willing to work with Filipino labor for the benefit of the HSPA. With such an endorsement from a high-level industry official, other sugar leaders also trusted Ligot.

In his reports to Governor General Wood, Ligot presented his initial plantation visits as a strategy to learn about worker conditions. But his notes from the evening gatherings with laborers in local movie theaters and recreational halls also demonstrated his support of plantation goals. Nine out of ten of his meeting agenda items provided guidelines on how to be better workers, emphasizing thirty-eight specific instructions on proper conduct.[51]

These points fell under the headings of mutual understanding and effective cooperation, mutual help among Filipino laborers, economy and thrift, religion and charity, patriotism, respect to authorities, and instructions on ethical, social, and educated living. The official's focus on compliance and collaboration with plantation management turned his meetings into sessions on moral training and obedience rather than opportunities for workers to file complaints. To Filipinos attending these town-hall style events, the light-skinned commissioner who wore Western-style white suits when visiting dusty plantations appeared more like a sugar industry advocate and elite government observer than an ethnic leader interested in the realities facing intra-colonial laborers. While Ligot was a paid representative for workers in Hawai'i, his elite style of dress, mannerisms, and attitudes established a class divide between him and the field hands he was supposed to represent.

Even though Filipino laborers in the islands effectively lobbied for an official local advocate, the commissioner they received became more accommodating to U.S. imperial and business concerns than to those of Filipino workers. Many of Ligot's reports included the paternalistic desire to civilize uncultured Filipinos in Hawai'i. He encouraged intra-colonials, "Watch your tongue and actions for our own sake . . . help the local officers to insure peace and order, pay your taxes timely to the government, and give due respect to the authorities and to every-body in order to be respected too."[52] The ethnic representative treated Filipinos in Hawai'i as children in need of his wise guidance. He was willing to help laborers as long as they were willing to abide by his Western imperial standards. As Vicente Rafael has shown, the Philippine ruling class viewed themselves as "the exclusive spokespeople for the rest of the nation, especially in relation to the United States."[53] Ligot believed he was the best person to make decisions for and represent the needs of the Filipino population in Hawai'i. Ligot was much like the *padrones* whom historian Gunther Peck described as "frequently portray[ing] themselves as paternalistic defenders of their compatriots, in large measure to offset the impersonal social distance that divided them from workers."[54] Sometimes elite ethnic representatives, like Ligot, used an authoritarian language of expertise to justify their roles of power among groups who might not trust them due to their differences in class background.

Ligot's position as a member of the upper class, as well as his Filipinization training, created major social barriers between him and intra-colonials in the islands. When sending a status report to Governor General Wood on his findings about these laborers in Hawai'i, Ligot described working-class Filipinos as a generally untrustworthy and devious group. His elitist perspective became clear when he delineated four classes of Filipinos in Hawai'i: bad leaders, honest and educated laborers and missionaries, humble workers easily fooled by charismatic labor leaders, and the shame of the Filipino race, or the criminal and immoral element which included loafers, rascals, gamblers, and rapists.[55] Ligot viewed Filipino laborers in an extremely negative light; he believed that most Filipinos in the islands were either being taken advantage of or were exploiting other Filipinos. He criticized immoral intra-colonials for ruining the reputation of upright and respectable Filipinos like himself. He lamented, "Such conduct gives very bad name to the Filipino people in this Territory, and lowers the honor and dignity of the Filipino race as a whole."[56] Such disapproving racializations demonstrated Ligot's class bias and further supported his self-positioning as a crucial guide and trainer for immature Filipino workers in Hawai'i.[57] Without his elite and Western-educated leadership, these U.S. colonials were bound to act inappropriately and get in trouble.

Ligot also freely created coalitions with haole elite to combat the activities of the poorer elements of intra-colonial Filipino society in Hawai'i. In an early report to Governor General Wood, he stated, "I secured also the cooperation of Governor Farrington, local authorities, and Managers of plantations with their policemen to eradicate vices among the Filipinos; and such cooperation was gladly given."[58] Ligot did not hesitate to use Anglo-American services to keep the wayward Filipino community in line.

Such deleterious and classist attitudes toward Filipino laborers in the islands often led Ligot to doubt the validity of their complaints. In the case of Victorino Laino's work accident, the labor commissioner did not try to get more information from Laino. He never met with Laino, spoke with the doctors who treated him, or conducted a personal investigation of the situation. Instead, Ligot fully trusted the plantation manager's explanation of the circumstances and was immediately appalled and embarrassed by the laborer's allegedly erroneous complaint. In a letter on October 6, 1923, Ligot told Ola'a manager A. J. Watt, "Of course you will understand that I have to comply my duty and there being no easier way to refer to you what the laborers say and complain than to write them to you, so there you have how I was misinformed by this man."[59] If his job did not require him to act on all complaints, Ligot would be more selective in the grievances he forwarded. He did not want to insult or be on bad terms with the plantation manager. Ligot even asked for forgiveness from the sugar leader for bothering him with this presumably false matter. He hoped this mistake would not reflect badly on him or hinder his own position within elite circles in the islands. In Laino's case and many others, Ligot's dismissal of Filipino claims demonstrated his greater faith in the word of Territory of Hawai'i leaders than that of the workers he was supposed to assist.

Since Ligot rarely believed worker claims, he had difficulty understanding situations from a laborer's standpoint. When he chose to look deeper into complaints, his findings usually sided with the HSPA. Ligot, like U.S. federal bureaucrats and Territory of Hawai'i officials in chapter 3, relied on information from the HSPA to evaluate work conditions. Through plantation manager reports, he found that Filipinos in Hawai'i "are more likely to break the contract by not working steadily 20 days a month as agreed. This is the cause of so often discharge [sic]."[60] If Ligot were to have obtained more information directly from field hands, he might have concluded that stringent plantation policies or subtle resistance strategies, not a lack of work ethic, motivated Filipino intra-colonials to leave their jobs. Instead, he depended on plantation manager reports that disregarded laborer perspectives.

Even when he did consider a worker's point of view, Ligot's reports still favored the HSPA position over those of Filipino intra-colonials. During a discussion about housing issues, he explained that "crowding is due sometimes to the custom of many Filipinos to get more and more relatives and friends living in the same house without the knowledge and consent of the Camp Boss or Policeman."[61] According to Ligot, Filipinos' cultural preference for communal living, not plantation procedures, caused overcrowding. Using this rationale, he believed that Filipinos created their own problems; he trusted that HSPA leadership acted properly and would never consciously approve or ignore living conditions that did not meet Western standards of hygiene and sanitation. But plantation managers had camp bosses to monitor life on plantation camps. They likely knew about congested conditions but chose to disregard the situation. Ligot had also received many complaints about crowded living conditions in camps from workers themselves but ignored such facts and failed to push HSPA leaders on these topics. He chose instead to fault Filipino workers rather than question the actions of the sugar industry. While Balmori's report presented a positive view of conditions on plantations, neither he nor the other short-term Philippine labor commissioners ever targeted Filipino laborers as the cause of their own problems in Hawai'i.

Ligot also blamed field hands for not making the most of the prospects given to them. When he requested and received a general pardon for Filipinos to resume work without repercussions for previously abandoned labor agreements, not as many intra-colonials took advantage of this opportunity as he had expected. Ligot found "many laborers remaining in the same condition as before, idling their time, loafing and gambling."[62] Such a perceived lack of gratitude and immediate action led Ligot to conclude that Filipino workers were lazy. While his efforts to provide employment for these U.S. colonial workers were well intentioned, the policy ignored the reality of plantation life. Ligot assumed Filipinos could not wait to start work in the fields again. He thought they just could not get jobs because of the HSPA moratorium on hiring former strikers. In fact, poor working and living conditions caused Filipinos to leave plantations. Most did not want to return until significant changes took place. Either unaware or unsympathetic to such perspectives, from his position of class privilege Ligot remained out of touch with laborer viewpoints and needs.

Even though Ligot's actions and rhetoric strongly portray him as an HSPA collaborator, he did not blatantly try to alienate his constituency. He attempted to make himself more accessible to Filipino workers by staying away from high-class locations and not openly fraternizing with plantation management during his 1923 tour. He refused to stay in a hotel or set up an office in the executive building where intra-colonial laborers might be intimidated or embarrassed to visit.[63] He would not dine, ride, or stay with plantation management, claiming that he "never accepted the kindness and courtesy of the Managers to be with them in their tables, to avoid misapprehension of the laborers."[64] He outwardly monitored his actions during the workweek. But when he was not meeting with laborers, Ligot reveled in socializing with elite leaders in Hawai'i.

During his residence in the Territory of Hawai'i, Ligot regularly associated with the haole ruling class. He spoke with pride about his invitations to exclusive meetings and events, regularly networking with influential government and business leaders. He even boasted, "I was the only person of other race invited by General Summerall, Commanding, Hawaiian Division, to be with the other Generals . . . in the grand stand to witness the Military Review."[65] Ligot became an accepted part of Hawai'i's elite, even appearing in the publication *Men of Hawai'i*, a biographical listing of important leaders in the islands, in 1930.[66] He clearly enjoyed establishing himself within the social and political hierarchies of power in Hawai'i. He could have also viewed his close interactions with haole elite as a way to become an effective labor commissioner. Regardless of his motivations, Ligot's personal success within upper-class circles and government structures ultimately did not serve the needs of Filipino laborers in the islands.

While he understood his responsibilities to manage work issues, Ligot's class status, imperial training, and colonial background prevented him from actually improving labor conditions in Hawai'i. True to his indoctrination through Filipinization, the commissioner willingly cooperated with U.S. business interests in the islands. He also invoked paternalistic rhetoric that consistently blamed the working class for their own issues. As a member of the Philippine elite, he looked down on laborers and remained unsympathetic to the daily perspectives and experiences of these intra-colonials.

When dealing with complaints, he became more sensitive to the pressures, challenges, and needs of sugar industry leadership than those of Filipino intra-colonials. Since he usually sided with the HSPA, his inability to help the Filipino working-class led to widespread protest against him and his programs.

Ligot's Slow Demise: Renewed Filipino Protests

The existence of a local Philippine government official did not guarantee community compliance with his policies or requests. As Peck has shown, worker support is central to the creation and maintenance of power for ethnic labor leaders.[67] Without worker approval, individuals trying to act as community representatives eventually fail. Ligot's extensive affiliation with regional haole elite, as well as his pro-plantation attitude, led Filipinos in Hawai'i to resist cooperation with the labor commissioner and his projects.

In October 1923, Commissioner Ligot initiated a fundraising campaign to fight tuberculosis in the Philippines. The HSPA enthusiastically supported this charity effort, immediately donating ten thousand Philippine pesos to the cause. Ligot told laborers, "This is the proper time to show up our dearest feeling towards our countrymen in the motherland. Give to the Manager, or his representative duly appointed, as much voluntary help as you can. . . . Do not forget the sincerest sympathy of the Hawaiian Sugar Planters to this cause, which is not theirs, but ours. We have to thank them with honest labor and sincere cooperation in the achievement of success in their enterprise. . . . let me thank you in advance for your early cooperation in giving support to this national cause of ours."[68] Ligot encouraged each worker to donate one-thirteenth of his or her salary, or about two dollars a month. With more than two thousand Filipinos at the Ola'a plantation at this time, he expected to raise $4,000 a month at this one location.

Despite Ligot's passionate and patriotic rhetoric, as well as his detailed plan for funding the campaign, Filipino laborers did not contribute widely to this program. About a month after the start of the campaign, Ola'a plantation manager A. J. Watt reported, "Filipinos are not very enthusiastic about subscribing."[69] Watt had informed Filipino leaders on the plantation about the fundraising drive and posted several copies of Ligot's statement on payday. Out of the 2,502 laborers at Ola'a, fewer than sixty Filipinos pledged $118.35 total for the months of October and November. Filipinos at two of the four work camps did not pledge anything at all. Just as Puerto Rican U.S. colonials in Hawai'i did not have to accept questionable labor investigations of their conditions, Filipinos did not have to support Ligot's agenda. Over time, most intra-colonial workers resisted participation in any activity that involved this representative. They learned that Ligot usually served HSPA interests over their own. Workers consequently became suspicious of and avoided any plan the commissioner endorsed. Without the trust of laborers, Ligot's campaign for tuberculosis fundraising was doomed.

Highlighting the central role and importance of plantation leadership in raising money for this campaign might have also deterred workers from donating their hard-earned wages to the project. Once again, Ligot's class perspective and imperial training prevented him from recognizing some obvious reasons his patronizing rhetoric and strategies might lead Filipinos to not participate in his programs. Laborers would likely not be motivated to act in a thankful way toward sugar leadership who kept wages low and resisted efforts to improve living or working conditions. If the HSPA had so much money to donate to a Philippine charity, why could the sugar industry not raise wages or provide better housing? Filipinos already believed they worked hard for poor treatment and did not want to support a cause funded by exploitative plantation managers and led by the dubious labor commissioner.

Unhappy with the actual use of the position they created, Filipinos in Hawai'i launched a movement to remove Ligot from office in January 1924. These U.S. colonials sent a scathing resolution to recall Ligot to Governor General Wood, the Philippine senate, and newspapers in Hawai'i and the Philippines. Just nine months after Ligot started his job, intra-colonial workers claimed that "all confidence in his ability, honesty, and integrity has been lost and his continued employment as labor commissioner is detrimental to the best interests of the Filipino laborers."[70] For Filipino intra-colonials in the islands, the removal of an official government representative was a better alternative than working with this co-opted leader.

To defend his actions, Ligot explained: "For the sake of the Filipino laborers, I doubled up my effort and energy to the risk of my health in placing the laborers in good terms with the Managers and capitalists; had I acted to the contrary I would have not been granted with the better treatments and housing conditions."[71] Ligot claimed his cooperation with sugar leaders was key to his success in obtaining plantation improvements. He also felt he worked harder than required, or expected, for a person of his social and political position. He believed Filipinos in the islands should be grateful for his insightful and diligent work on their behalf.

The petition to remove Ligot from office stated, "Ligot has refused to cooperate with the Filipino Laborers in Hawaii in their efforts to improve working conditions and to provide for their general welfare, and has deprived them of the opportunity of presenting their grievances."[72] Filipinos disapproved of Ligot's blatant cooperation with the HSPA and wanted to end his ineffective and detrimental work there. This petition claimed that 905 individuals unanimously supported the resolution at a mass meeting held at 'Aiea on January 10, 1924. A second petition was sent to the Philippine director of labor in May that same year, using similar rhetoric and citing 138 signatures. As a representative of the Higher Wages Movement, Manlapit also sent letters that spoke out against Ligot to the Philippine government on October 10.[73]

In response to these complaints, Governor General Wood asked Territory of Hawai'i governor Farrington to conduct an investigation of the accusations. While Filipino intra-colonial workers expressed extreme distrust of the commissioner, Ligot's haole government and business allies fully defended him. Farrington's investigation of Ligot did not uncover anything negative about the labor representative. Farrington claimed, "I have failed to find an instance that would justify me in concluding that commissioner Ligot has neglected his duty . . . I have always found him to be gentlemanly and businesslike. . . . [He] has done very well."[74] Ligot's continuous prioritization of Philippine and Territory of Hawai'i administrative goals and business interests motivated Anglo-American leaders to strongly defend his character and actions, as well as protect his government position. As part of the U.S. imperial hierarchy, Ligot was expected to work closely with businessmen and government officials. He acted as desired by elite leaders in the interconnected political, economic, and social hierarchies of Hawai'i. With the positive report and endorsement from the territorial governor of the islands, the Philippine government did not have any solid evidence to recall Ligot from office.

Even though Filipino U.S. colonials did not succeed in removing Ligot in 1924, they continuously resisted cooperation with him and his programs. The strike of 1924 became another major example of worker opposition to Ligot's efforts. If Filipino laborers in Hawai'i trusted this leader and believed he could advocate for real change, they would not need or want to go on strike. But they did. The 1924 work protest developed after Ligot failed to address labor issues that remained unresolved since the 1920 strike. When the presence of a local government representative did not improve their most basic experiences, Filipino workers took it upon themselves to demand better work and living conditions.

The 1924 strike started on April 1 and lasted eighteen months, involving more than five thousand workers on twenty-six of the forty-five plantations on the islands.[75] Led by Manlapit, the protest, also known as the Filipino Piecemeal Strike, aimed to obtain two extra dollars for an eight-hour work day, an end to the bonus system, and better housing. When Ligot visited plantations in an attempt to calm down workers, "rumors of Ligot's arrival caused uneasiness" among Filipino laborers.[76] Instead of comforting and reassuring workers, the commissioner's presence increased tensions.

On September 15, 1924, in an attempt to end or at least curtail the strike, Ligot issued a statement to Filipinos translated in multiple Philippine dialects. He discussed how "the authorities in the Philippines are in thorough support of your labor commissioner here, whose advice to you has been continuously to conduct yourselves with respect to law and to obey and respect the Representatives of the Government. . . . I call upon you all to disband as strikers, go back to work wherever you may find it, and to work faithfully in restoring the good name of Filipinos in Hawaii. . . . I call upon you to follow this action at once. Return to work quickly."[77] Ligot explained that the Philippine government empowered him to manage intra-colonial labor issues. As their official labor leader, he wanted workers to follow government and business expectations and go back to the fields. Ending the strike would maintain a positive reputation for Filipinos in the islands. Ligot's appeal, based on pleasing Philippine authorities and the U.S. public, was ineffective. Filipinos ignored his collaborationist directives and continued to strike. Without the trust or support of workers, this commissioner's anti-protest attempts did not alter the course of the labor stoppage.

During the 1924 strike, local plantation managers also started to lose faith in Ligot's ability to influence Filipino labor in the islands. Ola'a manager A. J. Watt explained how other managers would not believe Ligot when he declared the end of the strike: "He told us the same thing shortly before it occurred in July."[78] Local sugar industry leaders came to doubt Ligot's capacity to represent or control Filipino workers. Some plantation managers, like Filipino laborers, also started to actively avoid interactions with him. When the strike ended in 1925, Ligot played no role in resolving the situation.

As an elite and colonized ethnic representative, Ligot failed intra-colonial workers for the majority of his time as labor commissioner. He also became less useful to local plantation managers over the course of his tenure. However, Ligot continued to serve as an ineffectual labor commissioner until he was forced to leave his position by the Philippine government in 1933. Even though his main opponent, Manlapit, was arrested and imprisoned for his involvement with the 1924 strike, protests and controversy continued to surround Ligot. Emilio Parangan, a Filipino leader in Hawai'i, Filipino Reverend N. C. Dizon in Hawai'i, and Philippine leader Francisco Varona were among several other people who complained to the Philippine government about Ligot's performance in the islands in the late 1920s and 1930s.[79] Reverend Dizon stated that Filipinos in Hawai'i "have lost their confidence in the incumbent."[80] Parangan said, "We want and need a leader in Hawaii from the Phippine who is not inclined to be lured by the shining dollar . . .

we donn't want a Leader as Mr. caytano Legot who onl works for his benefit and not for his country and countrymen [sic]."[81] But Anglo-American Philippine governor general H. L. Stimson liked Ligot and fully supported him throughout the late 1920s. He stated, "Mr. Ligot is doing fine work in Honolulu."[82] Despite multiple protests against him, Ligot continued to fill the position of worker representative for the Philippine government.

When Theodore Roosevelt Jr. became Philippine governor general in 1932, he viewed Ligot's actions in Hawai'i as inappropriate. Roosevelt consequently abolished the position of resident labor commissioner in November 1932. The governor general asked Ligot to return to the Philippines to face charges of collusion with the HSPA and misinforming the Philippine government about the conditions facing Filipino laborers in Hawai'i. It was "specifically alleged that the commissioner, though fully aware of the local unemployment situation, failed to inform his government frankly and permitted much unauthorized recruiting of labor for jobs which did not exist.[83] But Ligot stayed in Hawai'i. While Roosevelt's legislation eliminated the government representative position, the act still allowed Ligot to collect a salary.[84] He viewed this loophole as a sign that he should continue his work in the islands, and he did just that.

In July 1933, Anglo-American Philippine governor general Frank Murphy also tried to end Ligot's work in Hawai'i. Murphy asked his lieutenant governor to initiate an investigation of ten years' worth of complaints against Ligot.[85] Since Ligot still remained in Hawai'i and continued to claim his role as a government representative, Murphy had to delineate an exact date for Ligot's dismissal: December 31, 1933. Only then did Ligot stop working in this capacity. Even after the end of his official employment, the former leader still received two years of retirement wages.[86] Despite losing the support of the workers he was supposed to represent, facing investigations that scrutinized his policies and actions, and having multiple governor generals dismiss him from office, Ligot continued to fill and get a wage for this unsupported leadership position from 1924 to 1933.

When he finally stepped down from his post as labor commissioner, Ligot still maintained a level of prestige in the islands. As a close HSPA and Territory of Hawai'i collaborator, Ligot's quality of life in Hawai'i remained comfortable for the rest of his days there. He continued to control *Ti Silaw*, the Filipino newspaper in the islands that he had maintained with HSPA money since 1927.[87] He also became the owner of a small general store and print shop in Honolulu in the late 1930s through the 1940s.[88] In 1947, he became director of the Territorial Filipino Council, which included International and Longshore Warehouse Union leaders. Even though he failed as an official advocate for Filipino workers before World War II, Ligot somehow gained a labor advisory position in the region fourteen years later. He returned to the Philippines in the last years of his life and died in 1973.

While the lack of approval from laborers often ended the careers of ethnic mediators (see Gunther Peck's work), Ligot's continued collaboration with Territory of Hawai'i business interests meant he received a certain level of protection and support throughout his time in the islands. When facing charges for misuse of his position, Ligot received only minor punishment with no long-term repercussions. Such cooperation with the regional elite bolstered his position in Hawai'i, but it rarely benefited everyday U.S. colonials. Filipinos, like Puerto Ricans in the islands, continued to suffer poor living and working conditions on Hawai'i sugar plantations.

Conclusion

As demonstrated by Ligot, the Filipinization of the intra-colonial labor complaint process in the Pacific did not result in improved conditions for the average Filipino. Despite Ligot's local residency in Hawai'i, as a seasoned and upper-class imperial official he ended up creating more problems than solutions for U.S. colonial workers. The commissioner had the potential to fill important advocacy roles and to take significant actions to improve the daily lives of the Filipino community in the islands. But instead of rallying behind intra-colonial workers, Ligot, with his class mannerisms, imperial training, and plantation sympathies, distrusted labor complaints and viewed Filipino workers negatively. He was generally not compassionate toward intra-colonial laborers and consequently had difficulty developing and maintaining support from the Filipino community in Hawai'i. While Ligot tried to be aware of situations that would alienate him from Filipino workers, his misguided efforts and inability to truly relate to laborers only further frustrated these U.S. colonials and led them to conduct more strikes, write additional complaints, and petition for the commissioner's termination.

While Ligot prioritized the interests of the HSPA, the Filipino workingclass did not have to act in similar ways. Many intra-colonial laborers protested within the colonial and plantation structures that restrained them. Their ability to create a Philippine resident labor commissioner position through formal petitions and government legislation displayed a moment of high influence with the Philippine administration. Filipino intra-colonials successfully pressured their home region, and subsequently HSPA officials, to accommodate their need for a local official.

When the resident labor representative failed to meet their expectations, Filipino workers actively resisted him and his programs. Intra-colonials even petitioned for Ligot's removal from office on multiple occasions. Despite numerous forms of colonial constraints, everyday Filipinos in Hawai'i exercised a measure of control over their individual practices and daily lives. Filipinos, like Puerto Ricans in Hawai'i, could not be forced to follow U.S. business or government expectations. However, the lack of effective official representatives for Filipino and Puerto Rican U.S. colonials in Hawai'i led both groups to rely on informal local community ethnic mediators to fill such leadership voids and deal with their daily issues, as will be seen in the next two chapters.

5. *Conflicting Convictions*

FILIPINO ETHNIC MINISTER INTERACTIONS
WITH THE PLANTATION COMMUNITY

In reaction to the low value of sugar in 1921, Hawai'i sugar plantations cut worker wages up to 20 percent. Before such pay reductions, intra-colonial Filipino laborers already struggled to save enough of their salary to send monetary remittances to their loved ones in the Philippines. These workers became upset at the change in wage scale and went on strike from 1924 to 1925. This labor stoppage, known as the Filipino Piecemeal Sugar Strike, was one of the largest protests of Filipinos in Hawai'i, as well as one of the most legally aggressive reactions by the HSPA during the first half of the twentieth century.[1]

On January 21, 1925, approximately two thousand strikers left the town of Hilo on the island of Hawai'i and headed toward the Ola'a plantation to enjoin Filipinos at that location to protest with them. Six miles out of town, the police drew a white line across the road and threatened to shoot anyone who crossed the threshold. Protestors stopped at this location and asked to speak with Filipino leaders at Ola'a. They spoke with Flaviano M. Santa Ana, who answered their questions without fear. Santa Ana stood his ground as an opponent of the strike.[2] After extensive questioning, the strikers dispersed and returned to Hilo "peaceably and seemingly in good humor."[3] Throughout the Piecemeal Strike, Santa Ana spoke on behalf of Filipino laborers at Ola'a. In addition to his role as community representative, Santa Ana worked as a member of the plantation special police, a unit of armed men paid by the plantation to maintain order during strike times. His conflicting responsibilities as labor spokesperson and plantation security became further complicated by his position as a Protestant minister for Filipinos at Ola'a.

Without permanent, trusted, and local Philippine officials to handle the daily issues of Filipino intra-colonials, the workers, plantation leadership, and Protestant church all looked to Filipino pastors to help them interact with each other. Multiple forms of social capital positioned Santa Ana and his replacement, Simeon Ibera, as influential middlemen for migrant laborers, sugar plantation management, and the Hawaiian Evangelical Association (HEA).[4] As religious leaders with fluency in English and Filipino dialects, both men had the cultural capital, or knowledge and skills, to negotiate on behalf of illiterate and non-English-speaking plantation workers.[5] These individuals also had social capital because they were members of the dominant religious institution in Hawai'i (the HEA), employees of HSPA plantation managers, as well as advisors for the Filipino community. Their combined social and cultural capital resulted in symbolic capital, or a degree of respect, influence, and consideration, that other informal community leaders could not access. Trust gained through symbolic capital led to the appointment of Santa Ana and Ibera as Filipino representatives for the plantation, as well as their development into Filipino community leaders. Workers and sugar managers both saw the cultural and social capital that HEA Filipino pastors had and targeted them for help with daily issues. Ultimately, these mediators gained their positions of power from the support and trust of the groups they served.

However, having one person fulfilling these diverse roles of leadership often resulted in suspicion over the loyalty of such a middleman. Santa Ana and Ibera constantly worked hard to convince Filipino workers that their loyalties lay with them over the plantation manager with whom they also closely worked. The association of these pastors with the HEA further caused Filipino workers to question the intentions of these individuals. In the end, Santa Ana and Ibera served important roles of mediation for all three groups. However, such positions of power were tenuous and frequently questioned by the people who placed them in these leadership roles.

Establishing Positions of Power

From the beginning of Protestant proselytization at plantation camps, Filipinos petitioned the HEA for a Filipino pastor at the Ola'a plantation. Even though Anglo-American Reverend Tommy F. Anderson had already worked with this ethnic group since 1914, Filipinos repeatedly asked for a minister of their same ethnic background. In 1915, plantation worker Leon Foronda wrote to Vincente Lionson of the Philippine Mission, stating, "No doubt you understand that what the Filipinos need in Hawaii is a leader, and we need one bad in Pahoa and Olaa . . . it seems as though this is the only way to save the situation at present, for who would want to sell his country or misrepresent his country [sic]."[6] Filipino workers in Hawai'i believed a Filipino minister could be trusted to take care of his ethnic community. The laborers wanted a pastor they could relate to: someone who looked like them, spoke like them, and came from the same culture. Workers believed an ethnic minister would have the cultural capital to be an effective leader for Filipinos at Ola'a. Such a push for the Filipinization of religious orders also had historic precedents in the Philippines.[7] In 1917, the HEA Board of Trustees, also known as the Hawaiian Board, assented to the requests of laborers and sent Flaviano M. Santa Ana to the Ola'a plantation to serve as the Filipino pastor. Santa Ana started work for intra-colonials in Hawai'i out of direct requests for local assistance and leadership from Filipinos themselves.

Both Santa Ana and Ibera provided Sunday services, Sunday school, prayer meetings, religious interviews, and other religious activities for the Filipino labor community at Ola'a. Their ministry also included a women's group, children's bible study, and choir meetings. If pastors did not provide a specific service, Filipino U.S. colonials proactively requested it. In February 1923, some church members wanted Santa Ana to baptize their children. But Santa Ana did not have the authority to conduct this ceremony because the HEA did not ordain ethnic ministers at that time. When Filipinos found out their minister could not provide this service, they did not hesitate to petition the HEA to empower Santa Ana to perform the services they expected and desired from a religious leader. Members immediately wrote the HEA to "send you our petition an occount of Mr. Santa Ana, Our Pastor of the said place. We know him that he could carry all necessary of the church, but we surprise that he could not be baptize of a Child, so there is no others that we much obliged to our petition is the one thing only we need of our Section to give him a faculty, so that we can get more Members at the future [sic]."[8] Church members did not believe a minister could effectively lead a church if he could not baptize a child. The petitioners also alluded to the fact that Santa Ana's expanded authority could lead to more church growth. The HEA granted this request. By July 1924, Santa Ana was a licentiate who could perform basic religious sacraments, such as baptisms and funerals.[9] This new level of authority and recognition from the HEA provided Santa Ana with increased social, cultural, and symbolic capital. Filipinos at Ola'a also likely appreciated the fact that the HEA was flexible enough to expand the duties of Filipino pastors since the Protestant church in the Philippines resisted Filipinization of the church until 1929.[10]

Filipino group outside Ola'a Filipino Evangelical church, Nine Mile Camp, Ola'a, Hawai'i, ca. 1920–1930. Photo by M. Koga, Bishop Museum.

Filipino laborers at Ola'a also relied on ethnic ministers for a range of nonreligious assistance. Even though Chinese, Japanese, Hawaiian, Portuguese, and Spanish-speaking labor groups also had ethnic ministers in the islands, the lack of official leadership for U.S. colonials in Hawai'i expanded the scope of topics Filipino ministers addressed on a daily basis.[11] Filipino workers asked ethnic ministers to help them with a variety of matters, including domestic disputes, financial issues, transport to the hospital, as well as interpreting and writing work and personal communications. For non-U.S. colonials, most of these matters could be handled by their country's consul general in Honolulu. Without a similar type of official government representative, Filipino intra-colonials at Ola'a looked to Protestant ethnic ministers to provide practical daily support and aid.[12]

Filipinos also had particular labor needs due to their status as U.S. colonials. As discussed in chapter 2, Filipinos were the only group in Hawai'i to gain return passage, as well as access to Paid Transport Applications (PTAs) and Recruit Transport Applications (RTAs). The paperwork for these programs could become complicated. Santa Ana frequently helped Filipino workers make sense of and succeed in applying for these highly specific and local HSPA recruitment and retention processes.[13] Santa Ana helped about seven people a week, or 405 people in a fourteen-month period. For twenty weeks he brought sick people to the hospital, for eighteen weeks he helped people apply for return passage to the Philippines and requested plantation jobs for Filipinos, for fourteen weeks he addressed the personal troubles of individuals, and for seven weeks he dealt with plantation-related issues.[14] Without permanent official leadership in the islands, about 40 percent of the approximately two thousand Filipinos at the Ola'a plantation went to Santa Ana for help with secular issues. These intra-colonials relied on this Protestant ethnic minister to negotiate with plantation managers, file a variety of paperwork, and assist with their personal needs. Santa Ana worked with plantation managers to champion work requests, and with individuals to address their private issues.

Ethnic Protestant pastors made concerted efforts to meet the needs of Filipino workers. Through regular contact with these laborers, Santa Ana and Ibera became familiar with Filipino expectations. They tailored their actions and practices to appeal to workers. Since Filipino laborers responded well to Santa Ana's individual assistance with personal and work matters, this ethnic minister focused on frequent, one-on-one interactions to develop Christianity among Filipinos at Ola'a. In one weekly report to the HEA, he stated, "My work now is going house to [house] every afternoon, doing personal work, [converting] the people as I can."[15] To free up more time for personal work with laborers, Santa Ana reduced the number of open-air meetings he conducted, a standard among evangelists at that time. He changed his HEA-prescribed daily routine to reflect and accommodate the needs of the Filipino labor community. Such flexibility was central to his development into a trusted leader among his compatriots.

By demonstrating his loyalty to workers and his prioritization of their needs over those of the church, laborers believed Santa Ana was working for their interests. Like the padrones in Gunther Peck's research, Santa Ana provided "vital cultural, economic, and political services" and "mediated the distance between immigrant workers and economic, cultural, and political institutions."[16] Through such consistent aid, the pastor gained symbolic capital as an accepted representative of Filipinos at Ola'a. Santa Ana's position of power in the community was consequently created through the sanction of the workers themselves. This ethnic minister maintained his role as an influential middleman by sustaining intimate, personal connections with workers and providing continuous useful assistance for the community.

The lack of effective Philippine government leaders in Hawai'i also meant that the sugar industry needed other trusted individuals to help them manage

Filipino issues. Olaʻa plantation leaders C. F. Eckhart and A. J. Watt looked to Santa Ana for assistance because he gained their trust through his ability to translate and work closely with Filipino laborers. These managers relied on Santa Ana so much that they hired him as a salaried employee of the plantation. They gave Santa Ana free housing, a partial salary, and free household amenities. For the church, both Eckhart and Watt supplied land at very low rent, offered discounted prices on construction lumber, and gave monetary donations for other needs.[17] In return, Santa Ana was responsible for addressing any and all Filipino issues that came to the sugar manager. He acted as a translator for the plantation office, met Filipino laborers upon arrival, and helped them get settled. He also distributed letters from the Philippines to workers in the camps, delivered contract cards for the plantation, and disseminated plantation communications to workers. During the 1924 strike, he was also expected to keep the peace in the Filipino camp where he lived.

Plantation managers also looked to ethnic pastors for advice on how to handle situations involving Filipino laborers. In 1928, Watt asked Ibera for his opinion on one Filipino family who requested financial assistance from the plantation. Ibera reported, "I can not recommend that family because I found out that the . . . poverty of the family is due to laziness. At any rate I'll try to make the husband work hard before I could recommend him to the plantation."[18] Ibera provided a truthful assessment about the status of this family and planned to work with these individuals to improve their situation for their own benefit, as well as the benefit of the plantation. Ethnic ministers became valuable sources of information about the Filipino community, as well as mediators for different policies and issues. The more loyalty and honesty these middlemen demonstrated to HSPA leadership, the more responsibilities and trust they gained.

Higher levels of plantation leadership also relied on Filipino ethnic ministers for insider information. In 1923, HSPA Director Butler asked Santa Ana to accompany Patricio Belen, a visiting representative of the Philippine fraternal organization *Dimas-Alang*. The sugar industry feared that Belen might be manipulated by strike leader Manlapit, so they asked Santa Ana to keep an eye on Belen as he traveled to various plantation camps across the Hawaiian Islands. While plantation head A. J. Watt did not trust Belen, he told Butler, "It is all right for Santa Ana to go to Maui if he can help out in any way. I feel sure you can depend on him."[19] Such trust from local and regional levels of the sugar management placed Santa Ana and Ibera in influential positions within the plantation hierarchy.

Plantation management also accepted ethnic ministers because of their social capital as members of the HEA, the powerful pro-plantation and pro-colonial religious institution in Hawaiʻi.[20] Historically, Protestant missionaries in the islands functioned as a significant part of the U.S. colonial project in the Pacific. According to historian Mark Gallagher, "The HEA's heritage as the dominant church in the Islands included a record of involvement in the affairs of the kingdom, an influence noticeable from the time of the first written laws of the 1820s."[21] Sugar leaders knew HEA ethnic ministers were supervised by and subject to the directives of like-minded Anglo-American leaders in the region. The close cooperation between the sugar industry and the HEA also "stemmed in part from the genealogical networking present by virtue of the Big Five [sugar] companies all having missionary descendants on their boards . . . [the sugar industry's] financial support of the Protestant Church further heightened the interlocking of the two groups. The Protestant Church regularly needed financial support above and beyond contributions of its membership."[22] But this level of cooperation between the plantation hierarchy and the Protestant church led to much suspicion from Filipino laborers. To maintain their positions of power on plantations, ethnic ministers had to constantly balance the interests and needs of the HEA, the Filipino community, and the HSPA.

As employees of the plantation, Santa Ana and Ibera found that their opinions and recommendations were more influential than those of other community mediators, like union leaders who did not have any direct affiliation with the sugar industry. In fact, local labor organizers were often closely monitored and harassed by plantation leaders and local police.[23] Labor commissioners from the Philippines also did not sufficiently address daily worker needs. Santa Ana and Ibera, in contrast, obtained the trust and support of both workers and plantation managers. Through their social, cultural, and symbolic capital, these useful mediators for sugar plantations, workers, and the Protestant church gained several diverse and powerful responsibilities at Ola'a.

Conflicting Roles

However, such positions of influence were not permanent due to the multiple and sometimes conflicting expectations, duties, and roles placed upon Santa Ana and Ibera. In Santa Ana's case, as a member of the plantation special police, he was expected to report any problematic workers to the manager. But as the pastor and ethnic leader for Filipinos, Santa Ana also had a responsibility to keep the affairs of his constituents confidential and to work ultimately for their benefit. Even though he was trusted to communicate with all three groups, Santa Ana was pulled to act in numerous directions. Plantation managers, laborers, and the HEA all worried that his loyalty lay with one of the other groups he worked for.

Soon after Santa Ana's multiple and seemingly contradictory roles at the Ola'a plantation came into sharp view during the 1924 strike, the HEA asked Santa Ana to focus on his religious activities and responsibilities. Santa Ana responded by stating, "About my connection in the Plantation I still had my Commission as a Special Police but they did not use me as the other Special, they use me as they use me before so I can use all my time in the religious work as I did before. But my dicision is to be a Missionary, and I have no any intention to be a Plantation helper [sic]."[24] While Santa Ana followed HEA instructions not to perform any more plantation office tasks, he continued to assist workers with many of the same personal and work needs as before. He continued to help bring sick people to the hospital, mediate personal troubles (such as domestic disputes and money issues), file applications for return passage, and submit requests for jobs or other plantation-related matters. Regardless of HEA directives to focus solely on religious services, Santa Ana prioritized and served the daily administrative requests of his Filipino community. As the best source of intra-colonial leadership in the area, he was a middleman who was serious about his role as mediator between migrant workers and the economic institution they worked for. When the HEA found out that Santa Ana had not stopped his nonreligious activities at Ola'a, and that he had no plans to cease such work, the organization acted more aggressively. The HEA decided to reassign the recalcitrant Santa Ana to a different church at another plantation on another island in 1928.[25] Santa Ana's transfer to another location resulted from his overly complicated and multiple roles at the Ola'a plantation that he was not willing to stop. He remained a loyal and dedicated representative for Filipino workers throughout his time on the island of Hawai'i.

After Santa Ana's departure, the HEA assigned a new Filipino minister to the Ola'a plantation: Simeon Ibera. This pastor also worked hard to help the Filipino labor community at this plantation. However, he was now constrained by the lessons learned by the HEA during Santa Ana's tenure. Ibera was prohibited from becoming a plantation employee, and he had to limit his activities with workers to religious outreach. However, the continued need for leadership in the Filipino intra-colonial community and his personal desire to help workers with their issues led Ibera to play a more involved role in labor issues and needs than the HEA wanted.

In 1928, a Filipino family wished to live closer to the church. Since the plantation did not have any employment or housing for them, Ibera allowed the family to move in with him temporarily. When his guests became too great a disturbance, the minister moved into another house. A few months later, the husband abandoned his wife and children. Another church member allowed the destitute woman and her children to live in her home. Norman C. Schenck, Ibera's supervisor in the Filipino department of the HEA, wrote to Ibera about this situation. Schenck advised, "No woman [should] be taken to live in your house under any condition whatever. It will only create situations in which gossip will do harm to you, as it has done in this case . . . [A] minister depends to a large extent upon keeping your name above reproach. As soon as you fail in this, you will fail in your job, and I warn you now that you will find very little chance to continue to work for the Hawaiian Board if you do not keep above suspicion in this particular respect."[26] Even though Ibera's superior reprimanded him for living with a woman, Ibera believed his actions were justified because he was helping new converts. Ibera explained, "The church feels that it is an ibligation to help the members who have been faithfully joined to the church, we the deacons and committees of the church took action right away and placed the mother four children in a house of our church member and give her support [sic]."[27] Since his congregation prioritized helping each other, Ibera acted as he felt his members wanted and expected him to. He proceeded according to the interests of his constituency. According to scholar Barak Kalir, evangelical churches usually provide "spiritual relief, a social network, a feeling of belonging, and some practical aid" for migrant laborers.[28] He claimed that the main function of such religious leaders and their institutions involved helping workers get adjusted to their host society and providing them with a community of support to listen to their struggles and to help in whatever way possible. Both Ibera and Santa Ana closely followed such patterns, goals, and activities, often to the dismay of their supervisors.

One of Ibera's main goals involved providing a permanent spiritual space for Filipinos at Ola'a to worship. In 1929, he explained, "I am planning the reorganization of our church . . . this year we will devote our time for membership campaign and next year for raising money to build our church. Sometimes our church building could not accommodate the people that want to attend our church services. So we looking forward to enlarge our building."[29] In addition to increasing the number of parishioners, Ibera wanted to provide an adequate and conducive building for his congregation and its long-term growth. By 1933, the majority of funds had been raised to erect a church structure.

When plantation leadership took a long time to decide which parcel of land to use for the church, Ibera authorized the start of construction without a finalized lease. Schenck chided Ibera: "I do not know where you got the idea that you could begin to build, until the land question was settled . . . I strongly urge you not to buy any lumber until the plans are approved by the Board."[30] Ibera knew his action would result in reprimands from the HEA. But he told the carpenters to begin work in March so he could raise the remaining funds for church construction during the peak of that year's harvest season. He believed workers would be less inclined to provide donations two months later, when their shifts and wages would be reduced to three days a week. Even after receiving Schenck's letter of reproach, Ibera defended his decision because Filipinos at Ola'a refused to provide additional donations until construction started.[31] Since these U.S. colonial laborers were withholding their financial support for the church building, Ibera initiated construction without plantation consent to regain cooperation from his congregants. Prioritizing the needs and attitudes of Filipino workers led to tensions for Ibera with both plantation and HEA leadership. However, he continued to choose the most effective ways to interact with laborers in favor of actions that would please the HSPA or the Protestant church.

Ibera also tried to help Filipino workers by organizing a union in 1937, called the Ola'a Filipino Labor League. Even though the HEA did not want ministers to get involved in plantation issues, he told Schenck, "I know you are surprise to hear and see me involved in labor problems and the Hawaiian Board does not approve my reaction toward better understanding between Filipino laborers and the plantation. But I did it with the intention of uniting the Filipinos to common understanding and to promote better relations between Filipino and plantation. It worked more than I expected and I am hoping the Olaa Filipino would realize what I have done for them [sic]."[32] Ibera claimed that he created this group to develop better relations between workers and plantation leadership. From his constant contact and familiarity with the Filipino community, he knew laborers themselves should be in charge of the organization and steer the direction of the group. Ibera also hoped the creation of a labor organization would boost the church's image among workers, as well as plantation leadership. He prioritized the collective interests of the laborers over that of the HEA and the HSPA. While this approach did not please his supervisor, such dedication and service led workers to trust Ibera as an ethnic mediator, at least at this particular moment.

Within two months of development, fourteen hundred Filipino workers joined the Ola'a Filipino Labor League. When strike leaders from Maui's Congress of Industrial Organizations came to Ola'a later that year, Filipinos at this location chose not to join them. According to Ibera, "Since the Olaa Filipino labor league offers better and direct way to settle their complains and grievances not one of them joined the Maui leaders."[33] Ibera's labor organizing could be interpreted as blatant collaboration with plantation managers. He even admitted that he created the group's constitution and bylaws to "please the plantation as well as the Filipino laborers."[34] By avoiding a strike, the union helped sugar industry interests. But this result was neither

Ibera's initial or ultimate motive. He simply wanted workers to have a useful way to address labor issues on their own.

Workers truly felt that Ibera helped them build an effective method of communication with plantation management. With his "ability to represent and provide services to working-class constituency," Ibera was able to address the needs of Filipinos as a class of unskilled workers.[35] As long as laborers believed Ibera worked in their interests and represented their perspective, they would continue to rely on this pastor as a trusted middleman. This position of endorsement was exactly what Ibera strived for as a representative for Filipinos at Ola'a.

Santa Ana and Ibera worked hard to provide all the services that intracolonial laborers requested or needed. Time after time, Filipino pastors disregarded HEA instructions in order to meet the desires and expectations of Filipino workers. Balancing the tensions between specific community needs and institutional directives became a daily part of the Filipino ministry at Ola'a. Both Santa Ana and Ibera became influential mediators at this location. But the trust freely given by the workers was just as easily taken away.

Suspicions Abound

Despite Santa Ana's and Ibera's close interaction and intense work with the community, the Filipino Protestant church at Ola'a did not have a large following during their careers. In 1915, Reverend Anderson commented that "Pahoa & Ola'a are the Biggest Filipinos camps I have yet seen and are realy needy fields the harvest is ripe [sic]."[36] Despite such a prediction, attendance and membership at the Ola'a church remained small compared to the number of Filipinos on the plantation. From 1924 to 1927, only about one hundred people out of an average of two thousand Filipinos on the plantation became members of this church.[37] Workers generally took advantage of the social services provided by these ethnic ministers, who had much social, cultural, and symbolic capital, but most did not feel obligated to join the Protestant faith. Even though U.S. colonials depended on ethnic ministers as one of the few influential local leaders for their community, the power and influence of Filipino ministers on the plantation generally remained secular. While they were successful at gaining the trust and sanction of workers to handle labor and nonreligious personal issues, these preachers did not fulfill their goals of widespread conversion in the Filipino community at Ola'a during the first half of the twentieth century.[38]

In the Philippines, the Protestant church was also unsuccessful in converting Filipino Catholics during this same period. Instead, these missionaries were seen as agents of the U.S. imperial government.[39] The Catholic religion had also established a strong foothold in the Philippines by the mid-seventeenth century.[40] With such historical contexts, few Filipino migrants at the Ola'a plantation flocked to the Protestant church for spiritual needs.

Filipino laborers in Hawai'i also had little interest in changing the belief system they grew up with and practiced in their home region. As intra-colonial workers, they moved, lived, and worked in Hawai'i as a temporary situation. These laborers did not go to the islands to settle or adopt a new faith. Instead, Filipino U.S. colonials participated in local processes that helped them meet their personal goals of making money in the islands and returning home. Laborers might have interacted with Santa Ana and Ibera to obtain essential forms of support and services, like getting rides to the hospital, writing letters to send home, and filing complaints to the plantation manager. However, workers usually viewed their time in Hawai'i as short term, as seen in chapter 2. Most laborers had families back in the Philippines, so there was pressure to return as a success. This desire to accrue enough money to support loved ones back home was the primary goal and focus of most Filipinos at Ola'a.

Plantation workers quickly became aware of the specific politics, as well as social and economic circumstances, guiding the realm of possibilities within the plantation hierarchy. They often looked to Santa Ana and Ibera to take charge and assist them with issues that came up in the workplace. In 1937, Filipinos at Ola'a wanted Ibera to negotiate between them and plantation leaders. Ibera responded by saying, "After organizing the Filipinos here I [said] . . . that it would be wise for me not to be a member of the Labor Union since I am not working for the [plantation]. After long deliberations they considered my requests and they are getting now closer to the plantation to discuss labor troubles in the field."[41] Laborers did not necessarily care how resolutions came about or who helped them. They just wanted their needs and interests to be addressed. Workers might have seen the HEA Filipino church as an influential organization with valuable ties to plantation leaders and the white community in general. These intra-colonials subsequently sought practical, daily assistance from these well-positioned ethnic ministers. Santa Ana's and Ibera's active support of workers made them attractive and effective middlemen for people of all religious backgrounds. However, most Filipino laborers chose not to adhere to the religious teachings of Protestantism.

At the same time that Santa Ana's and Ibera's connections with plantation managers and other white elite were seen as useful, workers also questioned their motives because of their close work and financial relationships with the sugar industry. Ethnic ministers constantly adjusted their interactions with Anglo-American leadership in the islands to avoid criticism from U.S. colonial laborers. In 1924, workers disapproved of Santa Ana's work as a member of the plantation special police. According to Santa Ana, "All the strikers and the strike leaders are against to all Filipino Pastor[s], and they call us a Plantation Cat, not only in one place they said this word but in all the place[s]."[42] Protestors believed someone who worked for the sugar industry could not also work for the interests of laborers. To avoid future entanglements, Santa Ana stopped working for the plantation. Once again, he prioritized the needs of Filipinos over the HSPA and the Protestant church, gaining credibility and trust among the worker community as their ethnic mediator.

In 1938, Ibera refused to accept direct donations from the plantation manager, saying, "The past has put the minister who receive direct help into many kinds of charges and suspicion by the Filipinos. To avoid this I told him to send to the Hawaiian Board the money he gave for the work."[43] Plantation contributions were vital to the daily function of the Ola'a Filipino church. At the same time, overt forms of financial support from the sugar industry were detrimental to the reputations of ethnic ministers within the labor community. Ibera consequently asked sugar management to provide funds in less obvious ways. The ethnic minister was completely willing to accept plantation money for his mission, but he also wanted to maintain his position of power and acceptance among Filipinos as their ethnic mediator. He consequently minimized his direct fiscal connections with sugar management to avoid negative worker reactions. Such measures demonstrated Ibera's skill at balancing the various interests and tensions involved in mediating multiple sides of the same situation. He had to exhibit loyalty and dedication to each group. Without clever tactics such as accepting money through the HEA board, Ibera would have lost credibility and influence over one or more of his constituents. The power of ethnic mediators was consequently always tenuous.

Even though the majority of the Filipino community at Ola'a did not attend their services or convert to Protestantism, Santa Ana and Ibera continued to provide practical administrative services to all laborers in hopes that such assistance would lead to future conversion. Since laborers knew that ministers would still help them, these U.S. colonials continued to avoid Protestantism. They did not need to join the Ola'a Filipino church to get Santa Ana and Ibera to help them communicate with loved ones back home, submit savings deposits, advocate for their issues with plantation management, and fill out return-passage applications. Conversion did not seem to provide any additional benefits for most Filipino workers.

The Converted, For Now

Among the minority of Filipinos at Ola'a who did convert to Protestantism, conflicting social expectations and questionable actions led many Filipino church members to give fragile loyalty to Ibera. In 1928, the Catholic church at Ola'a sent agitators to disrupt Protestant services. Protestant Filipino church members wanted these men arrested. Ibera chose to follow Christian ideals of patience, forgiveness, and peaceful action. Instead of calling the police, as some members requested, he ignored the interruption and moved forward with the service. The pastor explained the situation to Schenck, saying:

> With the crowd came three men of Father Alveriz a catholic priest of Olaa. These three in *our Bible* study disputed what was mentioned and then started a riot. I have not done any harm but hold him out of my church. I know my members were so angry and to avoid further trouble I tried to cool them off by ignoring the whole thing and proceed to continue our service. . . . My members wanted to call the police but I felt it was not a good thing to do although I have the right to make it so. For the police will not stop their scheme to suppress my work. I feel that we can stand in the long run by patience and humiliation and perseverance. I have been criticized so much by our members why I have not done any action for what they have done in our church . . . [yet] I believe that to settle these things through the procedure of law does not quench the fire of hatred and jealousy. I always let God settle these things with me.[44]

As scholars Jonas Nakonz and Angela Wai Yan Shik have found, many evangelical churches for Filipino workers preached patience, coping with one's circumstances, sharing with one another, and looking toward a higher, more long-term salvation to cope with the stresses of daily life. They explained how "most religious coping strategies used by the participants aim either at emotional adjustment to the (stressful) situation or at a relegation of responsibility to a higher entity, rather than at action to change the stressors."[45] Patience was highly valued in these churches. The religious reframing of problems advised laborers to be thankful for the problems that God put upon them. Workers were encouraged to develop "immense hope put into godly interventions to make things change for the better."[46] Ibera reflected a similar nonaggressive calm approach to the disruption at his church.

Ibera's perspective sharply contrasted with the anger of church followers. Members of the Filipino Protestant church wanted revenge and immediate action for the troubles caused by rival churches.[47] However, Ibera would not give into their desire for retaliation or vengeance. While teachings of patience and deference to God's will worked for the Filipina workers in Nakonz and

Shik's research in Hong Kong, this approach did not mollify the Filipinos at Ola'a. Such differences in attitude between the pastor and the community could have resulted in reduced or skeptical membership in the church.

Protestant limitations on the range of acceptable social activities created more tensions between Ibera and church members. The pastor complained about members who engaged in social dancing, an activity prohibited by this denomination at the time. The converted who participated in these recreational activities personally offended him:

> [I] sincerely believed that social dancing in the way the Filipinos take it was a degration of moral character. . . . Social dancing then for two years has not been allowed as a part of our social activities. . . . I did not pay attention to it until it affects the social life of our church. I told them I was hurt to see that the social evil that has caused many homes a failure come out again. They made a commence that a brother minister from Papaiku do not approve it and it is right morally to dance in social party so long it is not a commercialized dance. That hurts me more to hear that a brother minister encourage it since I am trying my best to help my [people] enjoy life free from social evil [sic].[48]

Ibera became deeply disappointed by church members who ignored his teachings. But the Filipino community did not see any problems with dancing. In such a difficult work environment and lonely social setting as plantations in Hawai'i, dancing was one way for people to relax and enjoy themselves on weekends. Even if Ibera acknowledged this fact, he chose to focus on the immoral nature of the practice over the benefits and comfort that dancing provided laborers. Ibera even chastised another Filipino pastor for allowing this form of entertainment among his congregants. Ibera's religious beliefs clashed with the goals and expectations of other Filipinos at Ola'a. Such tensions weakened his ability to serve as a trusted ethnic mediator for this group. These types of restrictions could have also deterred nonmembers from joining the Protestant church.

A general suspicion of Ibera also existed among church followers in his first year as pastor at Ola'a. Most members likely compared Ibera to Santa Ana, whom they greatly respected as a giving and dedicated community leader who was forced to relocate for prioritizing workers to the extent that he did. Some members criticized Ibera's actions as selfish just six months after he began working at the Ola'a Filipino church. In January 1929, he took a vacation from preaching without notifying his local congregation or the HEA. Church member Macario Eugenio wrote to Schenck asking if Ibera had received permission from the central office to leave. He had not. When Schenck asked Ibera to explain his actions, the ethnic minister stated that he left to contemplate his plans for the upcoming year.

The ethnic minister explained, "I regret to hear that my disappearance for a few days has created something that lead you to question me in regard to the work you entrusted me. It seems that I have overlooked that fact that I am not free as anybody else."[49] Ibera lamented his restricted position as both a Protestant minister and a community mediator. He was not an independent individual with freedom to travel as he pleased. Instead, he was a leader responsible and accountable to both the church and his ethnic group at the plantation. He had to consistently work hard to maintain a position of power and influence in the community.

Ibera's unapproved break from his responsibilities at Olaʻa actually had a positive outcome. In his absence, church members delegated various ministerial duties among themselves. Such teamwork displayed the congregation's dedication to keeping the church running with or without a spiritual leader. Ibera stated, "The church is reorganized and now the idle churchgoers are animated assuring their hearty co-operation for the advancement of the gospel."[50] This unexpected result actually pleased Schenck, leading him to chastise Ibera only mildly for leaving without informing anyone.[51] But this incident was just the start of church members' doubts over Ibera's actions, character, and ability to serve as leader of their community.

Around the same time as this incident, Ibera bought a car that he claimed was for church purposes. Both Schenck and Olaʻa church members questioned the logic of such an extravagant purchase. When Ibera requested help from the Hawaiian Board to pay for the license tax on the vehicle, Schenck replied, "You bought a huge car which cost a tremendous sum of money in the first place, and which uses up a lot of gasoline and tires, in the second place, it is not at all likely that the Hawaiian Board will be interested in paying the license tax on such a big car. Besides, you will remember that we pay you ten dollars a month for automobile expense."[52] The HEA acknowledged the need for a pastor vehicle, especially to travel the long distance among different plantations on rural islands with no reliable public transport. However, the allotted amount of ten dollars was not enough to cover the expenses of Ibera's large and costly car. Such an indulgence was not approved by either Schenck or Ibera's congregants. Eugenio also severely criticized Ibera's purchase of a car, telling Schenck,

> The church does not like to help him buy his tires and gasoline for his auto for the reason that he did not use his auto for the church. He used it for his personal concern. He used it once a week for the church while he used it six days for his leisure. Now if we helped him bought his tires and gasoline he might have gone further and further away from the church and he might have gone as far as the Devils' Land.... If he might have used his car more for the church than for his then that would have been different.[53]

Such accusations of self-serving actions were exactly how ethnic leaders lost their support and power in a community. As soon as social distance and lack of loyalty to the community were displayed, laborers often worked hard to remove the mistrusted ethnic mediator.[54] In fact, Eugenio's letter continued to ask, "Is the Rev. Righteous? Do you think it is fair for any Pastor to do that toward his members? Or to treat the church in that way? We don't consider that fair, but the worst kind of treatment since we entered the church."[55] Church followers completely questioned Ibera's actions, intentions, and integrity. He would never become an effective ethnic mediator at Ola'a without their trust and support.

Such vocal and strenuous conflict between a pastor and his congregation was quite problematic for the HEA. In late July 1929, Schenck led a two-day conference to address the issues between Ibera and the Ola'a Filipino church members.[56] An open discussion occurred during the weekend of meetings. At the end of the conference, church members felt satisfied with Ibera's explanations for his actions. Eugenio wrote to Schenck, explaining, "If only Rev. Ibera talked to us in an honest way before he left us, these trouble might have ended long ago. Instead of telling us the truth, he deceived the congregation. . . . I hope that Rev. Ibera will be more faithful to the congregation and work with energy, loyalty, and spirit and devote most of his time for his duty."[57] Again, mediators had to work hard to build community confidence and prove their fidelity to their constituents. Even though Ibera was the appointed leader of this church, his position was not solid or guaranteed. Instead, he had to nurture and develop relationships with the community to truly be accepted as the leader of this group.

Church members slowly came to trust Ibera after a tumultuous first year at Ola'a. In fact, Ibera was able to learn from his early mistakes and develop his position as ethnic mediator to work successfully at this plantation for thirteen years before the HEA transferred him to another location in 1941.[58] But Ibera's rocky start underscores the general suspicion that existed in the Filipino community about the trustworthiness of Protestant ministers. Such a difficult beginning also highlights the temporary nature of power and influence that ethnic mediators, even those in assigned positions, hold over their communities. Without the approval of their constituents, be they workers, the HEA, or the HSPA, leaders would have no traction to lead anyone.

Conclusion

Ethnic ministers tried to fill the void in effective local leadership for U.S. colonials in Hawai'i. When these pastors served the welfare of their ethnic community, they increased their credibility among Filipinos. As demonstrated by Peck, workers mistrusted ethnic mediators at every opportunity: it was "the worker, not the padrone or corporate manager, who possessed, however briefly, the final and decisive word over who was or was not a legitimate defender and protector of workers' interests."[59] Santa Ana and Ibera constantly had to convince workers and church members of their sympathetic intentions. When they demonstrated concrete actions that supported the Filipino community, they were treated as the leaders of the community. When they acted in a suspicious or questionable manner, even at a basic or minor level, Filipinos immediately voiced their disapproval.

The multiple roles ethnic ministers filled often resulted in problematic and tense situations. They had to abide by the requests of the HEA, represent the interests of workers, as well as help facilitate and mediate negotiations and policies for the HSPA. They gained power through each interaction with the HEA, the HSPA, and the workers. But this delicate balancing act often fell short on one, if not multiple, ends. Santa Ana and Ibera had to juggle these conflicting interests constantly to maintain their position of influence among workers and plantation management. Ethnic ministers' power on plantations remained tenuous and impermanent because their position depended on their continual support of multiple interests.

Overall, Filipino Protestant ministers succeeded in providing many secular and religious services for their community. Both pastors were motivated to work with Filipino intra-colonials by their sense of moral duty and obligation to serve their ethnic community, the HEA, the Protestant church, and God. They focused on providing the best services for Filipinos at Ola'a, with hopes to also convert them to Protestantism. Santa Ana and Ibera helped build missions and churches, created local labor organizations, and facilitated daily communication between the labor community, the plantation, the surrounding community, various levels of government, and their home region. Usually, the efforts of ethnic ministers prioritized workers. Sometimes their actions also benefited the plantation. And other times their own personal ministry or broader church principles took precedence over accommodating their ethnic communities on the plantation. Even though large scale conversion did not happen among Filipinos at the Ola'a plantation, Filipino ethnic ministers did what they felt was best for their constituency. This approach resulted in their long-term tenure and success as endorsed ethnic middlemen at Ola'a.

6. *Limited Leadership*

ROLES OF PUERTO RICAN LABOR AGENTS
IN THE PLANTATION COMMUNITY

In 1901, many Puerto Ricans on the island of Hawai'i approached Florentin Souza for help. He said, "Knowing their country, their habits and their language, the Porto Ricans have found their way to me, with a great variety of requests."[1] As Spanish speakers in the English-speaking U.S. Territory of Hawai'i, Puerto Ricans needed mediators to help them navigate local labor practices. As we have seen in chapters 4 and 5, having a local ethnic community leader in close contact with plantation leadership could result in regional improvements and immediate resolutions to worker issues. Like Filipinos, Puerto Rican intra-colonials did not have foreign consul generals in Hawai'i. But unlike Filipinos, Puerto Ricans in the islands never obtained an official local ethnic representative willing to address their issues or handle their complaints. These intra-colonials only had a handful of individuals to fill their lack of leadership in the region. There were a few sporadic community ethnic mediators in various professions. There were also self-initiated labor agents who marketed themselves to Puerto Ricans and plantation leadership. This chapter will examine both types of middlemen on the island of Hawai'i during the first half of the twentieth century. Without as many local advocates to publicize their issues, Puerto Rican intra-colonials became an invisible population in the political, social, economic, and religious life of Hawai'i.

All but one of the ethnic mediators in this chapter chose to serve in a leadership role for the Puerto Rican community on their own volition. The ethnic minister Joseph Pagan directly contacted the Hawaiian Evangelical Association (HEA) for a position. The HEA was happy to hire an enthusiastic self-starter to serve the Puerto Rican community for the first and, as it turns out, only time. The labor agents examined in this chapter, Florentin Souza and Alberto E. Minvielle, approached plantations and promoted themselves as influential negotiators among Puerto Rican laborers. Just as with Filipino workers, the HSPA welcomed anyone who could help them work with labor groups and make them more efficient. A local plantation worker, who also served as the community baker at Ola'a, became an informal ethnic mediator for Puerto Ricans at this plantation. However, Juanito Rosario did not actively pursue such a position of power. Instead, he grew into the role of trusted leader through his individual and consistent assistance to different members of his community over time.

Like Filipino Protestant ethnic ministers in chapter 5 and the Philippine resident labor commissioner in chapter 4, Puerto Rican labor agents had to balance the needs and expectations of sugar management and the ethnic community to maintain their positions of influence in the islands and successfully fulfill different aspects of their responsibilities. Pagan had to cooperate with HEA supervisors and work within church guidelines while attracting Puerto Rican converts. As a plantation worker, Rosario could not be overly aggressive with plantation leadership because he could lose his job and home in the plantation camp. The power of all these ethnic mediators in the U.S. Territory of Hawai'i changed and fluctuated over time. But their authority always lay in each middleman's ability to provide useful services and gain the endorsement of their constituents, be they workers, the HEA, or the HSPA.

Except for Rosario, none of these mediators held long-term positions of leadership in the Puerto Rican community. The HSPA stopped paying for Puerto Rican labor agents after a few years because the migration of this ethnic group to the islands ended after a year and a half. Souza transitioned into other profit-oriented pursuits in the islands in December 1901. While Minvielle continued to work for the HSPA and Puerto Ricans in Hawai'i until 1906, after being laid off from his position that year he moved back to Puerto Rico. Pagan became discouraged by his small number of converts and quit missionary work after three years of proselytizing from 1915 to 1918. Even though Rosario lived on the island of Hawai'i from the turn of the century until the end of his life, his role as an independent and informal ethnic mediator meant he did not have any official connections, hence strong influence, with plantation management. He did not have the same kind of cultural, social, and symbolic capital in local institutions of power as labor agents and ethnic ministers.

The short duration of Puerto Rican recruitment was ultimately detrimental to those who remained in the islands. Since most of these intra-colonials transitioned out of plantation work as soon as possible, the HSPA had no need for Puerto Rican–specific mediators long term. The HEA could also assign Spanish-speaking ministers of other ethnicities to proselytize among this smaller population. According to anthropologist Claudio Lomnitz-Adler, power brokers build ties "between the locality and state and private institutions."[2] These go-betweens have special access to or knowledge of political, social, and/or economic power structures. Their monopolization of certain values and processes becomes essential to their positions as influential community mediators. These leaders also help migrant groups adjust and succeed in their new environment. The lack of ethnic mediators with connections to the sugar industry and other Anglo-American institutions of power deprived Puerto Ricans of assistance and forms of coping that other labor groups had more access to in Hawai'i. As permanent settlers with no support to return home, this intra-colonial group was stuck in the middle of the Pacific Ocean with no official representatives and rare contact with local middlemen who could listen to their concerns in Spanish and then transmit them in English to Anglo-American leaders in the islands. Such an absence of influential ethnic leadership to advocate for their issues contributed to the general invisibility of Puerto Ricans in Hawai'i.[3]

Sporadic Puerto Rican Mediators

From 1916 to 1918, Joseph Pagan served as a Spanish-speaking ethnic minister for Spanish and Puerto Rican groups in the Hilo region. He was a devout, ambitious, and intense man of God. In one letter to HEA leadership, Pagan expressed, "Many people are rejoicing to heard the word of god preaching. Souls are coming at the feet of Jesus and many poor people they expect to see on the future some good thing from our works [sic]."[4] While Pagan believed there was a great need for his religious preaching in the Puerto Rican community, his hiring was an anomaly. Before and after this preacher's short service, the HEA had no intention of hiring Puerto Rican–specific ethnic ministers. Puerto Rican recruitment ended in 1901, making this group relatively small compared to other communities in the islands.[5] The HEA consequently placed this group of intra-colonials under the jurisdiction of a general Spanish-speaking minister who worked among all Hispanics in the region.[6] The diminutive population of these U.S. colonials in Hawai'i often became the justification for not providing a Puerto Rican-specific ethnic mediator for this group; among multiple institutions of power in Hawai'i, they were not seen as significant enough to devote dedicated resources to.

The HEA only hired Pagan because he offered his services to them of his own volition. He had already initiated a Sunday school and a mid-week service at the Makiki Experiment Station near Hilo when he requested a job through the HEA in the fall of 1915. Pagan explained how he wanted "to do the will of our father which is in heaven and trying to do the best I can to please him. Every day's in his service . . . with my determination in order to put this works under the control in conection with the board if they are . . . to have Spanish speaking workers on the field [sic]."[7] In response to this letter, HEA secretary H. P. Judd stated that they could not offer him a position but they morally supported his "work of preaching the Gospel to the Spanish and Porto Ricans of this city."[8] Pagan's excitement to proselytize in this particular community eventually convinced the HEA to hire him in January 1916.

According to HEA Reverend T. F. Anderson, Pagan "is a good Porto Rico leader and knows the Bible well."[9] But in the same letter, Anderson stated, "Pagan would have to be kept under directions of another man in the Spanish work . . . otherwise he would get very proud and at times not use the best wisdom being full of zeal. Lacking the practical every day steadiness in time of tests and trials and low ebb."[10] On February 15, 1917, Pagan had a group of 120 attendees at Pahoa, part of the Ola'a plantation. But the next month, Anderson had to counsel Pagan "to be more energetic and to visit the people more than he has been doing and to not be discouraged because of small numbers but to be faithful with the two and the threes."[11] Pagan was extremely enthusiastic about his work, but he was also easily disappointed when his efforts did not result in large numbers of attendees. The HEA also worried that Pagan was spreading himself too thin. Judd counseled Pagan, "[Do] not scatter your forces too much, not attempt to cover so much ground that you will have to give up the work started at Pepeekeo, Hakalau and other places."[12] Despite his energetic and widespread efforts, Pagan seemed to be just as unsuccessful as Filipino HEA ministers in converting many intra-colonial Catholics to Protestantism in Hawai'i. On average, he had about forty-seven attendees at his services.[13]

Pagan eventually left this position in 1918 because of the difficult nature of preaching among Spanish-speaking plantation workers. He explained, "[Workers] don't believe that a man who is selling rice and beans as they use to say, may be aceptable as a preacher of word of god because use to say that all the store man must to robb and I subjected that this is what it mean disgrace the evangelization [sic]."[14] For the most part, laborers suspected Pagan's intentions and resisted his conversion efforts. His lack of success led him to abandon his work in the region. After the minister's departure, no replacement was made. Puerto Ricans on the island of Hawai'i consequently did not have steady access to their own Protestant ethnic minister, as did Filipino intra-colonials. Religion became one of multiple areas where Puerto Ricans lacked a local mediator to advocate for their needs and issues.

Some Puerto Rican labor recruits in Hawai'i also filled unofficial leadership roles on plantations. According to Gus Villaneuva, who was born and raised at Ola'a, "Every [Puerto Rican] camp had their own elder. Everyone looked up to them."[15] Juanito Rosario, or John Sr., was both a plantation worker and a local baker at the Ola'a plantation. Rosario took care of the camp stove oven and filled an informal leadership role. Rosario's son Vincente remembered working as his father's assistant selling *bojito*, little bread rolls, in the Filipino camps at Ola'a.[16] Since most plantation workers did not have much money, his father was willing to take IOUs for purchases. Vincente would keep track of those debts in a book. Rosario's sympathy and kindness to workers resulted in their respect for him and contributed to his overall social capital among plantation laborers. Vincente also stated that his father was a well-known man in the area and that his nickname was *Papacito*. Such symbolic capital was augmented by the fact that Juanito also knew Spanish, English, and "lenge trapo," or pidgin English. Such cultural capital meant that Rosario had all three major forms of capital skills needed for an effective ethnic mediator. Juanito became greatly admired in his camp, with many Puerto Ricans relying on him for advice and assistance with daily issues. Rosario was an important and constant leader in his community who could help with activities like translation and advice on personal problems.

But as a worker himself, he had little traction within the HSPA and the Anglo-American power structure in Hawai'i. Rosario did not have formal relationships or great influence with white leaders, like local labor agents and ethnic ministers. His ability to enact change was therefore more limited than ethnic mediators with direct connections to the HSPA or the HEA. Regular community members, such as Rosario, could not develop the same type of influence and power to promote Puerto Rican issues as other, more connected middlemen, like Florentin Souza and Alberto Minvielle.

Puerto Rican Labor Agents

Local labor agents became the other major group of mediators who tried to fill the leadership vacuum for the Puerto Rican community in Hawai'i. Businesspeople, like Florentin Souza and Alberto E. Minvielle, played important roles in the daily lives of this group. In the first years of the twentieth century, these men were paid by the HSPA to facilitate communication between workers and plantation leadership about a variety of Puerto Rican labor issues. Spanish-speaking intra-colonial workers and English-speaking sugar management relied on these labor agents to interpret and convey their concerns to each other. Such dependence placed these mediators into prominent positions within this ethnic group and the plantation hierarchy. While Minvielle and Souza entered into such roles for self-profit, they also effectively voiced worker concerns and obtained some improvements for the Puerto Rican labor community at the Ola'a plantation. However, the attenuated nature of Puerto Rican recruitment to the islands meant the HSPA would not pay for dedicated labor agents for this small and diminishing ethnic labor group long term. Souza and Minvielle only mediated issues for this community for a short period.

Souza

As a manager for the Hawaiian Business Agency in Hilo, Florentin Souza handled real estate, collections, accounting, and general commission projects. He was familiar with both U.S. business practices and Puerto Rican culture. He was also fluent in Spanish and English.[17] This broad skill set of cultural and social capital positioned Souza as a powerful and much-needed mediator for Puerto Rican workers and local sugar management in the first years of the twentieth century.

The cases Souza mediated indicated the kinds of issues that concerned intra-colonial laborers in Hawai'i at the turn of the century. In a letter to Ola'a plantation manager F. B. McStocker in 1901, Souza stated that Puerto Ricans at this location wanted "medical attention, [with] others wishing better employment." He said, "I have helped them in both matters, and in doing so I have not in the least intended to harm any particular interest, but simply to aid those coming to me, and to aid myself."[18] This message informed the plantation manager that this labor group prioritized health services as well as good jobs. This judicious statement also let McStocker know that Souza was a neutral party simply providing a requested service. He was not a lackey of the Puerto Rican community fighting against the sugar industry. Souza was an independent agent filling existing needs and working unapologetically for self-profit.

Puerto Rican workers also wanted to receive comparable and fair wages. In 1901, Souza successfully increased wages for Puerto Ricans at the Pepeekeo, Hakalau, and Ola'a plantations (see map of Hawai'i in the introduction). As a smart and savvy businessman, Souza used the information he gained from one plantation manager to support his requests for higher wages at neighboring locations. Within a week, he wrote to all three plantation managers. His first letter went to H. Deacon, the Pepeekeo manager, on June 26. He explained how Puerto Ricans who recently left Pepeekeo "would probably all go back . . . but they say that the wages of $15.00 per month are not enough because they can not live on them."[19] They would return if they received eighteen dollars per month. Since the HSPA needed laborers at that time, Deacon agreed to increase wages the next day so the workers would return as soon as possible. On June 28, Souza wrote Hakalau plantation manager George Ross, stating that Puerto Ricans at his plantation needed a fixed rate of eighteen dollars per month. Ross responded that he already paid Puerto Ricans between seventeen and twenty dollars a month based on their productivity. On June 29, Souza wrote Ola'a manager McStocker that other local plantations paid Puerto Ricans eighteen to twenty dollars a month. Even though this amount had just increased at Pepeekeo as a result of his recent communications with the other HSPA managers, Souza used this new wage rate to convince McStocker to pay at least twenty dollars a month to Puerto Ricans. In this series of letters, Souza leveraged his knowledge of all three plantations to obtain higher wages for Puerto Rican laborers in the entire region.[20] His symbolic capital, or trust from plantation managers, gave him access to private wage information. This data combined with Souza's cultural capital skill of negotiation to economically benefit Puerto Rican laborers at all three plantations.

While not a government representative, Souza wielded significant power over the wage-labor situation in this region. Since Puerto Rican intra-colonials had no official local ethnic mediator, both laborers and plantation managers became dependent on Souza for information about the other group. Workers entrusted their complaints to Souza. HSPA leadership also relied on this middleman to help retain these U.S. colonial workers whom they had paid a lot of money to transport to Hawai'i. However, plantation managers did talk to each other after this set of wage negotiations. McStocker questioned the role Souza played in labor unrest, asking if the middleman had encouraged workers to move to other locales. Souza responded, "I have never been to any Plantation camp nor written to any Porto-Rican laborers inducing them to leave any Plantation."[21] Instead, Souza worked hard to cultivate a belief among both plantation management and laborers that he possessed the skills and influence that they needed for a good work environment.

Souza contacted the Pepeekeo, Hakalau, and Ola'a plantations on June 28, offering his "services for all matters in connection with Porto-Rican laborers . . . to help the Plantations to keep them."[22] In a follow-up letter to McStocker on July 17, Souza stated, "I could devote my time to serve the Plantations in the districts of Hamakua, Hilo and Puna, by visiting them whenever required, and if all the sugar enterprises in those districts would agree to pay me according to the number of Porto Ricans employed, it would make a very small expense to each."[23] Souza presented a logical and profit-oriented case for why plantations should hire him. He also explained, "The small remuneration that each Plantation would pay me, would be much more than compensated by the value of my assistance, not only to induce them to remain, but to help in many details which would bring advantage to the employers."[24] He consistently spread the message that his work would focus on enriching plantations and himself.

Souza also used subtle innuendo to suggest the possible negative outcomes of not hiring him. In the same letter to McStocker, Souza said, "If the Plantations refuse to accept my offer, and the Porto Ricans come to me, I feel that I have a perfect right to procure employment for those willing to pay for my services."[25] He was willing to work on behalf of anyone who paid him and would not hesitate to send Puerto Ricans from nonpaying plantations to locations that gave him money.

During this same period, Souza also demonstrated his ability to control Puerto Rican labor flow to plantations. On July 12, he wrote McStocker: "Fearing that you may be short of houses, I have suspended sending laborers, please inform me as soon as you are ready for more."[26] Presenting the situation in diplomatic rhetoric, Souza informed the plantation manager that his Puerto Rican labor supply would cease if the industry did not provide proper accommodations for them. Tacit threats and value-based financial justifications became two major aspects of Souza's business strategy to get hired by the HSPA.

Souza understood the demand, value, and importance of a Spanish-speaking labor liaison for both intra-colonial Puerto Rican workers and regional plantation management. Both groups needed a local representative to help them with their issues with each other. He said, "[Puerto Ricans] come to me for assistance to procure better employment, not as much regarding wages, as regarding treatment. Many of them come for something to eat and I do not like to refuse to give them something when I see that they are hungry. In some cases, I have helped them to obtain employment, in others, I have advised them to return to the Plantations from which they came."[27] He was a trusted leader in the community who sometimes helped intra-colonials engage in mobility among plantations and at other times encouraged workers to stay at their assigned location.

Ola'a plantation manager McStocker also acknowledged that an interpreter was needed for future interactions with Puerto Ricans. He knew poor translation could lead to frequent labor disputes, stating, "If we wish to avoid misunderstanding and consequently trouble, an intelligent interpreter of their needs medical and otherwise is required."[28] Sugar leaders sought an educated individual to help them maintain a stable and amiable Puerto Rican labor force on plantations. Despite questions over Souza's role in the June labor unrest, McStocker hired Souza to work with Puerto Ricans at Ola'a as a result of the intra-colonial leadership vacuum in the region.

Souza happily filled this mediator position for the right price. As an independent contractor, he received good compensation for such work. He charged plantation managers a twenty-five-dollar flat rate for the mediation of all Puerto Rican issues in communities of fewer than one hundred laborers. Since the sugar industry highly valued a stable labor force, and Puerto Rican intra-colonial laborers had a tendency to move from plantation to plantation when they were unhappy with working conditions, Souza felt justified in charging thirty-five cents for each laborer that worked steadily on plantations with more than one hundred laborers. With forty-eight Puerto Ricans at Hakalau, thirty-four Puerto Ricans at Pepeekeo, and 249 Puerto Ricans at Ola'a, Souza earned $137.15 per month. This salary was $117 more than the monthly earnings of an average Puerto Rican field laborer who completed back-breaking agricultural labor ten hours a day, six days a week. In addition to these payments from the sugar industry, Souza also charged intra-colonial workers when he obtained jobs on their behalf. Souza created an extremely profitable niche for himself based on the needs of both the intra-colonial Puerto Rican plantation community and the sugar industry.

While Souza provided services for personal gain, he also effectively voiced worker concerns and obtained some improvements for the Puerto Rican labor community. The Ola'a plantation employed Souza to work with Puerto Ricans from June to December 1901. In August 1901, Souza wrote Ola'a manager McStocker concerning twelve men who abandoned the Mountain View camp. After his investigation of the situation, Souza believed these laborers stopped work either because one of the laborers incorrectly translated information for the entire group or because the *luna* (field overseer) had a short temper. Souza stated that the impromptu translator told the others that "the luna called one of them 'S-of-a-B' and moved as if to strike him."[29] This makeshift translator also told his fellow workers that the luna disliked all of them and planned to fire them at some point. Since Puerto Ricans often refused to stay at plantations where they were mistreated, these laborers abandoned their work to avoid further abuse. Souza spoke to these laborers and promised to get them a new Spanish-speaking luna if they promised to return to work. He also explained the misunderstanding to McStocker and requested a new supervisor. Souza helped Puerto Ricans adjust to the work environment in the islands and educated employers about the perspectives of their new laborers. Both sides of the workplace believed he could act as their representative and manage their specific needs. Since McStocker and the workers trusted Souza, he was able to provide beneficial and essential services for each group while making money for himself.

At a basic level, Souza worked in the Puerto Rican community because he received a good salary for his services. Souza readily admitted his self-centered motivations in Puerto Rican affairs. In one letter to the Pepeekeo plantation manager, he stated, "I must be frank in saying that I also wish to do something for myself and I feel sure of my influence with these people."[30] Since four-fifths of his monthly monetary commission was dependent on the number of Puerto Ricans who remained on each plantation, Souza had extreme self-interest in making Puerto Ricans happy, or at least steady, workers.

This goal was exemplified in his creation of the Porto Rican Association. Generally, mutual benefit societies involved a nominal yearly membership fee in return for burial services and other types of financial aid during times of crisis.[31] Souza acknowledged that he created the association as a way to get Puerto Ricans to stay on their assigned plantation. He said,

> I have told every one of them, that if they leave your plantation, I will never give them any assistance, and that they will also lose all their rights to the protection of the "Porto-Rican" Association, which object is to better their condition in every way, providing that they obey the instructions of the Association. This has so far had the very best influence to make them stay in one place. They all want to be registered in the Association and have it as their protection in case of any trouble. As I have the sole management and control of the Association and I only send those registered in it.[32]

If there were other viable ethnic mediators widely available at that time on the island of Hawai'i, Souza's threatening tone might have resulted in Puerto Ricans abandoning him and working with someone else. Since Souza was the only middleman available to these intra-colonials throughout this region, except for Ola'a, these laborers felt dependent on Souza for protection through the Porto Rican Association.[33]

Like the padrones of Peck's research, Souza "gained power from [his] clients' marginal status . . . and often times exploited their ignorance of the English language and of North American political customs."[34] Souza saw the great need for a Spanish-speaking leader or organization to represent Puerto Rican interests and created an imagined community where he was central to workers' communications with plantation management.[35] He portrayed his assistance as the only way laborers could keep their jobs and be shielded from employer abuses. Ultimately, Souza created and managed the Porto Rican Association to develop a stable workforce that would provide him with even more profits. He controlled both the work process and social organization that Puerto Rican laborers relied on for support and coping on a daily basis. Such total control over this labor group resulted in coercive labor relations.

Once workers became part of the association, Souza used this community's desire for local protection and advocacy as a way to control their movement. If they moved to another location, he would stop helping them. Puerto Ricans likely felt they had few other options than to follow Souza's directions. Not able to communicate issues on their own to non-Spanish-speaking Anglo-American leaders in Hawai'i, intra-colonial workers submitted to Souza's control in exchange for a source of leadership, guidance, knowledge, assistance, and advocacy. While they trusted his ability to wield his social and cultural capital in the workplace, they might not have liked Souza on a personal level. In contrast, Filipino intra-colonials had multiple sources of leadership in the islands. If they had issues with Filipino Protestant ethnic ministers or the Philippine resident labor commissioner, they could complain to the supervisors of these individuals or work with local ethnic labor organizers for alternative support and assistance. With a lack of other sources for help in Hawai'i, Puerto Rican U.S. colonials were subject to Souza's personal profit motivations and coercive labor policy to stay on one plantation.

Throughout his time as a labor agent for the HSPA, Souza focused on bringing all Puerto Ricans on the island of Hawai'i under his supervision and control. For Puerto Ricans employed at plantations that paid him a salary, Souza worked to keep them happy and stable at the same location. He met with intra-colonial laborers as needed, fielded their complaints, and tried to resolve their issues with plantation management. For Puerto Ricans who did not work at a plantation that paid him a salary, Souza tried to place those individuals at a location that did. Souza was extremely skilled at figuring out unique and diverse ways to profit from the specificities of the Puerto Rican labor situation in Hawai'i, especially from their frequent mobility and their need for a local leader to advocate for their issues.

Keeping these workers at the same job for the long term was difficult to accomplish since Puerto Ricans readily changed jobs if they were ill treated or their issues were not quickly resolved, as seen in chapter 3. The HSPA hated such an attitude toward work mobility because the sugar industry wanted a permanent and stable labor force for cane production. The frequent self-relocation of Puerto Ricans from plantation to plantation also caused problems for Souza, who got paid based on the number of Puerto Ricans who worked consistently at the same location over time. Souza's overall ability to keep this ethnic group at one plantation was a huge accomplishment that HSPA management recognized and rewarded with payment.

Since Souza could not stop all workers from moving, he developed a creative way to capitalize on such mobility. He made sure he got credit for placing transient workers at a different HSPA plantation that he also worked for and got commission from. He also encouraged Puerto Ricans not under his management to work with him so they would have full access to his much-desired services and to the Porto Rican Association. He received one dollar for each new laborer he brought to a plantation.[36] While Puerto Rican labor mobility was inconvenient for the abandoned plantation, Souza was still able to benefit from such movement and maintain influence over these ambulatory workers.

Souza's for-profit motivations also led him to offer non-ethnic-related services to plantation management. Travel at the turn of the twentieth century between rural plantations on the east side of the island of Hawai'i and the region's main town of Hilo required the costly use of horses or hours of walking by foot. As a resident of Hilo, Souza told plantation managers he was willing to conduct business in town on their behalf. He stated, "Outside of Porto-Rican affairs, you may have some other errands to which I could attend, and as to the salary, I would accept whatever you would consider right."[37] Souza hoped the social, cultural, and symbolic capital he developed and demonstrated as a Puerto Rican labor agent could pave the way for plantation managers to rely on him for a variety of other services. He wanted to become the go-to man for sugar industry leaders. Such an expanded position would also provide Souza with additional sources of income. He believed plantation managers had such a great need for this type of service that he let them decide on the appropriate amount of money to pay him. Souza was a confident and aggressive local middleman who always looked for new ways to make a profit.

As an independent agent, Souza felt no obligation to remain loyal to Puerto Ricans. Souza worked with these intra-colonials only if he was getting paid. In fact, his devotion fluctuated with changes in the most profitable means to make money. In February 1901, Souza explored the recruitment of other labor groups. Regarding Mexicans, Souza told McStocker, "[They are] very good laborers from South California, they are of a much better class than the Porto-Ricans . . . they could be brought direct to Hilo and at much less expense than the Porto-Ricans. I would very much like to have you to make an experiment, because I am sure that they would give you entire satisfaction."[38] He explained that Mexicans would work harder for less than Puerto Ricans. He likely recommended this labor group because he wanted a monopoly on this untapped labor source. To promote his latest and greatest recruitment proposal, Souza willingly criticized the very group he was supposed to be advocating for, Puerto Rican intra-colonials.

While Souza was not a fully dedicated advocate for Puerto Rican workers, he was also not a pawn of plantation leaders. When plantation managers complained that Souza employed laborers who still had debt at other plantations, Souza defended himself: "I don't know that they do owe when they come to me."³⁹ Souza claimed it was not his job to check the background of workers he was hiring. He focused only on the gathering of steady workers to fill job vacancies. Like Ligot in chapter 4, Souza did not deem his actions as excessive, unfair, or unfree. Instead, as Peck has described, padrones believed they were "part of a contractual exchange that benefited both immigrant workers and himself."⁴⁰ In the context of a free labor market, agents like Souza and Ligot were only doing what was proper in a wage-based economy. In the end, Souza favored profit over plantation policies and labor rights.

Souza's ability to straddle both the Spanish-speaking world of Puerto Rican intra-colonials and the English-speaking realm of Anglo-American leadership in Hawai'i placed him in a powerful position of leadership in the islands. But Souza did not fill these roles for long. When Puerto Rican labor recruitment ended in 1901, the sugar industry focused its attention on the recruitment of Japanese, Filipino, and Korean workers. With Puerto Ricans becoming less central to the plantation workforce, Souza knew that his profits would diminish or vanish altogether. He therefore used his knowledge of both the plantation system and the Puerto Rican community to start his own cane-cultivation venture in December 1901. Contract cane cultivation involved independent farmers raising sugar cane in a designated area on behalf of the plantation. Payment would occur after harvest; monetary compensation would be based on the total weight of cane supplied. Souza hired around one hundred dissatisfied Puerto Ricans who wished not to return to their original plantations.⁴¹ He financed the costs of planting and managed the workers in return for a percentage of the total payout at harvest time. In this way, Souza continued to profit from both the intra-colonial laborers and the sugar industry. But his move away from general work mediation among multiple plantations left a huge gap in leadership for other Puerto Ricans in the region.

Minvielle

Fortunately for Puerto Rican intra-colonials at Ola'a, they had another labor agent they could turn to in Souza's absence. Alberto Minvielle worked for the Ola'a plantation at the same time as Souza.⁴² After Souza became a contract cultivator in December 1901, Minvielle became the sole labor mediator for Puerto Ricans at the Ola'a plantation. Unlike Souza, who worked throughout the east side of the island of Hawai'i, Minvielle focused his work in the Puerto Rican community at Ola'a. While Souza prioritized providing services that resulted in high-yield profits, Minvielle worked on improving the daily lives and social perceptions of Puerto Rican experiences in Hawai'i and their home region. Both men helped these intra-colonial laborers in their own ways.

Minvielle first came to Hawai'i as an employee of Wolters, a third-party Puerto Rican recruitment agency, in 1901. Born to a Puerto Rican mother and an Anglo-American father, Minvielle served as a translator for Puerto Ricans as they traveled from the Caribbean to Hawai'i. While in Hawai'i, Minvielle's boss accepted another job to run a plantation in Puerto Rico. Instead of returning to the Caribbean, Minvielle decided to seek employment in Hawai'i. In June 1901 he contacted the Hawai'i sugar company B. F. Dillingham and offered to help recruit Puerto Ricans from other areas of the Hawaiian Islands to work at their plantations. Minvielle claimed he could lure Puerto Ricans from other locations: "We can soon get all the Porto Ricans we want from the other Plantations."[43] Since B. F. Dillingham and other sugar companies were working to unify the sugar industry under the centralized leadership of the HSPA during this same period, Elmer Paxton, vice president of B. F. Dillingham, could not condone Minvielle's overt recruitment of workers away from other plantations. Paxton explained, "If we join the Association, we do so under an agreement not to employ any Porto Ricans from another Plantation, unless he has an honorable discharge."[44] Paxton thought Minvielle could better serve the company by recruiting laborers in Puerto Rico. The vice president suggested that Minvielle could "import a ship load of Porto Ricans either in connection with the Planters Association or independent of them."[45] McStocker agreed that Minvielle would be helpful if he could travel with new recruits from Puerto Rico. He could use information from his daily interactions on the ship to pick the best laborers for Ola'a. But Minvielle did not end up accompanying new recruits on their voyage from the Caribbean to Hawai'i. After speaking with a few members of the HSPA Board of Trustees, Paxton did not believe he could convince these leaders to allow Minvielle and the Ola'a plantation to get the first pick of Puerto Rican laborers arriving in the islands.

Paxton and McStocker still thought hiring Minvielle would benefit their business dealings with the Puerto Rican community. He had strong social and cultural skills in the Puerto Rican community that the HSPA wanted to take advantage of. Within ten days of his first communication with B. F. Dillingham, Minvielle was hired by McStocker on June 27, 1901, to serve as a hospital assistant, interpreter, and general helper for the Ola'a plantation.[46] Minvielle also investigated offers for new Puerto Rican labor from independent recruiters. He tried to make sure new laborers were good workers who were not taken from neighboring plantations. Like Filipino Protestant ethnic ministers Flaviano Santa Ana and Simeon Ibera, Minvielle became a respected and reliable mediator for the HSPA and was incorporated into the daily function of the Ola'a plantation. Souza, in contrast, remained an independent labor agent who offered piecemeal services to multiple plantations.

Though Minvielle was not officially hired as a specific Puerto Rican representative, he focused on providing useful services for this intra-colonial group that had no official leaders in Hawai'i. Puerto Rican workers used Minvielle mainly for his cultural capital of translation skills and social capital of connections with plantation management. As with Souza, these laborers looked to Minvielle for complaint mediation and defense of legal rights. They also asked him to help with personal affairs, such as arranging funerals.

Since Minvielle also lived on the plantation, he became the perceived leader among Puerto Ricans at Ola'a. One Sunday morning Puerto Ricans woke Minvielle up at 2:30 because they wanted him to get the police to arrest someone who had stabbed another Puerto Rican at a party.[47] Instead of directly contacting the police, community members relied on Minvielle to act as their liaison with authorities. Puerto Ricans at Ola'a came to view Minvielle as a sentinel for their issues. With such symbolic capital, Minvielle gained mediation power from the confidence that workers instilled in him to manage their affairs. He became a middleman for this community because they endorsed him in this position of leadership.

Minvielle took this responsibility seriously. He held regular meetings with Puerto Rican laborers to discuss their concerns. At one gathering, on January 16, 1902, he informed workers about the possibility of entering into cultivation contracts. Puerto Rican laborers felt the system of payment by weight of cane was too confusing. Instead, the laborers suggested their own plan. They wanted Minvielle to sign a contract and hire them to work for him. The intra-colonial laborers also wanted payment according to individual amounts of production. Unlike Souza, Minvielle chose not to become a contract cultivator. But he did tell McStocker about the cultivation contract modifications proposed by the workers. The Ola'a manager did not fully embrace the plan, stating that "a better plan would be to divide men off into gangs classified accordingly to ability of work."[48] While McStocker did not adopt the Puerto Rican plan in its entirety, he did consider their request for compensation based on work completed. Minvielle's work as a trusted ethnic mediator among both workers and plantation management resulted in Puerto Rican opinions influencing the content and form of plantation policies and practices toward cane cultivators.

As the sanctioned local representative for Puerto Ricans at Ola'a, Minvielle also took it upon himself to contact the plantation manager when he felt intra-colonials were being mistreated. In August 1901, Minvielle wrote

McStocker about problems between twenty laborers and their luna, Mr. McRae.[49] Minvielle discovered that these workers had to wait around for at least half an hour before McRae showed up to give them instructions. The mediator worried such unprofessional behavior would upset workers and lead to trouble. To prevent a potential walkout, Minvielle notified the plantation manager about the situation. While Souza was always quick to react to problems presented to him and figure out solutions, Minvielle, like Filipino ministers Santa Ana and Ibera, proactively engaged in preventative actions to protect the intra-colonial community.

Minvielle also shared his own suggestions to improve the Puerto Rican social environment with McStocker. At least twice he recommended that payday be moved to Sunday. Saturday paychecks tempted workers to skip that day's shift, drink heavily, and hold evening house parties, which often ended with violence. As Walter Basque Sr. stated, "If someone gets cut, (if) there's blood, it's a party!"[50] House parties were a primary vehicle for the Puerto Rican community to socialize and relax in the Territory of Hawai'i. Since unmarried Puerto Rican females could not leave the house without parental supervision, house parties became the only venue for these girls to see their friends and meet boys. Usually, females would gather in the bedroom; males would stay in the living room. Unless married, each woman could dance only with one man at each party. If she declined to dance with one man, she was not supposed to dance with anyone else the rest of the night; if she accepted another man's request, the first suitor was considered to have a legitimate reason to get jealous and start a fight. This process was understood by everyone in the Puerto Rican community. With this knowledge, Minvielle suggested the change in payday to maintain safety in the plantation camps and avoid alcohol-induced disturbances during the workweek. Through his intimate knowledge of this community, Minvielle was able to provide preventive advice in addition to reactive assistance for these intra-colonial workers and the sugar industry.

Minvielle's close work with both Puerto Ricans and plantation management required him to balance the interests of both entities. In April 1904, McStocker asked Minvielle to provide a list of unsatisfactory Puerto Rican workers at Ola'a. After careful consideration, Minvielle identified eight men whom he deemed unacceptable laborers. But before providing these names, Minvielle prefaced the information with a discussion of how the Puerto Rican camp had become a refuge for non-Ola'a employees. He stated how he has "seen PtRicans in said camp . . . ten days laying . . . lunas go in the camp and see so many men and not knowing if they belong to this plantation . . . think that they are our regular men, but they are not."[51] Minvielle continued to explain how, on a regular basis, about ten transients sojourned at the

Puerto Rican camp. The lunas who saw these men sleeping at the camp during the workday assumed Puerto Ricans were too lazy to go to work. But since they did not work for the plantation, these individuals did not need to wake up at any particular time. Most of the perceived lazy Puerto Ricans were not plantation employees.

The presence of these drifters perpetuated negative stereotypes about Puerto Ricans as poor workers. To counter such portrayals, Minvielle acknowledged there were a few bad workers, but he claimed that the majority of Puerto Ricans at the Ola'a plantation worked hard. Most people who lingered in camps during the day were not employed by the HSPA. Minvielle also defended sickly workers. While they frequently stayed home due to illness, he asked McStocker to retain these laborers because they worked hard when healthy and would have no other means for livelihood outside the plantation. Minvielle explained, for example, "#1720 is one of our men but he is sickly and I would recommend not to send him off as he is harmless, he works when he can and he is willing to do what he can and he will land in jail if he sent off [sic]."[52] Minvielle tried often to balance intra-colonial Puerto Rican interests with plantation needs.

Minvielle also blamed the misrepresentation of Puerto Rican workers on the camp boss. Minvielle believed the reason the Puerto Rican camp was used "as transit Hotel, is on account of the Camp Boss not been acquainted very well with the faces of the PtRicans, he might see one of those that are in transit and he could not tell different of the regular working men."[53] The camp *luna* could not distinguish between Ola'a employees and outsiders. If this supervisor made an effort to become familiar with Puerto Ricans in his area, he could easily identify trespassers and kick them out. According to Minvielle, such changes would immediately rectify the troublesome situation and vindicate the reputation of the Puerto Rican community at Ola'a. In his report, Minvielle balanced his obligation to provide plantation management with an honest evaluation of the quality of workers with his desire to support and improve the Puerto Rican community at Ola'a.

Unlike Souza and Philippine resident commissioner Ligot, who both probably would have just answered McStocker's request without worrying about the impact that such a report would have on intra-colonials, Minvielle always tried to present Puerto Ricans in the best light. While Souza focused only on developing profitable ventures, Minvielle worked hard to protect the interests of this ethnic community. Minvielle held a significant position of power among workers because his actions demonstrated his ability and willingness to consistently advocate for their interests. Such reliability led laborers to strongly support his role as their ethnic leader. Through his honest communications and evaluations, Minvielle also had a large degree of influence over the policies that plantation managers developed for Puerto Ricans. Throughout his work at this plantation, Minvielle developed symbolic capital of recognition and respect from both plantation managers and laborers to become a dominant local mediator at Ola'a.

Minvielle in Puerto Rico

Just as Minvielle wanted to fill the leadership gap in the Puerto Rican intracolonial community in the Territory of Hawai'i, he also wanted to be seen as the authority on this group for those in Puerto Rico. According to Peck, the padrones in his study "gained power first as labor market entrepreneurs in North America and only subsequently reached back to the villages in Europe."[54] Minvielle worked for the HSPA for several years and was able to develop a similar position of influence as a transregional ethnic mediator who connected plantation workers in Hawai'i with loved ones and the general public back home. He created this link primarily through his development of a special relationship with *La Correspondencia*, the major San Juan newspaper of the time. Through Spanish-language news articles he wrote for this paper, Minvielle positioned himself to become the voice of intracolonials and the HSPA in Puerto Rico.[55]

In his communications with *La Correspondencia*, Minvielle frequently highlighted his importance within the Hawai'i plantation system. In one article he stated, "Many of our countrymen that are found at other plantations complain they are badly treated and want to come to Ola'a because I am here to improve who's in charge of them."[56] While lots of Puerto Ricans moved from plantation to plantation due to poor treatment, Minvielle bragged that most laborers wanted to go to Ola'a because of his presence and influence with plantation management.

Minvielle also claimed that he "is in contact with them [Puerto Ricans in Hawai'i] and knows them all."[57] He portrayed himself as the best way for those in Puerto Rico to communicate with their loved ones in the islands. *La Correspondencia* supported this image by encouraging people to send their letters to loved ones in Hawai'i through Minvielle at the Hawaiian Hotel in Honolulu. This newspaper article described how Minvielle was doing "a good deed that we owe him thanks."[58] Minvielle's relationship with *La Correspondencia* promoted his position as a valuable leader for Puerto Ricans in Hawai'i, as well as in Puerto Rico.

Most Puerto Ricans in Hawai'i were illiterate and had few opportunities to communicate and maintain contact with their families and friends after settling in the Pacific. Few ever returned to the Caribbean. In his journalism pieces, Minvielle often mentioned the name and hometown of newsworthy individuals. In September 1905, he reported how a child of Jacinto Colondre from Adjuntas married Marlin Elizarry.[59] Even if they had no direct contact or personal connection to the mentioned individuals, Puerto Ricans in the home region could stay updated on notable occurrences among Puerto Rican intra-colonials who originated from their town.

Minvielle's articles transmitted images and ideas about Puerto Rican experiences in Hawai'i to loved ones, interested parties, as well as the general public in Puerto Rico, assisting in the creation of a transregional Puerto Rican community. Even though most readers had no specific relationship to the individuals reported on from Hawai'i, Minvielle helped them imagine a nationalistic emotional tie to people who had come from their region.[60]

Between 1900 and 1901, Minvielle also wrote Puerto Rican news stories to dispel negative reports about movement to Hawai'i and to promote intra-colonial recruitment to the Pacific.[61] Newspapers would paraphrase his letters into short news articles that often promoted the sugar industry. In response to the rumors of poor treatment during Puerto Rican transport to Hawai'i, Minvielle stated that "the events did not have the importance attributed to them in letters and clippings."[62] He explained that the accusations of insufficient food were false and that only one minor disturbance occurred during the last shipment of Puerto Rican workers. He assured the newspaper and those in Puerto Rico that "our brothers are well treated and they found better circumstances than in their native land."[63] Minvielle also promoted the benefits of plantation work in Hawai'i for Puerto Ricans. He described how many migrants "wanted to go to 'Olaa,' where I am, to improve their situation and take care of them."[64] All of Minvielle's correspondence with Puerto Rican newspapers positively portrayed Puerto Rican experiences in Hawai'i. Such descriptions buttressed HSPA recruitment efforts in the Caribbean region and endeared Minvielle to industry leaders in Hawai'i.

Even though HSPA recruitment efforts in Puerto Rico ended in 1901 and no additional programs developed until 1921, Minvielle continued to work for plantation management and the Puerto Rican community at Ola'a for several more years. He also continued reporting on events in the Puerto Rican community in Hawai'i for *La Correspondencia* until he was laid off by the HSPA in 1906. In fact, in the fall of 1905 Minvielle became an official correspondent for that Puerto Rican newspaper. Such a position further augmented his efforts to become a transregional ethnic mediator for Puerto Ricans in Hawai'i and back home.

As an employee of *La Correspondencia*, Minvielle filed stories about general happenings at the Ola'a plantation, such as rain on the Fourth of July, local complaints, the labor situation, recent deaths, and crimes committed in the Puerto Rican community. He also provided detailed information on the sugar production process and boasted that the Ola'a plantation had all the most modern conveniences, such as electricity and an icemaker. This advanced environment made "work comfortable and easy" at Ola'a.[65] Life in Hawai'i seemed ideal in Minvielle's articles.

In addition to reporting general news, Minvielle also addressed moral issues and community problems. He offered specific directives to community members in the Pacific and Puerto Rico. When Antonia Martinez died in October 1905, she left behind a young child. Minvielle printed the name of the girl's father, Vicente Maldonado Roble, who still lived in Puerto Rico. Minvielle encouraged Roble to come to Hawai'i to take care of his daughter.[66] Since Minvielle viewed himself as the spokesperson for Puerto Ricans in the islands, he took it upon himself to express his personal expectations of this group in both the Pacific and the Caribbean. He seemed to enjoy serving in this multiregional position of power and leadership.

While Minvielle liked living and working in Hawai'i, such employment became a lower priority for the Ola'a plantation after the end of Puerto Rican recruitment. In 1906, his work for the sugar industry ended and he returned to Puerto Rico. But when the HSPA attempted to recruit more Puerto Ricans in 1921, Minvielle willingly and enthusiastically worked with the HSPA once again. He communicated with local newspapers in Puerto Rico, providing encouraging stories in Spanish about the opportunities in Hawai'i, especially compared to overpopulation in the Caribbean. Minvielle explained, "In 1901, we weren't tactful with our selection. We obtained men in error but fortunately despite a lack of experience most Puerto Ricans became excellent workers and moral, admirable citizens. . . . [J]ust a few . . . created difficulties."[67] He acknowledged how early Puerto Rican recruitment, in which he played a role, had been haphazard. Minvielle also addressed and countered the negative stereotypes of those who did move intra-colonially. There were just a few troublemakers who ruined the reputation of upstanding Puerto Ricans in Hawai'i. According to Minvielle, most of those who migrated turned into good workers. Once again, Minvielle portrayed these intra-colonials in an optimistic way, despite their history of failed recruitment.

Minvielle admitted that there had been problems in Hawai'i, such as "ostracism perpetuated by native laborers."[68] But he believed the economic opportunities in the islands outweighed such past negative experiences in Hawai'i. For the current recruitment campaign, he and the HSPA would be more selective in their choices. They wanted "calm, loyal and strong" workers.[69] Minvielle also claimed that the HSPA was the most generous employer of all labor recruiters in Puerto Rico. He commented on the "kindness of the company recruitment . . . different from the majority of ads for work."[70] To encourage people to sign up for work in the islands, Minvielle highlighted how new HSPA work agreements had the backing of the Puerto Rican Bureau of Labor and were developed to protect workers. "Immigrants are guaranteed a contract backed by a notary for all their legal requirements and the honored officials of the department of labor will make sure there is compliance with the rules established between the two parties."[71] He trusted that the Puerto Rican Bureau of Labor would provide enough regulations and oversight to facilitate the success of new recruitment efforts. While this employment push resulted in only one ship of 683 Puerto Ricans going to Hawai'i, Minvielle did his part to encourage and sustain Puerto Rican labor recruitment for Hawai'i sugar plantations through positive rhetoric. He continued to show loyalty to the HSPA and Puerto Ricans in Hawai'i despite his move back to Puerto Rico and several years of alternative employment.

Minvielle's comments in 1921 closely reflect the general perspective of the U.S. government at that time. As discussed in chapter 1, U.S. leaders believed in the need to funnel Puerto Ricans away from their overpopulated home region. Bureau of Insular Affairs chief Frank McIntyre was concerned with the "surplus of people in Porto Rico that could not be supported by what is produced in the island and that the only way in which the people of Porto Rico could live comfortably there would be by a removal of the surplus in order that there should be a job for every man."[72] Minvielle also viewed immigration as "the solution to the problem."[73] Both the U.S. government and Minvielle believed migration could cure Puerto Rico's economic difficulties. Since Minvielle's ideas sounded similar to those of the U.S. colonists, Puerto Ricans in Puerto Rico might have viewed Minvielle's statements as U.S. government and plantation propaganda. Despite Minvielle's strong endorsement and efforts, the 1921 migration program failed to recruit more than one initial group of recruits.

Both Minvielle and Souza created positions for themselves to work with Puerto Rican U.S. colonials and address their daily issues at the Ola'a plantation. These two men had different approaches to the mediation of this group's concerns in Hawai'i. Minvielle lived and worked in the eight-mile camp of the Ola'a plantation. Souza lived in the town of Hilo, thirteen miles away. Minvielle focused on Ola'a-specific matters while Souza tried to work with as many plantations and labor groups as possible. Souza focused on quick solutions to keep the peace between workers and the sugar industry; Minvielle tried to figure out the best practices for both laborers and plantation management, as well as predict future needs or problems. Souza constantly changed or augmented his services to increase self-profit. Minvielle worked steadily for the Ola'a plantation for several years and created a transregional position of mediation for himself between Hawai'i and Puerto Rico. Even after leaving the industry and the Pacific in 1906, he continued to idealize the HSPA and Puerto Ricans in Hawai'i. Despite their different leadership styles, Minvielle and Souza served as important and accepted mediators for Puerto Ricans in Hawai'i, as well as plantation leadership, in the early twentieth century.

Both men tried always to balance the interests of Puerto Rican workers, plantation leadership, and themselves. These mediators could help translate and voice worker concerns and negotiate with sugar managers. Souza achieved wage adjustments for these U.S. colonial plantation laborers, and Minvielle transmitted Puerto Rican preferences for cultivation contract work to sugar leaders. Puerto Ricans relied on Souza for protection, especially through the Porto Rican Association. But he also used this organization to create a more stable and dependent—hence more profitable—workforce for him and the HSPA. As the assumed leader for Puerto Ricans at Ola'a, Minvielle provided McStocker with insider information on workers but also blamed the camp boss, not intra-colonials, for problematic transients. In divergent ways, both men provided critical services for Puerto Rican intra-colonials who had few other sources for leadership and representation in the islands.

Regardless of the combination of altruistic and selfish interests that drove them, these ethnic mediators' early retirement from labor leadership brought an end to a brief and unique opportunity for the Puerto Rican community to enjoy advocacy at a high level in the islands. Puerto Ricans in Hawai'i had constantly struggled to obtain fair representation and positive acknowledgement in the islands, as seen in chapter 3. Without local community leaders like Souza and Minvielle, who had the trust and attention of plantation management and Anglo-American elite in Hawai'i, there was a lack of attention to Puerto Rican issues in the region and a consequent invisibility of these intra-colonial Puerto Ricans in Hawai'i throughout the twentieth century.

Conclusion

Despite similar needs for leadership due to the lack of effective local government representatives for intra-colonials, unofficial Puerto Rican and Filipino ethnic mediators had different lived experiences. Religious ethnic mediators felt a moral obligation to serve their community, the HEA, and God. Their willingness to help members of their ethnic community, as well as their association with the dominant religious institution in the islands, made Filipino preachers long-term ethnic mediators for their community. Labor agents for Puerto Ricans, on the other hand, sought mostly to benefit themselves. Two short periods of Puerto Rican recruitment, from 1900 to

1901 and in 1921, led these labor agents to fill mediator positions temporarily in the sugar industry. Once employer needs for such brokers dissipated, labor agents moved on to other profitable opportunities. This disparity in purpose and institutional support for Puerto Rican labor agents, compared to Filipino Protestant ethnic ministers, affected the longevity and success of each mediator's involvement in their intra-colonial ethnic community.

Puerto Ricans' permanent settlement in Hawai'i made the presence of local leaders more important for these intra-colonials than Filipino laborers, who often flowed back and forth between Hawai'i and the Philippines. Intra-colonial Puerto Ricans, who became U.S. citizens in 1917, never obtained a local ethnic representative willing to address their issues or handle their complaints in the Hawaiian Islands. Filipinos, in contrast, who were on the path to eventual independence from the United States, also gained access to local labor organizers, short-term labor commissioners, and a resident labor commissioner in 1923. Overall, Puerto Rican intra-colonial laborers in Hawai'i had less access to influential local community leaders than did Filipino intra-colonials.

Outside Hawai'i, few people know about the history of Puerto Rican migration to and labor in the islands. Filipinos, by contrast, are seen almost as synonymous with plantation labor in Hawai'i, with close to one hundred community organizations in the islands. Such discrepancies in contemporary Filipino and Puerto Rican visibility in Hawai'i can be linked to each group's differential access to local mediators who could fill the leadership gaps that were products of their in-between political-legal status as U.S. colonials in a second colonized space. Without as many local advocates to publicize their issues and struggles, Puerto Ricans in Hawai'i became an invisible population in the political, social, economic, and religious life of Hawai'i.

Conclusion

CURRENT STRUGGLES AGAINST U.S. COLONIALISM
AND EMPIRE

Islanders in the Empire challenges studies of U.S. history to move beyond the standard narrative that centers on the forty-eight contiguous states. Most people view the history of sugar plantation labor in Hawai'i as an interesting sidebar to U.S. history. Such a marginalization of this chain of islands ignores the role of colonialism in the overall story of the nation. The practice of distinguishing sharply between continental versus overseas U.S. expansionism also shrouds early imperial histories. Some scholars claim that the expansion of a nation to contiguous continental areas made the takeover of American Indian, Mexican, as well as British, Spanish, and French territories in the Americas domestic issues. According to Charles Maier, "Fulfilling 'manifest destiny' reassuringly implied an exemption from empire, and the acquisitions were mentally relegated to the purely domestic dimension."[1] Accepting such expansion as a natural part of the development of a country directly feeds into ideas of U.S. exceptionalism.

No one would claim or believe that Hitler taking over other parts of continental Europe was just the natural outgrowth of contiguous continental expansion or a domestic German issue. American Indian lands, Mexico, and other European territories in nineteenth-century America were likewise foreign entities that were taken over by a colonizer through war or diplomacy. In addition to the political-legal status of such polities, these acquired regions were also just as economically and geographically substantial as other recognized nations at that time. Scholars need to move away from thinking about U.S. continental expansion as a normal and benevolent process toward a view of the United States as having an empire and the country's expansion as colonial.

Most scholars recognize that the United States ran the Philippines and was involved in other parts of the Caribbean and Pacific at the beginning of the twentieth century. But the size of these areas was small, the United States did not hold long-term control in the archipelago, and other regions eventually gained citizenship or some form of local autonomy. Some academics consequently do not see these histories as significant enough to characterize the United States as colonial or an empire.[2] James Kurth explained that Puerto Rico and the Philippines "never approached the levels of importance that the European dependencies held for the metropolitan nations of Europe."[3] Such attitudes, as Epeli Hau'ofa has suggested, are themselves part of Western domination and subjugation of those areas.[4] From this perspective, the classification of these regions as insignificant is itself an exercise of colonialism and empire, especially in light of the economic dependence of the United States on these colonial areas.

According to Maier, "an empire in the classic sense is usually believed, first, to expand its control by conquest or coercion, and, second, to control the political loyalty of the territories it subjugates."[5] Both U.S. continental expansion and U.S. control in the Caribbean and the Pacific have reflected such characteristics. Just because U.S. control in the Philippines lasted only fifty years does not nullify that period or its lingering effects, which have been pointed out in this book and by other scholars.[6] Puerto Rico, Hawai'i, American Sāmoa, Guam, and the U.S. Virgin Islands are also all still under U.S. control.[7] The acts and ramifications of U.S. expansionism were significant to these regions and continue to be so. Moreover, taken in accumulation, these colonized areas contributed significantly to the economic, social, military, and political position and role that this nation-empire holds in the world today.

Scholars and policymakers have also often separated imperial histories by time period, region, and group. Such segmentation portrays U.S. government actions as unique, productive, and often beneficial for each subjected group. While ground-level practices were particular to each set of U.S. colonials, the examination of these experiences as part of a consistent policy shows the overarching imperial nature of expansionist actions by the United States government throughout its history. *Islanders in the Empire* has demonstrated how such imperialistic activities manifested in the daily lives of Puerto Rican and Filipino U.S. colonials in the second colonized space of the U.S. Territory of Hawai'i.

I will conclude by examining two significant ways that U.S. colonialism still has an active influence on the daily lives of Puerto Ricans and Filipinos. These examples are: the push for a change in Puerto Rico's temporary territorial relationship with the United States, and the quest for the return of the Balangiga church bells, taken as war booty in 1901, and currently displayed at a U.S. war memorial in Cheyenne, Wyoming.

Puerto Rican Plebiscite

The United States' political-legal relationship with an incorporated territory is a currently contested issue in Puerto Rico. According to President Barack Obama, there are "more than four million U.S. citizens who call Puerto Rico home and a nearly equal number of Puerto Ricans living on the mainland who travel back to Puerto Rico for business, vacation, or visits to see family and friends."[8] In a January 2, 2009, message to the people of Puerto Rico, President-Elect Obama pledged "to work with Congress and all groups in Puerto Rico to enable the question of Puerto Rico's status to be resolved during the next four years."[9] Such a goal has been much easier to proclaim than actuate. Puerto Rican efforts to change their region's political-legal relationship with the United States have been ongoing for years.

When Puerto Rico became an organized but unincorporated territory of the United States after the Jones Act of 1917, the region's governor's seat continued to be appointed by the president, and the president and Congress both had authority to override Puerto Rican legislation. In 1947, President Harry Truman allowed the people of Puerto Rico to elect their own governor through the Elective Governors Act (PL 80–362), with Luis Muñoz Marín becoming the first elected Governor of Puerto Rico in 1948. In 1950, Congress allowed Puerto Ricans to draft their own constitution for local matters under the Puerto Rican Federal Relations Act (PL 81–600), resulting in the July 25, 1952, creation of the Commonwealth of Puerto Rico, or the Estado Libre Asociado de Puerto Rico. Current relations between Puerto Rico and the United States continue to be dictated by the U.S. Constitution and the Puerto Rican Federal Relations Act. The local government is run by the elected governor and a bicameral legislature. National government matters, such as currency, defense, foreign relations, and interstate commerce, are within federal jurisdiction. Puerto Rico is represented at the federal level by a resident commissioner who serves in the U.S. House of Representatives as a nonvoting member.[10]

In 1967, the Puerto Rico legislature held a referendum to identify both "the interest of the people of Puerto Rico and the will of Congress to settle the political status debate."[11] That referendum resulted in 60.4 percent of voters supporting the Commonwealth option. In 1970 and 1971, an Ad Hoc Advisory Group on Puerto Rico met to investigate the viability of giving U.S. citizens in Puerto Rico the right to vote in presidential elections. While this committee recommended such a change, Congress rejected this policy. In September 1973, a second Ad Hoc Advisory Group examined "the extent of the applicability of federal laws and regulations to Puerto Rico in light of its commonwealth status."[12] This committee drafted legislation to provide Puerto Rico with greater autonomy, but the policy never made it out of congressional committee due to bipartisan opposition. While ad hoc groups and some presidential administrations supported the augmentation of Puerto Rican rights, bipartisan opposition in the U.S. legislature has prevented such changes from going into effect.

On November 30, 1992, President George H. W. Bush directed "all federal agencies to treat Puerto Rico administratively as if it were a State," except when it would cost money.[13] Such a policy would remain in effect until the status of Puerto Rico was determined. In 1993 and 1998, the Puerto Rico government enacted legislation to conduct plebiscites. The 1993 results had 48.6 percent of Puerto Ricans selecting the commonwealth option, 46.3 percent supporting statehood, and 4.4 percent asking for independence. In 1998, the "none of the above" option, supported by the Popular Democratic Party, gained 50.3 percent of the vote, with statehood getting 46.5 percent, independence having 2.54 percent, free association with 0.29 percent, and commonwealth with 0.06 percent.[14] According to the Task Force Report, this plebiscite became a moment of protest by the Puerto Rican people over several issues. Some were dissatisfied with the status choices provided. The Commonwealth Party did not agree with the definition of commonwealth on the ballot. Congress was also not obligated to act on plebiscite results.[15]

Despite such issues, voter turnout for both plebiscites was around 70 percent because "status remains of overwhelming importance to the people of Puerto Rico."[16] In their biyearly report in March 2011, the Task Force stated that the Puerto Rican government had discussed the possibility of holding a plebiscite in summer 2011 "to ascertain the will of the people of Puerto Rico concerning status."[17] This vote did not happen, but on December 21, 2011, the Puerto Rico House of Representatives approved Law 283 by a vote of 31–13.[18] This legislation, also approved by the Puerto Rico Senate earlier that month, decided that a plebiscite would be held on the same day as the U.S. general elections: November 6, 2012. Puerto Rican Governor Luis Fortuño signed the legislation into law on December 29, 2011.

On November 6, 2012, the first part of the status referendum asked voters whether they were satisfied with the current territorial status. The second part gave voters three options for change: statehood, independence, or sovereign free association (an as-yet-undetermined nonterritorial hybrid of commonwealth and independence). While the original plan, supported by the Presidential Task Force, involved a two-part vote—one ascertaining voters' desire to change commonwealth status and, if this won a majority, a second referendum held on a later date to decide on what change to endorse—Law 283 ultimately called for both votes to be held the same day: November 6, 2012.

There was much division among political parties in Puerto Rico about the best way to resolve the status question. Inter-political party rivalries and conflicts shaped organizational recommendations to their party members. The pro-commonwealth Popular Democratic Party (PDP) stated that its voting recommendation should be seen "as a vote against the current New Progressive Party (NPP) administration" and the pro-statehood position of the governor.[19] On February 12, 2012, the governing board of the PDP unanimously agreed "to protest the plebiscite (that did not include a commonwealth option) by urging voters to mark no in the first question about being satisfied about the current status, and to leave the second question blank, which asks voters to check their preferred status option."[20] This type of vote would mimic a none-of-the-above option. PDP president Alejandro García Padilla, also the party's gubernatorial candidate, complained that "neither the current commonwealth status nor an enhanced commonwealth are on the ballot."[21] Such absences, as well as the party's disapproval of the NPP, guided the PDP's voting recommendations.

According to an ABC/Univison news report on November 8, 2012, 54 percent voted no to the question "Are you satisfied with the current territorial status?" For the second question, 61.2 percent of 1.8 million voters favored statehood.[22] However, there were 466,337 blank votes to the second question "Which status do you prefer?" If blank votes are factored in, statehood only wins 45.1 percent of the total. If you add the Sovereign Free Associated State and the blank ballots together, they total 51 percent of the votes: results similar to the plebiscites of 1967 and 1993, and nearly identical to that of 1998, which was won by the PDP's "None of the Above" option.

The complicated outcome of the November 2012 vote is shaky ground for any request to the U.S. Congress for statehood. In fact, newly elected and incoming pro-commonwealth governor and PDP president García Padilla announced that he would hold a constitutional convention in Puerto Rico in 2014 and would seek a new plebiscite that would be approved by Congress. Clearly there is dissatisfaction in Puerto Rico with the current political-legal status. But a deep divide exists over how to move forward.

And even if the 2014 vote resolves the rifts among Puerto Ricans, the U.S. Congress must still approve any proposal. While President Obama has claimed that he will take any vote by the Puerto Rican people seriously, there is no guarantee that plebiscite consensus would result in actual status change. In fact, HR 2499, known as the Puerto Rico Democracy Act of 2010, was supposed "to provide for a federally sanctioned self-determination process for the people of Puerto Rico."[23] While the House passed this bill on April 29, 2010, the legislation died when it was never passed by the Senate. The controversies over changing Puerto Rico's political-legal relationship with the United States are manifestations of continuing U.S. colonialism in Puerto Rico today.[24]

The Bells of Balangiga

While the Philippines became officially independent from the United States in 1946, vestiges of U.S. colonialism still exist in the archipelago's economic, political, military, and social policies. Current controversies over the bells of Balangiga started in 1901, when the 11th U.S. Infantry Regiment took the church bells from the Philippine town of Balangiga as war booty. Such an act was part of a controversial set of conflicts between the United States and the Philippines in this Eastern Samar, Visayas location. Infamous events included a Philippine surprise attack on U.S. troops that started after the church bells were rung. In retaliation for the assault, U.S. troops returned the next day, razing the town and wounding or killing Filipinos throughout the region for the next several weeks.[25] This set of battles resulted in heavy casualties on both sides. Details of these events have been widely debated, but it is clear that violence and suffering occurred among all groups involved.

After the Balangiga incident, the town's church bells "accompanied the Eleventh Infantry to Fort D. A. Russell in Cheyenne, Wyoming, in 1904. When Company C mustered out of the state, it took one of the bells to its subsequent postings (Madison Barracks, New York; Fort Sam Houston, Texas; Fort Lewis, Washington; Fort Ord, California; and, since the early 1950s, near Tong Du Chon, South Korea), leaving two bells at the Wyoming base, which was later renamed F. E. Warren Air Force Base."[26] In 1911, Major General Franklin Bell questioned the "propriety of taking (even as a souvenir) a bell belonging to the Catholic Church."[27] In 1935, a survivor of the Balangiga incident, Eugenio Daza, also called for the bells' return, after which interest in them faded.[28] F. E. Warren base historian Gerald Adams maintains that base officials "wanted to get rid of them. . . . [The bells] just didn't seem to have any strong meaning" decades after the men who took them had left.[29]

According to scholar Sharon Delmendo, in 1986 Philippine secretary of defense Fidel Ramos requested a return of the bells.[30] In 1987, he also asked Secretary of Defense Dick Cheney, a former U.S. Congressman from

Wyoming on a routine diplomatic visit to the archipelago, about repatriating the artifacts.[31] While Cheney said he would look into the situation, no subsequent action was taken. Sustained diplomatic requests to return the bells started in 1994 as preparations for the 1996 centennial celebration of Philippine independence from the United States ramped up. Ramos, by then Philippine president, asked President William Clinton during his 1994 state visit to return the bells as "a good gesture in 1998 to commemorate 100 years of U.S.-Philippine relations."[32] Once again, Ramos received a promise to investigate the situation with no results. Until 1997, discussions to repatriate the bells generally occurred at the diplomatic level.[33]

Public involvement with the bells began in 1997 when an article was printed in the *Gillette News-Record* in July about the visit of local Wyoming politician Jeff Wasserburger to the Philippines, where he was frequently asked about the return of the bells of Balangiga.[34] By the end of his visit, he agreed to sponsor legislation to assist this goal. Philippine ambassador to the United States Raul Rabe visited Cheyenne a few months later in October. During a speech to the Greater Cheyenne Chamber of Commerce that dealt primarily with U.S.-Philippine cooperation and business collaboration, he briefly mentioned the bells, angering some veterans in the audience. According to Joe Sestak, Wyoming commander for the American Legion, this veterans group "is not inclined to dismantle war memorials to our own troops to give to other countries."[35] Reaction to Rabe's visit initiated a firestorm of debate among multiple groups in the United States and the Philippines about the status and purpose of the bells of Balangiga.

Some Filipino and U.S. citizens wanted the bells returned to their original location in the Philippines. Since 1999, the Catholic diocese in Eastern Samar, with the support of the Catholic diocese in Cheyenne, has claimed that "the Diocese of Borongan, to which the Parish of Balangiga belongs, lays rightful ownership to the Bells of Balangiga.[36] Since the artifacts were church property, religious officials believed the bells should be returned to the Philippines. According to Sylvester Salcedo, a Filipino from Boston, the repatriation of the bells was "an important moral issue ... Americans do not desecrate other peoples' houses of worship."[37] Rodger McDaniel, a Cheyenne resident, also said that "I think we would do greater honor to the real values of our nation ... by graciously returning [the bells] to a people to whom such a gesture would say a great deal about who we are."[38]

Others believed the bells represented the sacrifices of the U.S. military and should remain part of an existing war memorial to recognize and respect the contributions of U.S. soldiers to the country. Retired Air Force general Robert Scott stated that "if you want to return the bells, that is a breach of faith and honor to men who lost their lives."[39] Wyoming State

Representative Barbara Cubin also stated, "The Bells of Balangiga memorial represents the blood and sweat invested by America to secure an independent Philippines."[40] Kenneth Steadman, executive director of the Veterans of Foreign Wars, discussed how "the Bells serve as a permanent memorial to the sacrifice of the American soldiers from Fort D. A. Russell (Wyoming) who gave their lives for their country while doing their duty. ... To return the bells sends the wrong message to the world."[41]

James Helzer, a Cheyenne businessmen and member of the Warren base's civilian advisory board, expressed a middle-of-the-road opinion. He said, "You sort of accept these monuments for what they are ... but what we have are bells looted from a Catholic church during an event which is worse than what happened in the My Lai massacre in Vietnam."[42] People from both countries have expressed passionate and varied opinions about the location and meaning of the Balangiga bells. For some U.S. citizens, these bells represented the veneration of U.S. military service personnel. For some Philippine citizens, the return of these bells represented the acknowledgement of the wrongs of the U.S. occupation and war in the Philippines.

Several compromises have been proposed in response to this controversy, including making replicas of the two bells and sending one original and one copy to the Philippines. Another suggestion involved cutting both bells in half so each location would have one half of the two real bells and the other half would be reconstructed.[43] However, according to Delmendo, a small group of mostly Wyoming veterans with no direct connection to the bells blocked any changes, even temporary removal for replication purposes.[44] In 1998, Wyoming branches of the American Legion, Veterans of Foreign Wars, United Veterans Council, Veterans Affairs Council, and the Special Forces Association all passed resolutions opposing the compromise. According to Bob Nab of the American Legion, "We feel very strongly that the minute those bells went off that morning, they became an instrument of war."[45] Kenneth Weber, commander of the Veterans of Foreign Wars Department of Wyoming, said, "Any compromise that would allow the return of a pair of bells taken from the Philippines as a war memorial and trophy in 1904 must be rejected."[46]

At one point it was believed that only one bell was taken from Balangiga and that the other artifact was actually in South Korea.[47] In light of such claims, in 1998, Senator Craig Thomas of Wyoming expressed his willingness to help return the bell in Korea to the Philippines in exchange for keeping the other two bells in Cheyenne. However, President Ramos refused to give up his desire for the return of all the bells. These artifacts, regardless of their provenance, came to represent ideological and patriotic struggles for certain groups in both the Philippines and the United States. National pride and ego became heavily invested in the future of these bells.

By September 28, 2004, Eastern Samar governor Ben Evardone stated that the Balangiga Research Group found that all three bells, the two in Cheyenne and the one in Korea, were from Balangiga.[48] In 2005, "Wyoming veterans voted to return them [the bells], but the governor of Wyoming blocked their return, claiming they represented 'a significant part of Wyoming's military heritage,' though no one from Wyoming served at Balangiga."[49] On February 15, 2011, U.S. Representative Bob Filner of California introduced House Congressional Resolution 18. This bill, referred to the House Committee on Foreign Affairs on the same day, planned to urge "the President to authorize the return to the people of the Philippines of two church bells."[50] The bill died in committee.

In June 2011 the Philippine House of Representatives passed HR 112, requesting the United States government to return the bells. The bill's sponsor, Representative Teodoro Casiño, expressed "hope that the Barack Obama administration will address this important resolution by the 15th Congress and heed calls to return the bells of Balangiga."[51] In September 2011, Jean Wall, one of the daughters of the survivors of the 11th Regiment, also stated: "I have always felt that church bells were meant to be hung in their house of worship (and) not used as a memorial to a bittersweet incident in our history that so few are aware of today and even less, no doubt, in the future."[52] In October 2011, Philippine vice president Jejomar Binay "expressed confidence . . . that the U.S. Congress will approve the return of Balangiga Bells to the Philippines."[53] While most people seem to support the return of the artifacts more than 110 years after their removal, as of this writing the bells remain in Cheyenne and no resolution has emerged.

The controversies surrounding the location of the bells of Balangiga and plebiscites on the future political status of Puerto Rico both demonstrate current, continual ramifications of U.S. colonialism in each of these regions. United States empire is not just an artifact of the past. It continues to function today. Colonized peoples still remain under U.S. authority in the twenty-first century. To fulfill U.S. ideals of democracy and equality, scholars and policymakers alike should acknowledge the existence and significance of past and present colonial relationships.

Currently, the disassociation of American Indians and Native Hawaiians from Chicanos, Filipinos, and Puerto Ricans maintains images of U.S. democracy and equality while masking U.S. federal officials' exertion of authority over unwilling peoples. Studying the qualities that connect and distinguish all U.S. colonials throughout the course of U.S. history on the continent and beyond can also highlight the patterns, trends, and possible future directions for U.S. government policies and actions.

U.S. colonials, like Filipinos and Puerto Ricans, have faced different administrative structures and government policies than those experienced by citizens or foreigners. Intra-colonials have also experienced colonial management and local leadership distinct from U.S. colonials living in their home region or the continental United States. Filipino and Puerto Rican interactions with local ethnic mediators, U.S. colonial government bureaucracies, and HSPA recruitment and retention programs all provide important examples of unique intra-colonial mobility experiences, as well as the everyday particularities of U.S. colonial lives.

Within government and labor systems, U.S. colonials have exercised a degree of control and choice over their mobility and work environments. They maneuvered through complicated bureaucratic structures that tried to manage and regulate their actions. At different moments in time, Filipino and Puerto Rican intra-colonials in Hawai'i could move where they wanted, write what they wanted, and resist when they wanted. They could prioritize and act upon their personal hopes, family aspirations, and community goals despite government regulations and employer preferences. But they were also limited and constrained by ever-present, even if distant, imperial officials and policies. A combination of structural and personal circumstances ultimately shaped the labor and migration experiences of U.S. colonials. Overall, in-between legal statuses created by U.S. colonialism provided Filipinos and Puerto Ricans with unique challenges, as well as opportunities.

Looking beyond regional and chronological boundaries, the connections and differences in U.S. colonial experiences and imperial government practices also provide new perspectives to interpret and understand United States history. A broader view of expansionism as a continuous ideology in the federal government shifts our perceptions of Hawai'i, Puerto Rico, and the Philippines: they are not satellites to the story of a republic but central components in the narrative of American empire.

NOTES

Introduction

1. *Gonzales v. Williams*, No. 225, 192 U.S. 1, 12. Also see Erman, "Meanings" and Burnett, "'They Say.'"

2. Puerto Ricans gained U.S. citizenship in 1917, but such status did not result in much change in their treatment in the Territory of Hawai'i. They could access higher paying government jobs, but most local government officials and members of the public continued to look down upon this population. A general ignorance of Puerto Rican citizenship status was prevalent in Hawai'i throughout the twentieth century. For more discussion of such struggles, see chapter 3.

3. Faye Caronan Chen, Julian Go, and Lanny Thompson have conducted the most recent studies of both groups, focusing on the political and social impact of U.S. colonialism in these regions and its people.

4. Scholars such as Rick Baldoz, Catherine Choy, Yen Le Espiritu, Dorothy Fujita-Rony, Dawn Mabalon, and Robyn Rodriguez have connected U.S. rule in the Philippines with Filipino labor migration to the United States, while scholars such as Elizabeth Aranda, Jorge Duany, Juan Flores, Gina Pérez, and Carmen Whalen have described the effect of U.S. colonialism on Puerto Rican mobility to the country.

5. For example, the annexation of Hawai'i was overseas expansion that eventually resulted in the same outcome as domestic expansion: statehood.

6. The relatively small number of American Indians, Native Hawaiians, Chicanos, and Alaska Natives during time of incorporation, compared to the high value of their lands, facilitated the granting of full U.S. citizenship to these groups. Other U.S. colonial groups, such as Filipinos, Puerto Ricans, and American Sāmoans, were either too distant, too populous, or not profitable enough to become fully incorporated as full-fledged citizens and states of the nation.

7. Throughout this work, the terms colonial and imperial are used interchangeably. A debate exists on which countries have engaged in colonialism versus imperialism. According to generally accepted definitions of colonialism, my focus on people who have come under direct U.S. authority is colonialism. While I look specifically at U.S. colonialism, I use imperialism as an alternative moniker for the exercise of United States influence and authority over extraterritorial groups and places. See Boot, "Case for American Empire"; Boot, *Savage Wars*; Ferguson, *Colossus*; Kennedy, "Essay and Reflection"; Kramer, "Power and Connection"; and Steinmetz, "Return to Empire."

8. The HSPA was the governing body of the Hawai'i sugar industry, with a director, multiple committees, and board that oversaw plantation policies and procedures. See Beechert, *Working*, 179–81.

9. Of course, not all citizens gained access to the same kinds of protections, such as women, African Americans, and U.S. born-Chinese. For examples, see *Minor v. Happersett, Plessy v. Ferguson,* and *Wong Wing v. United States.*

10. "Treaty of Peace between the United States and Spain; December 10, 1898," Avalon Project: Documents in Law, History and Diplomacy, Yale Law School, Lillian Goldman Law Library, available at http://avalon.law.yale.edu/19th_century/sp1898.asp (accessed April 4, 2012).

11. Starting with the Chinese Exclusion Acts of the 1880s and culminating with the 1924 National Origins Act, the immigration of non-Western Europeans into the United States was greatly curtailed until 1965. People from the Western Hemisphere were excluded from the 1924 act, but they needed to pay for expensive visas and passports to enter the country. Such requirements were cost prohibitive for most migrants from this region. For more information, see Ngai, *Impossible Subjects* and Salyer, *Laws Harsh as Tigers.*

12. For discussion of the variability in colonial policies within a single empire, see Cooper, *Colonialism in Question*; Cooper and Stoler, *Tensions or Empire*; Go, *Patterns of Empire*; Kennedy, "Essay and Reflection"; and Steinmetz, "Return to Empire."

13. For more information about debates over the Philippines, see Baldoz, *Third Asiatic Invasion* and Zwick, "Anti-Imperialist League." For general reading on anti-imperialist debates, see Bouvier, *Whose America?* and Foster and McChesney, *Pox Americana.*

14. Chapter 4 explains how Filipinos had a resident labor commissioner from 1923 to 1932. However, he was ineffective as a worker advocate because he often collaborated with the U.S. government and sugar plantation industry.

15. See Baldoz, *Third Asiatic Invasion* and Aranda, *Emotional Bridges.*

16. Scholars such as Frederick Cooper, Amy Kaplan, and Ann Stoler have examined the effects of the colonizer in the colonized region, the influence of colonization on the culture of the metropole, and the impact of colonialism on the identity of the colonized. César J. Ayala and Rafael Bernabé examined the economic effects of colonialism in Puerto Rico. Eileen Findlay focused on U.S.-imposed changes in gender and marriage regulations. Efrén Rivera Ramos studied the effect of colonial laws on Puerto Rican identity. Warwick Anderson studied the intersection of medicine and colonialism in the Philippines. Paul Kramer analyzed the influence of colonial racial discourse on Philippine political development. Michael Salman examined the influence of U.S. anti-slavery rhetoric on Philippine labor policies. Alfred McCoy and Francisco Scarano's *Colonial Crucible* provided a compilation of studies about U.S. colonialism in Puerto Rico or the Philippines, as well as other imperial locations like Cuba and Hawai'i.

17. Roopnarine, *Indo-Caribbean Indenture*, 5. For more information on experiences of intra-colonial Indian British colonials, see Kale, *Fragments of Empire*; Kaplan and Kelly, "On Discourse and Power"; Lal, *Girmitiyas*; Look Lai, *Indentured Labor*; and Roopnarine, "Return Migration." For a general comparison of British and U.S. empires, see Go, *Patterns of Empire.*

18. See Wenzlhuemer, "Indian Labour."

19. After completing labor contracts, some Indian British colonials returned to India and re-migrated back. See Carter, *Voices.*

20. Scholars such as Donna Gabaccia, Madeline Hsu, and Jonathan Okamura, as well as Nina Glick Schiller and Georges Eugene Fouron, have discussed how individuals maintain active contact and affiliation with their home nation while living and working in another country.

21. McKeown, *Melancholy Order*, 1.
22. For examples of global studies across time and space, see Go, *Patterns and Empire*; Maier, *Among Empires*; Pagden, *Peoples and Empires*; and Abernethy, *Dynamics of Global Dominance*.
23. Bankoff, "Wants," 61. Steinmetz typified U.S. imperialism as focused on "democratic tutelage, neoliberalism, or human rights . . . often present themselves in the universalizing language of economics or human nature." Steinmetz, "Return to Empire," 341.
24. For studies of U.S. exceptionalism, see Bender, *Rethinking*; Fredrickson, "From Exceptionalism"; Go, *Patterns of Empire*; Kaplan, "'Left Alone'"; Nolan, "Against Exceptionalisms"; Perez, *War of 1898*; Rodgers, "Exceptionalism"; and Winks, "American Struggle."
25. See Maier, *Among Empires*, 80.
26. For two examples, see Maier, *Among Empires* and Steinmetz, "Return to Empire." For a more in-depth discussion, see the conclusion.
27. See Go and Foster, *American Colonial State*. Cooper, Kramer, and Stoler also talk about the interchange among different empires. But clearly there were differences in overseas scope and length of time. Cooper, *Colonialism in Question*; Cooper and Stoler, *Tensions*; and Kramer, "Empires." Also see Hempenstall, "Imperial Manoeuvres."
28. Kramer, "Empires," 1327. Dale Kennedy and Maya Jasanoff also claimed the United States built and managed their empire based on British structures and ideas.
29. Schmidt-Nowara, "Spanish Origins," 33. Juan Guisti-Cordero claimed that "American interests in the Philippines and Puerto Rico lay in not overturning—and indeed in strengthening—the land and sugar-mill configurations that had developed under Spain." Guisti-Cordero, "Compradors or Compadres?" 194.
30. According to Mariano Negrón-Portillo, the U.S. government portrayed the Spanish regime in the colonies as "an authoritarian, repressive, and backward form of colonial domination with no positive political legacy to be remembered by." Negrón-Portillo, "Puerto Rico," 45.
31. "In comparison with Anglo-Saxons, Hispanics were singularly susceptible to corruption, brutality, laziness, and greed." Hess, "John Philip Sousa's *El Capitan*," 5.
32. Williams, *Northwest Ordinance* and Duffey, "Northwest Ordinance."
33. *Downes v. Bidwell*, 182 U.S. 244, May 27, 1901. The Insular Cases are composed of *DeLima v. Bidwell*, 182 U.S. 1, *Goetze v. United States*, 182 U.S. 221, *Armstrong v. United States*, 182 U.S. 243, *Downes v. Bidwell*, 182 U.S. 244, and *Huus v. New York and Porto Rico S.S. Co.*, 182 U.S. 392.
34. Silva, *Aloha Betrayed*; Osorio, *Dismembering L'ahui*; Maier, *Among Empires*, chapter 4; Merry, *Colonizing Hawai'i*.
35. Archer, "Remedial Agents."
36. This citizenship was forced upon them. Native Hawaiians had no say in their incorporation into the United States. Prior to this legislation, Native Hawaiians protested annexation and territorial status by signing petitions and lobbying members of the U.S. Congress. See Silva, *Aloha Betrayed*, 123–204.
37. As Peggy Choy has said, the "wider context of colonial domination cannot be ignored." Choy, "Anatomy of a Dancer," 291.
38. An example of requests for the exemption of the Territory of Hawai'i from the application of general U.S. policies involves Section 8A1 of the Philippine Independence Act, discussed in chapter 2. Anglo elite in Hawai'i lobbied for this loophole through multiple letters and passionate testimony to Congress. These leaders

emphasized the uniqueness of the racial and labor situation in the islands and the desire for continued Filipino migration to the Pacific despite the anti-Filipino sentiment and violence in the continental United States.

39. Kauanui, *Hawaiian Blood*; Sarannillio, "Colliding Histories"; Scott-Smith, "Symbol of Division"; Trask, *From a Native Daughter*; Whitehead, *Completing the Union*; and Ziker, "Segregationists Confront."

40. See Brewer, *Shamanism* and Rafael *Contracting Colonialism*.

41. Ileto, *Pasyon and Revolution*.

42. Perez, *War of 1898*.

43. For more information of the anti-imperialist debates, see note 13.

44. See Kramer, *Blood of Government*; Go, *American Empire*.

45. Filipinization is discussed in chapter 4.

46. See Baldoz, *Third Asiatic Invasion*; España-Maram, *Creating Masculinity*; Fujita-Rony, *American Workers*; and Mabalon, *Little Manila*.

47. Francia, "Rind of Things."

48. See Morales Carrión, *Puerto Rico* and Picó, *History of Puerto Rico*.

49. See Ayala and Bernabé, *Puerto Rico* and Ayala, *American Sugar Kingdom*.

50. Findlay, *Imposing Decency* and Briggs, *Reproducing Race*.

51. Rodriguez-Silva, *Silencing Race*, chapter 4. Rodríguez-Silva also discussed how silence about blackness among Puerto Ricans allowed leaders to avoid discussions of racial conflict in the region. Ayala and Bernabé also explained the diversity of approaches to race in Puerto Rico at the turn of the twentieth century. Some political and labor groups ignored the issue of blackness while others embraced African slave roots in labor, political, and social movements. Overall, blackness became a negative identification in Spanish- and U.S.-controlled Puerto Rico. Ayala and Bernabé, *Puerto Rico*, chapters 3–5.

52. Despite their categorization as white, Puerto Ricans in Hawai'i were still treated as inferior members of society. They faced negative stereotypes as a lazy and violent people. See chapter 3 for more details. Briggs also discussed how Puerto Ricans have historically been stereotyped as problematic members of society due to their family structure. Briggs, *Reproducing Empire*, 3–6. Even after becoming U.S. citizens in 1917, leaders in Hawai'i resisted acknowledging this change in legal status. As will be discussed in chapter 3, Puerto Ricans in Hawai'i had to file a court case to gain the right to register to vote in Honolulu.

53. See Rivera Ramos, *Legal Construction of Identity* and Burnett and Marshall, *Foreign in a Domestic Sense*.

54. See Negrón-Muntaner, *None of the Above*. This issue is also discussed in the conclusion.

55. Hawaiian Sugar Planters' Association, *Sugar in Hawaii*, 22–23. Increased capital from duty-free sales enabled plantations to upgrade their milling technologies and irrigation systems, dramatically increasing their output.

56. See Hawaiian Sugar Planters' Association, *Sugar in Hawaii* and *Facts about Hawaii's Largest Industry*.

57. See Beechert, *Working*; McGowan, "Industrializing"; and Takaki, *Pau Hana*.

58. Fujikane and Okamura, *Asian Settler Colonialism*, 17.

59. For more information on the concept of total institutions, see Mize and Swords, *Consuming Mexican Labor* and Goffman, *Asylums*.

60. Hawaiian Agriculture Research Center, History, available at http://www.harc-hspa.com/index.php?section=research&page=HARCHS11#HSPA (accessed June 9, 2013). For

the most recent history of the HSPA, see Heinz and Osgood, "History of the Experiment Station." Other names for the sugar industry in Hawai'i include the Big Five, referencing the five major sugar companies in the region (Alexander and Baldwin, C. Brewer and Company, Castle and Cook, American Factors [formerly Hackfeld and Company], and Theo. H. Davies), as well as Merchant Street, the road in the Honolulu financial district where these companies had offices. Gallagher, "No More a Christian Nation," 201.

61. The only time all ethnic groups interacted and integrated with each other were in rural, one-room elementary school classrooms. From my oral history interviews, I found that even in this environment, children still gravitated toward others of their same ethnic background during their free time. This lack of horizontal relationships lasted until after World War II, as explained by Jung in *Reworking Race*.

62. Along with the closing of all but two sugar plantations on Kaua'i and Maui in 1996, the HSPA changed its name to the Hawaii Agriculture Research Center (HARC) that same year. This new organization, which still exists today, focuses on crop research, pesticide registration work, and other agricultural response and lab services.

63. See Beechert, *Working*; Reinecke, *Filipino Piecemeal Sugar Strike*; and Takaki, *Pau Hana*, 145–76.

64. See Gordon, "Agrarian Question." Guisti-Cordero also found that "in Puerto Rico as elsewhere in the Caribbean, field labor in the cane remained overwhelmingly manual into the 1950s." Guisti-Cordero, "Labor Ecology," 894.

65. Matrana, *Lost Plantation*, 50, and Guisti-Cordero, "Labor Ecology," 895. The classic work by Charles Roland (*Louisiana Sugar Plantation during the American Civil War*) compared the plantation system to an army. "The master was the commander, and the overseer his lieutenant. From the overseer the chain of command ran through first and second drivers, who performed the functions of sergeants, to the common hands—the private soldiers of the slave company. The plantation bell was to the Negroes what the bugle is to troops. It was rung in the morning by the first driver as the quarter's reveille; meals were announced by its tolling; and at night it sounded taps to send the laborers to their cabins." Roland, *Louisiana Sugar*, 13.

66. Reidy, "Mules and Machines," 183–84.

67. Ibid., 184.

68. Ibid. Plantation leaders sought to create a balance of "industrial innovation and social stability within a framework of paternal hierarchy" on turn-of-the-twentieth-century Louisiana sugar plantations.

69. For a classic example, see Genovese, *Roll, Jordan, Roll*. For a more recent example, see Follett, *Sugar Masters*.

70. Reidy, "Mules and Machines," 184.

71. Look Lai, *Indentured Labor* and Wenzlhuemer, "Indian Labour."

72. I also embrace this concept because it includes experiences beyond the conventional binary of citizens and foreigners.

73. Garfield, "Tapping Masculinity," 276.

74. On forms of social capital, see Bourdieu, *Outline of a Theory of Practice* and "Forms of Capital."

Chapter 1. Letters Home

1. Bergad, *Coffee*, 209.
2. Santiago-Valles, "*Subject People*," 94.

3. See Erman, "Meanings."
4. Interview in Aina Haina, June 27, 1978, Norma Carr Collection, 2.
5. García-Colón, "Buscando Ambiente," 43.
6. Hawaiian Sugar Planters' Association, *Story of Sugar*, 10, and Hawaiian Sugar Planters' Association, *Facts About Hawaii's Largest Industry*, 2.
7. Once aware of the departure of underage kids for Hawai'i, recruiters worked to return these unaccompanied children and prevent further exits of this kind. For an example, see Carmelo Rosario Natal, "Temas históricos de Puerto Rico," *El Mundo*, March 20, 1983. Translation in Puerto Rican newspaper articles folder, Blase Camacho Souza collection, CENTRO archives, Hunter College, CUNY, New York, New York.
8. "De Yauco," *La Correspondencia*, March 23, 1901, *Documentos de la Migración Puertorriqueña*, No. 1 (New York: Centro de Estudios Puertorriqueños, 1977), 27. Hereafter listed as *DMP1*.
9. Santiago-Valles, *"Subject People,"* 78.
10. Ibid., 80.
11. Ibid., 56.
12. Edward J. Livernash, "Record-Breaking Run to Be Made by Exile Train," *San Francisco Examiner*, December 12, 1900.
13. This quote also alluded to fears over racial violence in the United States. Livernash, "Porto Ricans Enticed from Their Homes by Promises of Luxury and Wealth," *San Francisco Examiner*, December 11, 1900.
14. Ibid.
15. Manuel Romero Haxthausen, "Braceros á las islas Haway," *La Correspondencia*, August 4, 1900.
16. Carr, "Puerto Ricans in Hawaii," 177–78.
17. "Porto Rican Prisoners in Railway Cars," *San Francisco Chronicle*, December 7, 1900. Another negative article in English can be found in "Porto Ricans in Hawaii," *New York Times*, May 29, 1901. Examples of negative Spanish-language articles include "Cablegramas de hoy," *La Correspondencia*, January 4, 1901, *DMP1*, 20; "Cablegramas de hoy," *La Correspondencia*, January 26, 1901, *DMP1*, 22; and "Emigrados q: regresan," *La Correspondencia*, April 17, 1901, *DMP1*, 31.
18. "Puerto Ricans Pass through Los Angeles," *San Francisco Call*, December 14, 1900. A *New York Times* article also reported "the happy bearing of the emigrants, who all seemed anxious to leave Porto Rico. Out of the entire shipment, only four changed their minds after boarding the ship, while all were given the chance to go ashore if they wished . . . the four men who yesterday decided not to make the trip on the Californian were no sooner put ashore than their places were filled from a party of 200 who were anxious and waiting to go. No more could be taken, however, as the ship was crowded." "The Porto Rican Exodus," *New York Times*, April 4, 1901. Positive Spanish-language articles include "Yauco. Emigrantes al Hawaii," *La Correspondencia*, March 27, 1901, *DMP1*, 29, and "Carta del Hawaii," *La Correspondencia*, April 25, 1901, *DMP1*, 34.
19. "First Annual Report, Charles H. Allen, Governor of Porto Rico," *DMP1*, 10–11.
20. See Carr, "Puerto Ricans in Hawaii," chapter 3, and Souza and Souza, *De Borinquen a Hawaii Nuestra Historia*, 25–26.
21. For more information on Puerto Ricans who stayed in the San Francisco Bay area, see Medina, "Rebellion in the Bay."
22. "Porto Rican Prisoners in Railway Cars."

23. "Cablegramas de hoy," *DMP1*, 22.
24. Ibid, 20.
25. "The Porto Rican Exodus."
26. Medina questions whether more clothing was actually provided to recruits by comparing photos of migrants boarding boats in Puerto Rico and San Francisco. Medina, "Rebellion in the Bay," 88–89.
27. "Emigrados q: regresan,"*DMP1*, 31.
28. Between December 1900 and October 1901, the HSPA spent $564,191.68 to transport Puerto Rican U.S. colonials to Hawai'i. Porto Ricans, Ref. Report of the Commissioner of Labor on Hawaii 1902, Centro de Investigaciones Históricas, rollo 5, RG 126, Documentos Sobre Emigración de Puertorriqueños a los Estados Unidos y a Otros Países en las Décadas del 1930–50, 2. Hereafter listed as *CIH*, rollo 5, RG 126.
29. "Porto Ricans in Hawaii," *New York Times*, May 29, 1901.
30. "Porto Ricans in Hawaii, 1933," *CIH*, rollo 5, RG 126, 2.
31. Report of the Attorney-General of Hawaii to the Governor of Hawaii, In re Complaint of Porto Rico Laborers Resident in Hawaii (1919 Report), Records of Governor Charles James McCarthy, Attorney General, GOV5–6, Hawai'i State Archives, Government Records, 59.
32. "Report of the Commissioner of Labor on Hawaii," *DMP1*, 44.
33. Center for Oral History (COH), *Kona*, 108.
34. COH, *Waialua and Hale'iwa*, 83. Also see Carr, "Puerto Ricans in Hawaii," 171–72.
35. Bergad, *Coffee*, 228, 230.
36. The HSPA only considered concessions after major labor strikes. Of all the strikes on plantations, only protests from 1900 resulted in a wage increase from eight dollars to ten dollars a month. Takaki, *Pau Hana*, 150.
37. "Una carta del Hawaii: Lamentaciones tardias," *La Correspondencia*, December 4, 1901, *DMP1*, 40.
38. Federico Degetau to Secretary of State, April 23, 1902, Hawai'i State Archives, Governors Papers, GOV1 v. 3, Dole letterbook #3, Hawai'i State Archives, Government Records Collection, 356A.
39. Negrón-Portillo, "Puerto Rico," 44.
40. Ibid.
41. Julio Agostiny et al. to Frederico Degetau, September 25, 1902, Archivo General de Puerto Rico (AGPR), Caja 17, Oficina del Gobernador, Correspondencia General, Emigración e immigracion, Hawaii, 1–2.
42. Statement from Antonio Gil et al., enclosure #4 of Sanford B. Dole to Secretary of Interior, September 4, 1902, 20, Hawai'i State Archives, Dole letterbook #3.
43. For more information on the close ties between agriculture businessmen and government officials in Hawai'i, see Fuchs, *Pono*; Ralston, *Grass Huts*; McGowan, "Industrializing"; Merry, *Colonizing Hawai'i*.
44. Also see "Dos Puertorriqueños que se fugan de Hawaii," *La Correspondencia*, December 5, 1901, *DMP1*, 41.
45. "Braceros á las islas Haway," *La Correspondencia*, August 4, 1900, *DMP1*, 15.
46. M. Romero Haxthausen, "Compentencia Al Hawaii," *La Correspondencia*, February 27, 1901, *DMP1*, 23.
47. "Causa principal de la emigración y medio de contrarestaria," *La Correspondencia*, March 26, 1901, *DMP1*, 28.
48. Ibid.

Notes to Chapter 1

49. Ayala and Bernabé, *Puerto Rico*, 180.
50. Carr, "Puerto Ricans in Hawaii," 88.
51. Rivera, "Will the 'Real' Puerto Rican Culture Please Stand Up?" 217–18.
52. Flores, "Diaspora Strikes Back," 215.
53. Duany, "Nation and Migration," 52.
54. Ibid., 58.
55. The FLT, translated as Free Federation of Laborers, was a workers coalition founded on June 18, 1899. This organization led a series of labor challenges in Puerto Rico at the turn of the twentieth century.
56. Santiago Gonzales to the Governor of Puerto Rico, February 2, 1904, AGPR, Caja 17, September 1903–1905.
57. Maria Torres to Governor of Puerto Rico, February 2, 1904, AGPR, Caja 17, September 1903–1905.
58. Assistant Secretary to Judson L. Underwood, October 31, 1904, AGPR, Caja 17, Folder 3, Puerto Ricans in Hawai'i, 1421–185.
59. Belen Frasinete y Rios to Governor of Porto Rico, February 10, 1905, AGPR, Caja 17, September 1903–1905.
60. "Puerto Rican classified as White from 1910 to 1930 and as a separate race in 1940 and 1950." "Table 26. Hawaii - Race and Hispanic Origin: 1900 to 1990," available at http://www.census.gov/population/www/documentation/twps0056/tab26.pdf (accessed February 14, 2012). For a discussion of Puerto Rican views and uses of whiteness, see the introduction.
61. Memorandum for General Parker, March 24, 1931, File 2876/34, Bureau of Insular Affairs General Records Relating to More Than One Island Possession, General Classified Files, 1898–1945, Record Group 350 (RG 350), Puerto Rican Labor to Hawaii; National Archives College Park (NACP), 4.
62. "A General Staff Study," August 7, 1925, File 2876/30-A, Puerto Rican Labor to Hawaii, 6.
63. Frank McIntyre to Horace N. Towner, June 25, 1923, File 2876/20, Puerto Rican Labor to Hawaii.
64. Duany, "Transnational Colonial Migration," 227.
65. Porto Ricans, Ref. Report of the Commissioner of Labor on Hawaii 1902, *CIH*, rollo 5, RG 126, 1.
66. General Conditions of Labor and Industry, Resident Labor, Third Report of the Commissioner of Labor of Hawaii, 1905, *CIH*, rollo 5, RG 126.
67. Lai, "Fifty Aged Puerto Ricans," 27.
68. See Lee, "Cultural Factors of Desertion"; Mizuta, "Some Aspects of Public Welfare"; and Brooks, "Hawaii's Puerto Ricans."
69. "Hawaii Seeks Labor Here," *Porto Rico Progress*, April 30, 1931, File 2876–26a, Temporary Press Clippings re P.R. Immigration to Hawaii. For examples of Puerto Rican government involvement in other migrations, see Duany, Transnational Colonial Migration," 228; Lapp, "Managing Migration"; and Bonilla and Campos, "Up by the Bootstraps."
70. The General Staff Survey reported two hundred Puerto Ricans came to Hawaii in 1907 ("A General Staff Study," 6).
71. See House Concurrent Resolution No. 38, Joint Resolution (J.R.) 158, June 20, 1921, Hearings of the House Committee on Immigration and Naturalization, June 21, 1921, J.R. 171, J.R. 82 and "Report of Hawaiian Labor Commission, Part II: Explanatory Notes and Corroborative Exhibits," Labor Commission, Confidential Report, Labor

Commission, Hawaii Emergency, (GOV6–16), Hawai'i State Archives, Hawai'i State Archives, Governors Papers, Government Records Collection.

72. See chapter 2 for details on Filipino recruitment.

73. "Copy of Agreement made in 1921," File 2876/24-l, Puerto Rican Labor to Hawaii, 2–3.

74. Manuel Soto Rivera to mother, March 13, 1922, File 2876/9a, Puerto Rican Labor to Hawaii, 1. Gavina Ortiz also stated how her daughter and two children in Hawai'i were "in great troubles and sufferings is anxious to return to this Island." Gavina Ortiz to Governor of Puerto Rico, April 3, 1922, File 2876/9b, Puerto Rican Labor to Hawaii.

75. E. R. Kinney to all plantations, May 18, 1922, HSPA archives, Lihue Plantation Company (LPC) 8/15B, Bureau of Labor and Statistics (BLS), HSPA 1922–1923, 1.

76. J. K. Butler to Patrick Hurley, October 14, 1931, File 2876/30-A, Puerto Rican Labor to Hawaii, 2.

77. Frank McIntyre to Horace Towner, May 16, 1924, File 2876/24, Puerto Rican Labor to Hawaii.

78. Form of agreement submitted to Governor Towner, February 18, 1924, File 2876/25-B, Puerto Rican Labor to Hawaii, 5.

79. Memorandum for General Parker, March 24, 1931, 3.

Chapter 2. Flexible and Accommodating

1. COH, *Kalihi*, 983–92. Unless specified, all oral histories of Filipinos in this study were conducted in English. If recruits had any education in the Philippines after 1902, they would have learned English in school.

2. Ward, "Contract Labor Recruitment," 273.

3. Junasa, "Filipino Experience in Hawai'i," 80. According to Sister Mary Dorita Clifford, 125,947 Filipinos came to Hawai'i between 1909 and 1946. Clifford, "Filipino Immigration," 42.

4. Exhibit B in the Report of Hawaiian Labor Commission, Part II: Explanatory Notes and Corroborative Exhibits, Labor Commission, Confidential Report, GOV6-16, Hawai'i State Archives, Government Records Collection, 19. There were 1,330 unskilled Puerto Rican laborers at the same time, about 3 percent of field labor force.

5. William Haywood to Secretary of War, October 25, 1901, File 3037/2, Filipino Laborers to Hawaii, RG 350; NACP, 1–2.

6. In the classic work by John and Leatrice MacDonald, chain migration is defined as the process by which likely in-migrants "learn of opportunities, are provided with transportation, and have initial accommodation and employment arranged by means of primary social relationships with previous migrants." MacDonald and MacDonald, "Chain Migration," 82. Also see Menjívar, *Fragmented Ties* and Yu, *Chain Migration*.

7. John Watt to Royal D. Mead, June 7, 1907, HSPA archives, Puna Sugar Company (PSC) 18/3, Sundry letters (SL) 1904 to 1908.

8. COH, *Koloa*, 1135.

9. COH, *Kona*, 1398–99.

10. See Angeles, "Political Dimension" and Vellema, "Agrarian Roots."

11. COH, *Kona*, 1401.

12. COH, *Kona*, 388.

13. Aguilar, *Clash*, 2.

14. Migrants from the Visayas also might not have begrudged the plantation owners for their positions of dominance and control. But workers did get upset if they were mistreated or lied to. For examples of Filipino complaints about life in Hawai'i, see chapter 4.

15. COH, *Koloa*, 557.

16. Ward, "Contract Labor Recruitment," 284.

17. Palloni, "Social Capital," 1264.

18. COH, *Stores and Storekeepers*, 558.

19. Address of Mr. A. W. T. Bottomley, November 17, 1930, enclosure in Lawrence Judd to David A. Reed, December 1, 1930, File 9-4-17, Records of the Office of Territories, Record Group 126 (RG 126), Office of Territories Classified Files 1907 to 1951; NACP, 16.

20. Butler to all plantation managers, September 10, 1926, PSC 32/5, HSPA BLS, 1925–1926, 1.

21. Alcántara, *Sakada*, 9.

22. Personal interview, Waipahu, O'ahu, February 1, 2004.

23. For more on health inspections of Filipinos headed to Hawai'i, see Poblete, "S.S. Mongolia Incident."

24. Pruitt, "For the Advancement of the Race," 435.

25. COH, *Stores and Storekeepers*, 585.

26. Goss and Lindquist, "Placing Movers," 403–4.

27. A. J. Watt to Whom it may concern, November 18, 1921, PSC 23/1, SL, 1924.

28. Domingo Ombon to Ola'a Sugar Company (OSC), May 2, 1939, PSC 33/14, HSPA BLS, 1939.

29. W. Pflueger to OSC, June 27, 1933, PSC 124/4, HSPA BLS, 1933–1934.

30. Butler to all managers and agencies, January 6, 1932, PSC 124/3, HSPA BLS, 1932.

31. Ibid.

32. Director to OSC, March 13, 1923, PSC 23/8, SL, 1923.

33. H. A. Walker to HSPA, April 30, 1926, PSC 32/5.

34. According to Clifford, agents "were paid five peso for every adult male recruited from Manila or seven pesos from the Ilocos and Visayan provinces; they received from the HSPA 20 pesos for every family they were able to recruit." Clifford, "Filipino Immigration," 43.

35. John Watt to Bishop and Company, January 9, 1911, PSC 60/5, Bishop and Co. letters 1911, 2.

36. See Stasiulis and Yuval-Davis, *Unsettling Settler Societies*.

37. España-Maram, *Creating Masculinity*, chapter 4; Mabalon, *Little Manila*, chapter 3; and Parreñas, "White Trash."

38. "Through 1979, 43,171 men, 4,856 women, and 7,369 children returned to the Philippines under this contractual obligation." Heinz and Osgood, "History of the Experiment Station," 5.

39. Sharma, "Pinoy in Paradise" and Cariaga, *Filipinos in Hawaii*.

40. COH, *Kona*, 475.

41. Pflueger to OSC, February 4, 1928, PSC 32/7, HSPA BLS, 1928.

42. Pflueger to OSC, May 6, 1929, PSC 32/7.

43. Butler to OSC, January 15, 1930, PSC 124/1, HSPA BLS, 1929–1930.

44. Claudio Danlag to Butler, September 3, 1933, PSC 124/4.

45. Butler to all plantations, October 13, 1927, PSC 32/6, HSPA BLS, 1927.

46. H. A. Walker to OSC, April 9, 1926, PSC 32/5.
47. Francisco Varona to Filipinos in the Territory of Hawaii, LPC 8/15A, HSPA BLS, 1921.
48. A. J. Watt to Bureau of Labor, March 9, 1934, PSC 32/10, HSPA BLS, 1934.
49. See PSC 32/10-12, HSPA BLS, 1933–1938.
50. H. A. Walker to OSC, July 2, 1924, PSC 24/3, SL, May to November 1924, A-B.
51. Pflueger to OSC, March 6, 1934, PSC 124/4.
52. A. J. Watt to Bureau of Labor, September 9, 1932, PSC 32/9, HSPA BLS, 1931–1932.
53. Goss and Lindquist, "Placing Movers," 403.
54. See PSC 32/7 to 32/12 and PSC 124/2 to 124/4, HSPA BLS, 1927–1933.
55. H. A. Walker to Ola'a plantation, December 7, 1923, PSC 23/10, SL, 1923.
56. For more on U.S. standards of a nuclear family, see Garrison and Weiss, "Dominican Family Networks," Chan, *Hmong Means Free,* and Grasmuck and Pessar, *Between Two Islands.*
57. S. O. Halls to OSC, January 27, 1928, PSC 32/7.
58. Cortezan report, Hawaiian Evangelical Association (HEA) Archives, Filipino Department, General, 1914–1946.
59. COH, *Kona,* 1402.
60. A significant amount of women seemed to have come to Hawai'i as the fake wives of their relatives. See Ligot to Hermenegildo Cruz, September 12, 1923, Filipinos in Hawaii (FIH) folder, Manuel Quezon Presidential papers, Filipiniana Division, National Library of the Philippines, Ermita, Manila.
61. Jean Kim talks about transnational families created by male Filipino migration to Hawai'i. Kim, "Objects, Methods, and Interpretations," 212.
62. Butler to all plantations, March 7, 1928, PSC 32/7, 1.
63. Ibid.
64. Takai, "Family Networks," 373.
65. See PSC 32/7 and PSC 32/8, HSPA BLS, 1928 and 1929.
66. Pruitt, "For the Advancement of the Race," 447.
67. Fujita-Rony, *American Workers,* 132.
68. Butler to O. P. Austin, December 6, 1920, File 9-4-55, Part 2, RG 126; NACP, 6.
69. Butler to all plantations, June 17, 1929, PSC 32/8, HSPA BLS, 1929.
70. Baldoz, *Third Asiatic Invasion,* 65.
71. Ibid., 66.
72. Public No. 127, 73rd Congress, HR 8573, File 9-4-55, 8.
73. As J. M. Young, president of the Honolulu Chamber of Commerce stated, "Unless Hawaii permitted Filipinos [to] continue in field work . . . kindred industries of production will immediately suffer and [the] consequence will be to create unemployment of skilled semi-skilled and unskilled citizens, also deplete territorial finances and general depression which is just opposite of intention of measure." Naval Message from J. M. Young to Governor Lawrence Judd, November 26, 1930, File 9-4-17, RG 126; NACP.
While there was an active repatriation movement of Filipinos in the 1930s, the Territory of Hawai'i worked hard to keep as many Filipinos in the islands as possible to work on sugar plantations.
74. See Halpern, "Iron Fist" and Mandell, *Corporation.* Other drawbacks to HSPA recruitment and retention policies included the bifurcation of families through the perpetuation of male migration, as well as the potential coercion of HSPA agents, family, and friends in both the Philippines and Hawai'i to migrate.

Chapter 3. Indefinite Dependence

1. Honoka'a complaint, March 5, 1919, File 2876/4-B, Puerto Rican Labor to Hawaii, 2.
2. Interview, January 6, 1978, Norma Carr Collection, 30–31.
3. Interview in Kohala, January 20, 1978, Norma Carr Collection, 4.
4. Interview in Wailuku, May 30, 1978, Norma Carr Collection, 32.
5. Interview in Kapahulu, November 11, 1976, Norma Carr Collection.
6. In the matter of the petition of Manuel Olivieri Sanchez for a writ of mandamus c. David Kalauokalani, Clerk of the City and County of Honolulu, Territory of Hawaii, 24 Haw. 21; 1917 Haw. LEXIS 18.

This case also highlights a Native Hawaiian action against migrant groups. It remains unclear why Kalauokalani took this stance. However, as a delegate who took the anti-annexation petition to Washington, D.C., and formed the Home Rule party for Native Hawaiians, both at the turn of the twentieth century, Kalauokalani could have been resisting the inclusion of more non-Native groups into the region under the guise of territorial and/or federal government regulations.

7. According to 24 Haw. 21; 1917 Haw. LEXIS 18, Sanchez was born in Yauco, Puerto Rico, on January 20, 1888. His father was the mayor of a Puerto Rican town until at least July 1900. When his father died, thirteen-year-old Sanchez left Puerto Rico with his mother for Hawai'i. They arrived in the islands on September 22, 1901.
8. Ibid.
9. This ruling resulted in an ambiguous status for Puerto Ricans in Hawai'i. If neither Puerto Ricans nor U.S. citizens, what were they and whom did they belong to? Such questions were not discussed in these court cases.
10. 24 Haw. 21; 1917 Haw. LEXIS 18.
11. Ibid.
12. According to Carr, Sanchez felt "the wrath of the opponents of citizenship for the Puerto Ricans of Hawaii . . . [he] was able to find only occasional employment in Hilo. A few years later he moved to Oahu." Carr, "Puerto Ricans in Hawaii," 237. The 1919 Honoka'a complaint also discussed how Sanchez was "unpopular, not finding employment, and has been persecuted and freely insulted through the press." Translation of Senate Resolution, File 2876/4-B, Part 1, 3.
13. Interview in Honolulu, August 5, 1978, Norma Carr Collection, 51.
14. Interview in Kona on January 8, 1978, Norma Carr Collection, 26.
15. Honoka'a complaint, March 5, 1919, File 2876/4-B, 3.
16. COH, *Waialua and Hale'iwa*, 156.
17. Carr, "Puerto Ricans in Hawaii," 368.
18. Ibid., chapter 9.
19. Translation of Senate Resolution, File 2876/4-B, Puerto Ricans in Hawaii, Part 1, 1.
20. Ibid., 1.
21. Ibid., 4.
22. The Puerto Rican Senate passed a resolution on April 16, 1919 and the Puerto Rican House passed a resolution on April 30, 1919. Ibid., 4, and Translation of House Resolution, File 2876/4-A, Puerto Ricans in Hawaii, Part 1, 2.
23. Translation of Senate Resolution, File 2876/4-B, 1.
24. The Government of Porto Rico, Office of the Secretary, Administrative Bulletin No. 2, November 13, 1909, File 2159/2, Correspondence with Porto Rico Chambers, 1
25. See Foreign Government files in the Hawai'i State Archives.

26. See Luis Gil to OSC Manager, November 16, 1915, PSC 32/3, HSPA BLS, 1915–1916. More examples of Spanish and Portuguese consul correspondence exist in the same folder.

27. C. F. Eckart to Consul for Spain, November 19, 1915, PSC 32/3, HSPA BLS, 1915–1916, 1.

28. In response to a Spanish consul letter about several complaints at Ola'a, manager J. Watt addressed each point in detail and concluded his letter by "thanking you [Consul] for your communication, and calling my attention to these few points." J. Watt to Ignacio de Arana, August 16, 1912, PSC 32/3, HSPA BLS, 1915–1916, 3.

29. The needs of Native Hawaiians, who were theoretically citizens, often remained invisible or subsumed to Anglo American elite during this period. However, the technical existence and general acknowledgement of their U.S. citizenship provided Native Hawaiians with certain basic constitutional protections that foreigners and U.S. colonials had more difficulty accessing. Conflicts over rights for indigenous groups, who forcibly became U.S. citizens through annexation, and U.S.-born citizens from settler groups also developed. For a discussion of this issue, see Kauanui, "Colonialism in Equality."

30. Exhibit B in the Report of Hawaiian Labor Commission, Part II, 18–19.

31. Newton Baker to Secretary of the Interior, June 13, 1919, File 2876/4-A, Part 1.

32. Thos. Ryan to Governor of Puerto Rico, November 25, 1902, Caja 17, Folder 2, 1.

33. Mead to Pacific Sugar Mill, July 11, 1919, HSPA archives, Honokaa Sugar Company (HSC) 6/11, F. A. Schaefer and Co. 1919, 3.

34. 1919 Report, 50.

35. Ibid., 21.

36. Ibid., 10.

37. Ibid., 22.

38. For example, one Puerto Rican newspaper article discussed how those in the Pacific wanted repatriation. "Los puertorriqueños residents en las islas Hawaii." *La Democracia*, October 24, 1919.

39. 1919 Report, 23.

40. Interview in Aina Haina, June 27, 1978, Norma Carr Collection, 5.

41. Personal interview in Culver City, California, March 30, 2004.

42. COH, *Kalihi*, 738.

43. Interview, Norma Carr Collection, 56–57.

44. Mead to all plantation managers, November 19, 1901, PSC 2/2, B. F. Dillingham Co. Letters, 1901–1902, 3.

45. Elmer E. Paxton to F. B. McStocker, January 17, 1902, PSC 2/2, B. F. Dillingham Co. Letters, 1901–1902, 1.

46. Ibid.

47. Bergad, *Coffee*, 198.

48. 1919 Report, 24 and 32, respectively.

49. Interview in Hilo, January 19, 1978, Norma Carr Collection, 21.

50. Santiago-Valles, *"Subject People,"* 69.

51. 1919 Report, 9.

52. Reidy also found that plantation workers in turn-of-the-twentieth-century Louisiana took impromptu vacations as a way to control their labor situation. Reidy, "Mules and Machines," 192.

53. W. C. Smith to Acting Governor of Hawaii, May 22, 1902, Executive Book 5, 16. CIH, rollo 5, NACP, 1.

54. Ongais, Santana, and Trochez's oral histories can be found in the Norma Carr Collections. Danny Ongais interview in Wailuku, May 31, 1978, 19–20, John Santana interview in Kona, January 8, 1978, 23, and Andy Trochez interview in Kahuku, December 1, 1977, 19.

55. COH, *Kalihi*.

56. Foreign laborers could also be recruited to the continental United States, but the Territory of Hawai'i created a law in 1911 to block such movement and keep these workers for the sugar industry in the islands. See Act 69, "An Act Declaring, Establishing and Defining Legal and Equitable Remedies for Inducing, Enticing or Persuading, or Attempting to Induce, Entice or Persuade Servants or Laborers to Leave their Employment, or Aiding, Abetting or Attempting to Aid or Abet Such Leaving," *Laws of the Territory of Hawaii Passed by the Legislature at Its Regular Session, 1911*, (Honolulu: Bulletin Publishing, 1911), 92–93, and Act 90, "An Act to Protect and Safeguard the Interests of Newly Arrived Immigrants Into this Territory," *Laws of the Territory of Hawaii, 1911*, 121–22.

57. Maldanado, "Contract Labor," 115.

58. According to Senior, Puerto Ricans from Hawai'i settled "in San Francisco, Oakland and on farms in California. There is now [1954] a Puerto Rican community in Hawaii of some 10,000 persons, first and succeeding generations." Senior, "Patterns," 95.

59. Rodriguez, "Boricuas, African Americans, and Chicanos," 425. For more information on this movement as a result of the World Wars, see Maldonado, "Contract Labor," 203–4 and Senior, "Patterns," 95.

60. Krauss, "California mo' bettah."

61. Rodriguez, "Boricuas, African Americans, and Chicanos," 426.

62. Interview in Kahuku, 50–51.

63. Krauss, "California mo' bettah."

64. Interview in Kahuku, 14.

65. Puerto Ricans were often housed in the same area as Portuguese or Spanish workers, and inter-marriage among these ethnicities occurred. There are Puerto Rican-Filipino families in the islands, but such intermixing was not widespread during my period of study.

66. In my oral histories, I always asked interviewees if they interacted with other ethnic groups. The common answer was no. One interviewee stated that she sometimes traded lunches with classmates from other backgrounds. Outside of school, she and most children chose to play with other kids who lived in their own race-based plantation camp. A few oral histories conducted by Norma Carr discussed Puerto Rican children playing with Japanese or Filipino kids, but this circumstance was not prevalent.

67. There have been a few references to eight Puerto Ricans who joined the Filipino labor strike in 1924. Additional details, such as the names of these Puerto Ricans, their reasons for joining the strike, or the extent of their involvement, have not been found in available sources.

Chapter 4. Tensions of Colonial Cooperation

1. Ligot to A. J. Watt, September 26, 1923, SL, PSC 23/12, SL, 1923.
2. A. J. Watt to Ligot, October 4, 1923, SL, PSC 23/12.
3. Ligot to A. J. Watt, October 6, 1923, SL, PSC 23/12.

4. For more information on Filipinization, see Kramer, *Blood of Government*; Ngai, "From Colonial Subject to Undesirable Alien"; Go, *American Empire*; and Apilado, *Revolutionary Spirituality*, 99.

5. Even today, Puerto Rican labor standards are still subject to U.S. federal oversight.

6. See Rafael, *White Love*, 107; Friend, *Between Two Empires*; Cullinane, "Ilustrado Politics"; and Hutchcroft, "Colonial Masters."

7. Kaplan, *Anarchy of Empire*, 8. This fear could also be a result of anti-immigration sentiments of the time.

8. This attitude also reflects patriarchal approaches typical of Progressive Era reformism. From 1890 to 1930, members of the educated middle and upper class in the continental United States and throughout the world invested their time and money to teach indigenous, immigrant, and indigent groups Western-based moral principles and practices. See Muncy, *Female Dominion*.

9. Filipinization was also a way to compromise with some Philippine elite who demanded immediate independence. Cullinane, "Ilustrado Politics," 338. Also see Abinales, "Progressive-Machine Conflict."

10. Frank McIntyre to T. R. Manarriz, June 6, 1925, File 3037/92, Filipino Laborers to Hawaii, RG 350; NACP.

11. Devins, *Observer in the Philippines*, 70–1.

12. See Ignacio, *Forbidden Book*.

13. Ligot to Wood, May 22, 1923, FIH folders, 4.

14. Rafael, *White Love*, chapter 4.

15. Abinales, "Progressive-Machine Conflict," 153.

16. Ligot to A. J. Watt, August 11, 1923, PSC 23/12, 2. Workers likely submitted complaints verbally to labor commissioners in their native language and the officials or their counterparts probably translated these statements into English for submission to Anglo leaders in the Philippines and the Territory of Hawai'i.

17. Despite living in the same camps, the mostly male Filipino population was often located at the rear of housing areas. The visibly different quality of housing between Japanese and Filipinos in the same residential camps established and maintained a social division between these two groups that contributed to their lack of horizontal interrelations. Negative stereotypes about the aggressiveness of the predominately male Filipino population were also prevalent among Japanese families in the camps. In workspaces, Japanese often served as lunas over Filipino work gangs. Filipinos often complained about these Asian bosses and viewed them as socially and vertically separate from themselves.

18. COH, *Kalihi*, 897.

19. COH, *Koloa*, 406–7.

20. For the 1920 strike, see Beechert, *Working*; Takaki, *Pau Hana*; and Okihiro, *Cane Fires*. For the 1924 strike, see Reinecke, *Filipino Piecemeal Sugar Strike* and COH, *1924 Filipino Strike*.

21. The HSPA and Territorial Government of Hawai'i also ordered studies of plantations. The HSPA-sponsored Rodriguez report of 1921 was supportive of the sugar industry. The territorial government sponsored 1916 Lord report and the 1926 Duckworth-Ford report claimed that the main problem on plantations involved the lack of social activities in camps. Otherwise, working and living conditions were acceptable.

22. "Report on the Investigation Made by the Honorable Joaquin Balmori, about Conditions under which the Filipino Laborers are Working in Sugar Plantations in the Territory of Hawaii," Manila, February 1912, 3.

23. "Report of the Commissioner to Hawaii Regarding the Conditions of the Workers in the Territory," August 2, 1919, translated from Spanish by Edgar C. Knowlton Jr., 18. Remigio did not visit Kaua'i plantations due to financial constraints. He also believed his findings on other islands were representative of conditions he would find on Kaua'i, 1919 Remigio Report, 2.

24. Mead to E. D. Tenney, July 29, 1919, HSPA archive, Honokaa Sugar Company (HSC) 6/11, F.A. Schafer and Co, 1919, 1–2.

25. R. C. Walker to C. F. Eckart, August 1, 1919, PSC 12/6, AmFac Plantation Department, 1919.

26. Mead to Tenney, July 29, 1919, HSC 6/11, F.A. Schafer and Co, 1919, 2–4. Local managers did not always respond positively, with one taking "offense" and telling Mead he "was lecturing upon the essential things which everybody knows." Mead to Tenney, July 29, 1919, HSC 6/11, 4. Regardless of such reactions, high-level sugar industry leadership made it very clear to local managers that they had to treat Filipinos fairly.

27. 1919 Remigio Report, 32.

28. "Complaints and Claims Presented by Filipino Laborers to Labor Commissioner Francisco Varona," November 1920, PSC 12/9, AmFac Plantation Department, 1920, 3.

29. Thirteenth Annual Report of the Bureau of Labor for the Fiscal Year 1921 embracing the period from January 1 to December 31, 1921, P-2185, Manuscript Reports of the Governor General of the Philippines, 1916–1935, RG 350; NACP, 2797–8.

30. Ibid., 2797.

31. Kerkvliet, *Unbending Cane*, 16.

32. Ibid., 21 and 17.

33. W. K. Kilpatrick to Charles A. Appel, Jr. May 17, 1932, Records of the Office of the Chief of Naval Operations, Record Group 38, Records of the Office of Naval Intelligence; NACP.

34. Other Filipino leaders in Hawai'i included but were not limited to Carl Damaso, Nicolas C. Dizon, Francisco Carbonel, Manuel Fagel, Emigdio Milanio, Juan Biones Samiento, and Epifanio Taok. See Kerkvliet, *Unbending Cane*, 20–21 and 71. For more information on labor organizing in Hawai'i, see Jung, *Reworking Race*; Beechert, *Working*; and Reinecke, *Filipino Piecemeal Sugar Strike*.

35. Anglo-American labor leaders who worked with Filipino labor leaders included George Wright, William Bailey, and Jack Hall. They were also not effective in union organizing due to the strong centralized control of the oligarchy in Hawai'i, discussed in chapter 1.

36. Kerkvliet, *Unbending Cane*, 26.

37. Ibid., 38.

38. After the 1920 strike, workers received a "slight modification of the bonus system, a lessening of the racial differentials in pay, and an improvement in welfare plans." Beechert, *Working*, 208.

39. See Jung, *Reworking Race*.

40. See M. A. Fonseca to Manuel Quezon, May 29, 1922, Pablo Manlapit to Manuel Quezon, September 19, 1992 and Pablo Manlapit to Manuel Quezon, October 25, 1922, all in FIH folders.

41. Resolution signed by P. Victoria, August 13, 1922, FIH folders.

42. Manlapit, *Filipinos Fight for Justice*, 37.

43. Ibid.

44. For an example, read about the Gentleman's Agreement of 1907 in McFarland and Eng, "Japanese Question" and in Daniels, *Politics of Prejudice*.

45. Ligot to Wood, May 22, 1923, FIH folders, 1–2.
46. Ibid., 1.
47. Manlapit, *Filipinos Fight for Justice*, 38.
48. Ligot to Wood, September 10, 1923, FIH folders, 5–7.
49. Ibid., 6.
50. Butler to Plantation Managers, June 30, 1923, PSC 23/8.
51. Ligot to Wood, September 10, 1923, FIH folders, 3–5.
52. Ibid., 4–5.
53. Rafael, *White Love*, 107.
54. Peck, "Divided Loyalties," 55.
55. Ligot to Wood, September 10, 1923, FIH folders, 9.
56. Ibid., 2.
57. Worry over inappropriate actions also demonstrates Ligot's class-based concern for acceptance in mainstream society and protecting the image of the Filipino race over the plight of workers.
58. Ligot to Wood, May 22, 1923, FIH folders, 2.
59. Ligot to A. J. Watt, October 6, 1923, SL, PSC 23/12, 1923.
60. Ligot to Wood, September 10, 1923, FIH folders, 7.
61. Ibid., 6.
62. Ibid., 2.
63. Ligot's assumption that working-class Filipinos would not be comfortable at the executive building also demonstrates his class-bias.
64. Ligot to Wood, September 10, 1923, FIH folders, 3.
65. Ibid., 1.
66. Nellist, *Men of Hawaii*.
67. Peck, "Divided Loyalties," 55.
68. Ligot, October 4, 1923, PSC 23/10, SL, 1923.
69. Filipinos at Ola'a and Mountain View camps made pledges, but no pledges came from Pahoa or Kapoho. A. J. Watt to BLS, November 1, 1923, PSC 23/10, SL, 1923.
70. Resolution signed by C. Basan, January 10, 1924, FIH folders.
71. Ligot to Wood, September 10, 1923, FIH folders, 11.
72. Basan resolution.
73. Manlapit, *Filipinos Fight for Justice*, 44–48.
74. W. R. Farrington to Leonard Wood, October 6, 1924, in 1923 in FIH folders, 1.
75. Beechert, *Working*, chapter 11, and Reinecke, *Filipino Piecemeal Sugar Strike*.
76. William Searby to plantation managers, November 14, 1924, PSC 13/10, AmFac Plantation Department, 1924.
77. Ligot to Fellow Countrymen, September 15, 1924 in "A Statement Concerning the Sugar Industry in Hawaii; Labor Conditions on Hawaiian Sugar Plantations; Filipino Laborers Thereon, and the Alleged Filipino 'Strike' of 1924," A. W. T. Bottomley, HSPA, November 1924, FIH folders, 46.
78. Watt to Searby, December 4, 1924, PSC 13/10, AmFac Plantation Department, 1924.
79. For an example, see E. A. Taok to Manuel Quezon, March 4, 1938, FIH folders. Emigdio Milanio also wrote a letter stating that the "Labor Commissioner refuses to administer the Filipino Laborers present condition and sufferings." Emigdio Milanio to Leonard Wood, February 25, 1925, FIH folders.
80. Dizon to Quezon, July 24, 1928, FIH folders.

81. Emilio Parangan to Manuel Quezon, November 1, 1937, FIH folders.
82. "Ligot's Enemy in Hawaii Seeks His Dismissal," *Hawaii Hochi*, November 20, 1928.
83. "Ligot Called Back Home to Answer Quiz," *Hawaii Hochi*, August 29, 1932.
84. Ligot stated that he would keep his position until further notice. John Reinecke, *Filipino Piecemeal Sugar Strike*, 116. "Ligot Out December 31; 'Too Close to HSPA'" *Honolulu Star Bulletin*, January 17, 1932.
85. "Ligot May Be Called to P.I. for a Hearing" *Honolulu Star Bulletin*, July 7, 1933, and "Ligot Out December 31" *Honolulu Star Bulletin*, January 17, 1932.
86. See "Ligot Subsidized by HSPA Claim of P-I Government," *Honolulu Advertiser*, November 8, 1933, and Reinecke, *Filipino Piecemeal Sugar Strike*, 118.
87. According to Philippine governor general Frank Murphy, "The H.S.P.A. had paid $150 monthly to the paper [*Ti Silaw*] in 1927 . . . the subsidy was improper." "Ligot Out December 31," *Honolulu Star Bulletin*, January 17, 1932. Also see Reinecke, *Filipino Piecemeal Sugar Strike*, 117, and Chapin, *Shaping History*, 136.
88. Reinecke, *Filipino Piecemeal Sugar Strike*, 118.

Chapter 5. Conflicting Convictions

1. Reinecke, *Filipino Piecemeal Sugar Strike*, 35.
2. Ibid, 66.
3. A. J. Watt to American Factors, Limited, January 22, 1925, PSC 13/11, AmFac Plantation Department, 1925 (1–3), 1.
4. Santa Ana served at the Ola'a plantation from 1917 to 1928, and Ibera served from 1929 to 1938.
5. According to Pierre Bourdieu, there are several kinds of capital a leader may have. Cultural capital involves knowledge, education, and skills. Social capital includes connections to social networks and membership in groups. Symbolic capital involves honor, prestige, and recognition from the community. Bourdieu, *Outline*, section 3, and Bourdieu, "Forms of Capital," 241–58.
6. Leon Foronda to Vincente Lionson, March 25, 1915, HEA Archives, Filipino Department, Filipino Evangelist, T. F. Anderson, Hilo and Puna 1914–1917.
7. See Apilado, *Revolutionary Spirituality*; Clymer, *Protestant Missionaries*; and Jones, *Christian Missions*.
8. Portions of this quote were grammatically corrected for clarity. Carlos Austria et al. to Rev. J. P. Erdman, February 27, 1923, HEA Archives, Hawaiian Churches, Hawaii, Olaa, Ygloria Memorial Church (Olaa Filipino Evangelical Church), Reverend Santa Ana, 1920, 1924, 1925.
9. Santa Ana was not ordained as a full minister until 1932, seven years after he left Ola'a.
10. The United Evangelical church appointed its first Filipino general moderator in 1919. Apilado, *Revolutionary Spirituality*, 269.
11. Due to the smaller population of Puerto Ricans compared to Filipinos and most other ethnic groups in the islands, the HEA did not actively pursue the employment of Puerto Rican ministers. For information on the one Puerto Rican ethnic minister on the island of Hawai'i, see chapter 6.
12. While the majority of Filipinos at the plantations were Catholic, priests from that denomination did not fill the same kinds of diverse mediator roles as Filipino

Protestant ethnic ministers. I found sugar industry correspondence about the rental of plantation property for the Catholic church at Ola'a, but there was no mention of the use of Catholic priests as interpreters, special police, or plantation liaisons, as there was for Santa Ana and Ibera.

13. Sixteen out of forty-seven weeks between October 1924 and December 1925, Santa Ana helped workers with return-transport requests. Nineteen out of forty-seven weeks, Santa Ana helped workers request jobs on the plantation for themselves or their family and friends. F. M. Santa Ana, Weekly Report, October 1924 to December 1925, HEA Archives, Reverend Santa Ana, 1920, 1924, 1925. Ibera's weekly reports do not detail such activities, likely because the HEA pressured him to focus solely on religious work, as will be discussed later in this chapter. However, the lack of detailed reporting does not necessarily mean he did not continue to help Filipino workers with work-related issues. He simply might not have reported such activities to the HEA.

14. Statistics were averaged from forty-seven weekly reports filed by Santa Ana from October 1924 to December 1925. F. M. Santa Ana, Weekly Report, HEA Archives, Reverend Santa Ana, 1920, 1924, 1925.

15. F. M. Santa Ana, Weekly Report, July 13 to July 19, 1925, HEA Archives, Reverend Santa Ana, 1920, 1924, 1925.

16. Peck, "Divided Loyalties," 51.

17. In 1915, Ola'a manager C. F. Eckhart offered to donate the lumber for the Pahoa Filipino mission. In 1924, Watt recommended $2,400 in appropriations for the Filipino church. In 1932, Watt also recommended a five-dollar-per-year rental fee for land for the church. In 1936, Watt donated one hundred dollars for the church to purchase a bus for transporting members.

18. Simeon Ibera to Rev. Norman C. Schenck, April 20, 1928, HEA Archives, Churches, Hawaii, Olaa, Ygloria Memorial Church, 1920–1946.

19. A. J. Watt to Butler, March 3, 1923, PSC 23/8.

20. Founded in 1853, the HEA was the umbrella organization for the Congregationalist church in Hawai'i. This denomination was the first and dominant religious institution in the islands since 1850. Descendants of these early missionaries became Anglo business and political leaders in the islands and continue to hold positions of power in Hawai'i today. The primary purpose of this religious institution during the first half of the twentieth century involved "active evangelism in the community" to "spread the Christian message" and obtain as many converts as possible. Gallagher, "No More a Christian Nation," 98. During the plantation era, the HEA had many ethnic departments to proselytize to the diverse range of racial and ethnic labor groups working for the sugar industry.

21. Gallagher, "No More a Christian Nation," 226. Also see Grimshaw, *Paths of Duty* and Zwiep, *Pilgrim Path*.

22. Gallagher, "No More a Christian Nation," 202. Gallagher also talked about how the HEA rarely criticized the sugar industry. The Protestant church often encouraged laborers to work directly with plantation managers to solve their problems instead of going on strike. Ibid., 201 and 210.

23. See chapter 4.

24. Santa Ana to Schenck, October 22, 1924, HEA Archives, Reverend Santa Ana, 1920, 1924, 1925.

25. Santa Ana was relocated to the Waipahu plantation on O'ahu, where he continued to serve Filipino intra-colonial interests for the rest of his career. Even in the

twenty-first century, he is fondly remembered as a leader of the Filipino community in that area. Personal interview with Helen Nagtalon-Miller, Kaneohe, O'ahu, February 22, 2003.

26. Schenck to Ibera, February 6, 1928, HEA Archives, Ygloria Memorial Church.

27. Ibera to Schenck, February 3, 1928, HEA Archives, Churches, Hawaii, Olaa, Ygloria Memorial Church, Reverend Simeon Ibera, 1928–1933.

28. Kalir, "Finding Jesus," 131.

29. Ibera to Schenck, February 1, 1929, HEA Archives, Reverend Simeon Ibera.

30. Schenck to Ibera, March 7, 1933, HEA Archives, Reverend Simeon Ibera.

31. Ibera to Schenck, March 7, 1933, HEA Archives, Reverend Simeon Ibera, 2.

32. Ibera to Schenck, December 27, 1937, Ygloria Memorial Church.

33. Ibid.

34. Ibid.

35. Peck, "Divided Loyalties," 52.

36. Anderson to Judd, April 18, 1915, HEA Archives, T. F. Anderson.

37. Stats averaged from forty-seven weekly reports filed by Santa Ana from October 1924 to December 1925 and twenty-two reports filed by Ibera from May to October 1927. In 1926, the Filipino Department of the HEA reported 1,221 Filipino adults and 732 Filipino children at Ola'a. Summary of Weekly Reports, June 1926–May 1927, HEA Archives, Filipino Department Weekly Reports, Summaries of Church Attendance, 1925–1935.

38. In 1965, the Ola'a Filipino Protestant church merged with the Japanese Congregational church. This church still exists in a vibrant way to this day as the Puna Congregational Christian Church. For more information, see Nakasato, *75th Anniversary*.

39. According to Apilado, Protestant ministers in the Philippines supported U.S. colonial rule through missionary education aimed to "indoctrinate U.S. learning, cultural values and colonial rule." Apilado, *Revolutionary Spirituality*, 259.

40. According to the 1903 U.S. census of the Philippines, about 56 percent of Filipinos were Catholic. By the 1918 census, 91 percent of the population claimed Catholicism as their religion. Census of the Philippine Islands taken under the direction of the Philippine Legislature in the year 1918 (Manila: Bureau of Printing, 1920), 39.

41. Ibera to Schenck, December 27, 1937, HEA Archives, Ygloria Memorial Church.

42. Santa Ana to Schenck, July 21 1924, HEA Archives, Reverend Santa Ana.

43. Ibera to Schenck, March 10, 1938, HEA Archives, Ygloria Memorial Church.

44. Ibera to Schenck, February 16, 1928, HEA Archives, Reverend Simeon Ibera.

45. Nakonz and Shik, "Problems," 33.

46. Ibid., 34.

47. There were many opponents to the Ola'a Filipino Protestant church. Father Alveriz with the Catholic church in 1928, the Glad Tidings church in 1936, and Father Cordero with the Seventh Day Adventists in 1938 all came to Ola'a and clashed with the Protestant pastors in some way.

48. Ibera to Schenck, April 24, 1929, HEA Archives, Reverend Simeon Ibera.

49. Ibera to Schenck, February 1, 1929, HEA Archives, Reverend Simeon Ibera.

50. Ibid.

51. Schenck to Ibera, February 9, 1929, HEA Archives, Reverend Simeon Ibera.

52. Schenck to Ibera, March 19, 1929, HEA Archives, Reverend Simeon Ibera.

53. Eugenio to Schenck, July 3, 1929, HEA Archives, Reverend Simeon Ibera.

54. See chapter 4 for negative reactions to the mistrusted resident labor commissioner. In a similar way, the padrones in Peck's work quickly lost their position of power when workers no longer endorsed them as their representatives. Peck, "Divided Loyalties," 64.
55. Eugenio to Schenck, July 3, 1929, HEA Archives, Reverend Simeon Ibera.
56. Schenck to Eugenio, July 31, 1929, HEA Archives, Reverend Simeon Ibera.
57. Eugenio to Schenck, August 6, 1929, HEA Archives, Reverend Simeon Ibera.
58. Ironically, workers became so attached to Ibera that they strongly protested his relocation to another island in 1940.
59. Peck, "Divided Loyalties," 65.

Chapter 6. Limited Leadership

1. F. Souza to McStocker, July 17, 1901, PSC 17/6, SL, June to September 1901, 1.
2. Lomnitz-Adler, *Deep Mexico*, 283.
3. According to Carr, Puerto Ricans developed various associations throughout the twentieth century. However, this community stayed close to each other and remained generally closed off from non-Puerto Ricans. See Carr, "Puerto Ricans in Hawaii," chapter 6.
4. Joseph Pagan to H.P. Judd, May 1, 1916, HEA Archives, Filipino Department, J. Pagan, Hilo, 1915–1918.
5. According to the 1920 census, Puerto Ricans were the fourth-smallest population out of ten ethnic groups in Hawai'i.
6. Ernest G. Da Silva worked mostly among the Portuguese, but also among Spanish-speakers in the Hilo region at this time.
7. Pagan to Scudder, October 27, 1915, HEA Archives, J. Pagan.
8. Judd to Pagan, November 12, 1915, HEA Archives, J. Pagan.
9. Anderson to Theodore Richards, November 1, 1915, HEA archives, T.F. Anderson, 1.
10. Ibid., 2.
11. Anderson to Judd, March 1917, HEA Archives, T. F. Anderson.
12. Acting Secretary of the Board to Pagan, April 20, 1916, HEA Archives, J. Pagan.
13. "Report for May ending May 1916," HEA Archives, J. Pagan.
14. Pagan to Judd, November 7, 1918, HEA Archives, J. Pagan.
15. Personal interview with Gus Villaneuva at Hilo, Hawai'i, January 26, 2004.
16. Phone interview with Vincente Rosario, January 27, 2004.
17. No documentation demonstrates Souza's ethnic background. Such an ambiguous identity, and likely light-skinned appearance, could have contributed to Puerto Rican laborers' belief in Souza's understanding of and/or affiliation with the white race.
18. Souza to McStocker, July 17, 1901, PSC 17/6, 1.
19. Souza to H. Deacon, June 26, 1901, PSC 17/6, 1.
20. Plantation leadership also likely accommodated Puerto Rican demands for more pay because they greatly needed labor at that time.
21. Souza to McStocker, July 9, 1901, PSC 17/6.
22. Souza to Deacon, June 28, 1901, PSC 17/6.
23. Souza to McStocker, July 17, 1901, PSC 17/6.
24. Ibid.

25. Ibid.
26. Souza to McStocker, July 12, 1901, PSC 17/6.
27. Souza to McStocker, July 9, 1901, PSC 17/6.
28. McStocker to B. F. Dillingham Co, July 5, 1901, PSC 2/1 B. F. Dillingham Company Letters, 1901, 1.
29. Souza to McStocker, August 1, 1901, PSC 17/6.
30. Souza to Deacon, June 28, 1901, PSC 17/6.
31. See Bankoff, "Dangers," Geertz, "Rotating Credit Association," Ardener, "Comparative Study," and Beito, *From Mutual Aid*, chapter 5.
32. Souza to McStocker, August 4, 1901, PSC 17/6, 1.
33. Discussed later in this chapter, Alberto Minvielle's work with Puerto Ricans and the HSPA overlapped with Souza's. Minvielle, however, worked only at Ola'a. There were no labor agents for Puerto Rican at other plantations on the island of Hawai'i.
34. Peck, "Divided Loyalties," 53.
35. For an explanation of imagined communities, see Anderson, *Imagined Communities*.
36. Souza to McStocker, August 4, 1901, PSC 17/6.
37. Souza to McStocker, October 7, 1901, PSC 17/6.
38. Souza to McStocker, February 13, 1901, PSC 17/7, SL, 1902.
39. Souza to McStocker, July 17, 1901, PSC 17/6.
40. Peck, *Reinventing Free Labor*, 851.
41. See Souza to McStocker, December 23, 1901, PSC 17/6A, SL, 1901.
42. Multiple spellings exist for this name in the archives. I use the spelling based on his signature in a letter to Assistant Manager Hay in PSC 17/8, SL, 1902.
43. Paxton to McStocker, June 17, 1901, PSC 2/1, 2.
44. Paxton to McStocker, June 25, 1901, PSC 2/1, 2.
45. Paxton to McStocker, June 17, 1901, 2.
46. McStocker to B.F. Dillingham, June 27, 1901, PSC 2/1, 1.
47. Minvielle to McStocker, January 11, 1904, PSC 18/2, SL, 1904–1905, 2.
48. McStocker to Minvielle, January 18, 1901, PSC 17/7.
49. Minvielle to McStocker, August 22, 1901, PSC 17/6 (6-9), SL, 1901.
50. Phone interview, Hilo, Hawai'i, January 28, 2004.
51. Minvielle to McStocker, April 13, 1904, PSC 18/2, 1.
52. Ibid., 2.
53. Ibid.
54. Peck, *Reinventing Free Labor*, 851–2
55. All the translations for the Spanish-language articles in this chapter are by the author.
56. "Desde Hawaii," *La Correspondencia*, October 6, 1901.
57. "Modo seguro de comunicarse," *La Correspondencia*, February 20, 1901.
58. Ibid.
59. Minvielle, "Matrimonio puertorriqueño en Hawaii," *La Correspondencia*, September 21, 1905.
60. For discussion of the impact of print-capitalism and national print-languages, see Anderson, *Imagined Communities*, chapter 3.
61. "Para Hawaii," *La Correspondencia*, December 24, 1900, Nicolás Rivas, "Hacia Hawaii," *La Democracia*, May 16, 1921.
62. "Noticias de Hawaii," *La Correspondencia*, February 23, 1901.

63. Ibid.
64. "Desde Hawaii."
65. Ibid.
66. "Sentenciados en Hawaii," *La Correspondencia*, October 14, 1905.
67. Rivas, "Hacia Hawaii."
68. Ibid.
69. Ibid.
70. Ibid.
71. Ibid.
72. Frank McIntyre, War Department, Bureau of Insular Affairs, "Memorandum for the Secretary of War," April 17, 1917, Center for Puerto Rican Studies, *Sources for the Study of Puerto Rican Migration, 1879–1930* (New York: Research Foundation of the City University of New York, 1982), 110.
73. Rivas, "Hacia Hawaii."

Conclusion

1. Maier, *Among Empires*, 4.
2. According to Ravenal, "Far from being an 'empire,' or even an accomplished hegemon, America is better described (metaphorically) as the object of a multi-pronged 'siege.'" Ravenal, "What's Empire?" 21.
3. Kurth, "Migration," 6.
4. Hau'ofa, *We Are the Ocean*, 28–29.
5. Maier, *Among Empires*, 24–25. Maier provided several other potential characteristics of empire, such as ethnic and geographic differentiation (21–22), control of human resources at micro and macro levels (59), and control of territory abroad through continuing military presence (66). At least one, if not more, U.S. colonies, possessions, or territories have experienced such exercises of U.S. authority in their region.
6. Maier even acknowledged that length of time is not a requirement for empire, explaining how the Nazi empire only lasted twelve years. Ibid., 12.
7. The United States also has special defensive control over the affairs of the Republic of the Marshall Islands, the Republic of Palau, and the Federated States of Micronesia.
8. Letter from President Barack Obama, March 12, 2011, in "Report by the President's Task Force on Puerto Rico's Status," March 2011, available at http://www.whitehouse.gov/sites/default/files/uploads/Puerto_Rico_Task_Force_Report.pdf (accessed April 9, 2012).
9. Quote from the Puerto Rican Federal Affairs Administration website: available at http://prfaa.pr.gov/puertoricond2.asp (accessed April 9, 2012).
10. "Report on Puerto Rico's Status," 17–18
11. Ibid., 20.
12. Ibid.
13. Ibid.
14. Ibid.
15. For more information about conflicted Puerto Rican ideas over their political-legal relationship with the United States, see Negrón-Muntaner, *None of the Above*.

16. "Report on Puerto Rico's Status," 21 and 3. The Puerto Rican resident commissioner also stated, "Puerto Rico's political status has been—and remains today—the central issue in the territory's political life." Pedro Pierluisi, "Puerto Rico Status Referendum is Historic," *JURIST-Hotline*, February 17, 2012, available at http://jurist.org/hotline/2012/02/pedro-pierluisi-referendum.php (accessed April 9, 2012). Also see Rafael R. Díaz Torres, "Congressman Gutiérrez Questions Effectiveness of Local Plebiscite," *Daily Sun*, December 23, 2011.

17. "Report on Puerto Rico's Status," 3.

18. "Concluyen los trabajos de la Sesión Extraordinaria," December 21, 2011. http://www.camaraderepresentantes.org (accessed April 9, 2012).

19. Eva Llorens, "PDP to voters: Skip 2nd part of plebiscite," *Caribbean Business*, February 12, 2012, available at www.caribbeanbusinesspr.com/news03.php?nt_id=67972&ct_id=1 (accessed April 9, 2012).

20. Ibid.

21. Ibid.

22. Ed Morales, "Analysis: The Puerto Rico Plebiscite That Wasn't," *ABC/Univison*, November 8, 2012, available at http://abcnews.go.com/ABC_Univision/Opinion/puerto-rico-status-plebiscite/story?id=17674719 (accessed November 9, 2012).

23. "H.R. 2499 (111th): Puerto Rico Democracy Act of 2010," available at https://www.govtrack.us/congress/bills/111/hr2499 (accessed November 2, 2013.)

24. The Presidential Task Force also started to research and give recommendations on economic development, building competitive industries, and creating policies toward the island of Vieques. The task force and the president are all working under the assumption that the United States has and will continue to have a paternal responsibility and financial connection to Puerto Rico.

25. See Borrinaga, *Balangiga Conflict Revisited*; Couttie, *Hang the Dogs*; and Adams, *Bells of Balangiga*.

26. Delmendo, *Star-Entangled Banner*, 178–79.

27. Marguerite Herman, "Bells Signal Emotional Dispute," *Wyoming Catholic Register*, December, 1, 1997.

28. Eugenio Daza, "Balangiga," available at http://rcouttie.topcities.com/balangiga/Daza_%20English.htm (accessed April 10, 2012).

29. Robert Tomsho, "Death Toll: The Bells of Balangiga Have a Different Ring in Manila, Cheyenne," *Wall Street Journal*, November 19, 1997.

30. Delmendo, *Star-Entangled Banner*, 179.

31. Rodel E. Rodis, "The Bells of Balangiga," *San Francisco Examiner*, December 23, 1997.

32. Ibid. According to Robin Hemley, "President Bill Clinton was ready to send the bells back, but his then-impeachment proceedings diverted his attention." Hemley, "The Bells of Balangiga: A War in the Philippines That Has Not Been Forgotten," *Wall Street Journal Asia*, February 6, 2009.

33. According to Adams, "[The Philippine] Ambassador and his Political Affairs Office have carried on an active lobbying program and produced a steady stream of articles, letters and visits aimed at influencing the White House, Congress, the Department of Defense and the American public" to return the bells. Adams, *Bells of Balangiga*, 31–32.

34. Ann Franscell, "A Bell for Balangiga," *Gillette News-Record*, July 6, 1997.

35. Tomsho, "Death Toll."

36. Leonardo Y. Medroso, "The Bells of Balangiga," *Samar News*, September 30, 2005. Helzer also stated, "The taking of the Bells was, in fact, legally wrong in 1901, just as the taking of the bells would be wrong today.... The 1863 Lieber Code, the set of formal guidelines providing a code of conduct for the U.S. Army in effect in 1901, provided that 'property belonging to churches... is not to be considered public property' and that private property could 'be seized only by way of military necessity.'... There is no doubt that the bells were religious objects, the taking of which was clearly not demanded by any necessity of war." Helzer, "Taking the Bells of Balangiga Was Unlawful in 1901," *Wyoming Tribune-Eagle*, April 10, 1998.

37. Rodis, "Bells of Balangiga."

38. Rodger McDaniel, "Issue Deeper than Possession of the Bells," *Wyoming Tribune-Eagle*, April 10, 1998.

39. Tomsho, "Death Toll."

40. "Congressional Delegation Writes Bill to Protect Bells," *Wyoming Tribune Eagle*, April 2, 1998.

41. Kenneth Steadman to Douglas Bereuter, January 6, 1998, *United States of America Congressional Record: Proceedings and Debates of the 105th Congress*, 2nd Sess., Vol. 144, Pt. 4, 5512.

42. Tomsho, "Death Toll." Also see Helzer, "Time to Right Injustice of Balangiga," *Casper Star Tribune*, November 23, 1997.

43. Fidel Ramos, "Return the Balangiga bells," *Manila Bulletin*, August 2, 2009.

44. Delmendo, *Star-Entangled Banner*, 181.

45. Kerry Drake, "Vets Groups Oppose Resolution on Bells," *Casper Star-Tribune*, March 12, 1998. Joe Sestak also said, "The Bells are properly located where they are and what they are. They are a memorial on a military installation to men who served and died for their country in the uniformed services. They ceased to be property of the church when the church was used to garrison the bolomen of the Philippines on the Saturday night prior to the heinous attack that was signaled by the Bells." Sestak, "Don't Dismantle Memorial," *Casper Star-Tribune*, October 31, 1999.

46. "VFW Strongly Opposes Compromise on Bells," *Sheridan Press*, December 9, 1997.

47. Delmendo, *Star-Entangled Banner*, 190.

48. Ben Evardone explained how "the name of Father Agustin Delgado, the town's parish priest in 1889, is embossed on the 1889 bell displayed in Wyoming, and the name of Father Bernardo Aparicio, the town's parish priest in 1896, is embossed on the 1896 bell now in Korea." Evardone, "The Time to Return the Bells Is Now," draft of speech for the 103rd Balangiga Encounter Day, September 28, 2004, available at http://www.samarnews.com/Insight/insight9.htm (accessed April 10, 2012).

49. Hemley, "Bells of Balangiga."

50. House Congressional Resolution 18, 112th Congress, 1st Sess., available at http://www.govtrack.us/congress/bills/112/hconres18 (accessed October 8, 2013).

51. Ryan Ponce Pacpaco, "House to Obama: Return 3 Balangiga Church Bells," *Journal Online*, June 24, 2011, available at http://journal.com.ph/index.php/news/national/7958-house-to-obama-return-3-balangiga-church-bells (accessed April 10, 2012).

52. Joseph G. Lariosa, "Let the Balangiga Bells Ring," *Mabuhay Radio*, September 30, 2011, available at http://www.mabuhayradio.com/jgl-eye/let-the-balangiga-bells-ring (accessed on April 10, 2012).

53. Jose Rodel Clapano, "U.S. Congress to Approve Balangiga Bells Return," *Philippine Star*, October 18, 2011.

SELECTED BIBLIOGRAPHY

Archive Collections

ARCHIVO GENERAL DE PUERTO RICO, INSTITUTO
DE CULTURA PUERTORRIQUEÑA, SAN JUAN, PUERTO RICO

Oficina del Gobernador, Correspondencia General

AMERICAN HISTORICAL COLLECTION, ATENEO
DE MANILA UNIVERSITY, MANILA, PHILIPPINES

Documents Related to the Philippine Commission

ARCHIVES OF THE PUERTO RICAN DIASPORA, CENTRO
DE ESTUDIOS PUERTORRIQUEÑOS, HUNTER COLLEGE,
CITY UNIVERSITY OF NEW YORK

Blase Camacho Souza Papers 1899–2003

CENTRO DE INVESTIGACIONES HISTÓRICAS,
UNIVERSIDAD DE PUERTO RICO, RIO PIEDRAS

National Archives, RG 126, Rollo 5, Documentos Sobre Emigración de Puertorriqueños a los Estados Unido y a Otros Pasíes en las Décades del 1930–50
National Archives, RG 350, Rollo 5, Cuestionario de 1909 Sobre Diversos Temas

HAWAIIAN MISSION CHILDREN'S SOCIETY LIBRARY,
MISSION HOUSES MUSEUM, HONOLULU, HAWAI'I

Hawaiian Evangelical Association Annual Reports
Hawaiian Evangelical Association Archives

HAWAI'I STATE ARCHIVES, HONOLULU, HAWAI'I

Governor's Records
First Circuit Court Transcripts, 1887–1967

HAWAIIAN SUGAR PLANTERS ASSOCIATION ARCHIVES,
HAWAIIAN/PACIFIC COLLECTION, HAMILTON LIBRARY,
UNIVERSITY OF HAWAI'I AT MĀNOA

Honokaa Sugar Company Records
Lihue Plantation Company Records
Puna Sugar Company Records

NATIONAL ARCHIVES AND RECORDS ADMINISTRATION,
COLLEGE PARK, MARYLAND

Record Group 126: Records of the Office of Territories, Office of Territories, Classified Files 1907–1951
Record Group 174: General Records of the Department of Labor, 1907–1942
Record Group 350: Bureau of Insular Affairs General Records Relating to More Than One Island Possession, General Classified Files, 1898–1945

NATIONAL ARCHIVES AND RECORDS ADMINISTRATION,
PACIFIC BRANCH, SAN FRANCISCO

Record Group 85: Immigration and Naturalization Service, Honolulu District, Case Files of Filipino Applicants for Certificates of Citizenship-Hawaiian Islands (4800-a), 1934–1944.
Record Group 126: Records of the Office of Territories, 1944–1976
Case Files of the U.S. District Court for the Territory of Hawai'i, 1900–1927

NATIONAL LIBRARY OF THE PHILIPPINES,
FILIPINIANA DIVISION, MANILA, PHILIPPINES

Manuel Quezon Papers

PUNA CONGREGATIONAL CHRISTIAN CHURCH DOCUMENTS

Records of General Membership and Sacramental Events

Published Primary Sources

Census of the Philippine Islands Taken under the Direction of the Philippine Legislature.
Devins, John B., and American Tract Society. *An Observer in the Philippines: or, Life in Our New Possessions.* Boston: American Tract Society, 1905.
Documentos de la Migracion Puertorriqueña (1879–1901): Documents of the Puerto Rican Migration, No. 1, City University of New York, Centro de Estudios Puertorriqueños, 1977.
Hawaii Data Book, 1900–1940.
Immigration into Hawaii: Hearings before the United States Senate Committee on Immigration, Sixty-Seventh Congress, First Session, August 13 and 18, 1921.
Immigration into Hawaii: Hearings before the United States Senate Committee on Immigration, Sixty-Seventh Congress, Second Session, June 7, 1922.
INS Reporter 26, no. 3 (Winter 1977–78).

Labor Bulletin of the Bureau of Labor, 7, no. 25, Report of the Director of Labor to His Excellency the Governor General of the Philippines, Investigation of Labor Conditions and Employment of Filipinos in Hawaii, Manila, Bureau of Printing, March 1926.
Laws of the Territory of Hawaii.
Manlapit, Pablo. *Filipinos Fight for Justice: Case of the Filipino Laborers in the Big Strike of 1924.* Honolulu: Territory of Hawai'i, 1924.
Ola'a Plantation Annual Reports, 1900–1930.
Ola'a/Kurtistown Oldtimers Reunion (booklet), July 12–13, 1996.

Newspapers

La Correspondencia
La Democracia
Pacific Commercial Advertiser
Porto Rico Progress

Oral History Collections

CENTER FOR ORAL HISTORY, UNIVERSITY OF HAWAI'I AT MĀNOA

Closing of Sugar Plantations: Interviews with Families of Hamakua and Ka'u, Hawai'i
Kalihi: Place of Transition
Koloa: An Oral History of a Kaua'i Community
Social History from Kona
Stores and Storekeepers of Pa'ia and Pu'unene, Maui
Waialua and Hale'iwa: The People Tell Their Story

NORMA CARR COLLECTION

Twenty-eight oral histories conducted by Norma Carr from 1978 to 1979, stored at her home in Aina Haina, O'ahu. Interviews funded by a grant from the Ford Foundation New York–Puerto Rico Research consortium.

Personal Oral Histories

TAPED INTERVIEWS

McElrath, Ah Quon. Honolulu, O'ahu, November 5, 2003.
Mendez, Rudy. San Juan, Puerto Rico, March 6, 2004.
Nagtalon-Miller, Helen. Kaneohe, O'ahu, February 22, 2003, and January 31, 2004.
Nicolas, Tito. Waipahu, O'ahu, February 1, 2004.
Villanueva, Gus. Hilo, Hawai'i, January 26, 2004, and January 29, 2004, Ka'u, Hawai'i.

DETAILED NOTES OF UNTAPED INTERVIEWS

Agag, Melvin. Hilo, Hawai'i, January 30, 2004.
Arakaki, James. Hilo, Hawai'i, January 30, 2004.
Basque Sr., Walter. Kea'au, Hawai'i, January 28, 2004.

Case, James. Honolulu, O'ahu, November 3, 2003.
Fontes, Josephine. Kea'au, Hawai'i, January 26, 2004.
Matsumoto, Tsune. Kea'au, Hawai'i, January 26, 2004.
Sasan, Jay. Hilo, Hawai'i, January 29, 2004.
Soriano, Fred. Hilo, Hawai'i, January 27, 2004.
Thompson, Mitsui. Honolulu, O'ahu, November 7, 2003.
Wickman, Charles. Honolulu, O'ahu, November 3, 2003.

DETAILED NOTES OF TELEPHONE CONVERSATIONS

Rena (name changed for privacy purposes). January 27, 2004.
Rosario, Vincente. January 27, 2004.
Sumarnap, Filomena (Fely). January 29, 2004.

Secondary Sources

Abernethy, David. *The Dynamics of Global Dominance: European Overseas Empires 1415–1980*. New Haven, Conn.: Yale University Press, 2000.
Abinales, Patricio. "Progressive-Machine Conflict in Early Twentieth Century American Politics and Colonial State Building in the Philippines." In *The American Colonial State in the Philippines: Global Perspectives*, edited by Julian Go and Anne Foster, 148–81. Durham, N.C.: Duke University Press, 2003.
Adams, Gerald. *The Bells of Balangiga*. Cheyenne, Wyo.: Lagumo, 1998.
Adams, Romanzo Colfax. *Interracial Marriage in Hawaii: A Study of The Mutually Conditioned Processes of Acculturation and Amalgamation*. New York: Macmillan, 1937.
Aguilar, Filomeno V. *Clash of Spirits: The History of Power and Sugar Planter Hegemony on a Visayan Island*. Honolulu: University of Hawai'i Press, 1998.
Alcántara, Rubén R. *Sakada: Filipino Adaptation in Hawaii*. Washington, D.C.: University Press of America, 1981.
Alegado, Dean T. "The Filipino Community in Hawaii: Development and Change." *Social Process in Hawaii* 33 (1991): 12–38.
Aleinikoff, Thomas Alexander. *Semblances of Sovereignty: The Constitution, the State, and American Citizenship*. Cambridge, Mass.: Harvard University Press, 2002.
Anderson, Benedict. *Imagined Communities: Reflections on the Origin and Spread of Nationalism*. London: Verso, 1983.
——. *The Spectre of Comparisons: Nationalism, Southeast Asia, and the World*. London: Verso, 1998.
Anderson, Robert N., Richard Coller, and Rebecca F. Pestano. *Filipinos in Rural Hawaii*. Honolulu: University of Hawai'i Press, 1984.
Angeles, Leonora C. "The Political Dimension in the Agrarian Question: Strategies of Resilience and Political Entrepreneurship of Agrarian Elite Families in a Philippine Province." *Rural Sociology* 64 (1999): 667–92.
Apilado, Mariano Casuga. *Revolutionary Spirituality: A Study of the Protestant Role in the American Colonial Rule of the Philippines, 1898–1928*. Quezon City, Philippines: New Day, 1999.
Aquino, Belinda A. "The Politics of Ethnicity among Ilokanos in Hawaii." In *Old Ties and New Solidarities: Studies on Philippine Communities*, edited by Charles J. H.

Macdonald and Guillermo M. Pesigan, 100–116. Quezon City, Philippines: Ateneo de Manila University Press, 2000.
Aranda, Elizabeth. *Emotional Bridges to Puerto Rico: Migration, Return Migration, and the Struggles of Incorporation.* Lanham, Md.: Rowman and Littlefield, 2007.
Archer, Seth. "Remedial Agents: Missionary Physicians and the Depopulation of Hawai'i." *Pacific Historical Review* 79 (2010): 513–44.
Ardener, Shirley. "A Comparative Study of Rotating Credit Associations." *Journal of the Royal Anthropological Institute of Great Britain and Ireland* 94 (1964): 201–29.
Argüelles, María del Pilar. *Morality and Power: The U.S. Colonial Experience in Puerto Rico from 1898 to 1948.* Lanham, Md.: University Press of America, 1996.
Ayala, César J. *American Sugar Kingdom: The Plantation Economy of the Spanish Caribbean, 1898–1934.* Chapel Hill: University of North Carolina Press, 1999.
Ayala, César, and Rafael Bernabe. *Puerto Rico in the American Century: A History since 1898.* Chapel Hill, N.C.: University of North Carolina Press, 2007.
Baldoz, Rick. *The Third Asiatic Invasion: Empire and Migration in Filipino America, 1898–1946.* New York: New York University Press, 2011.
Bankoff, Greg. "The Dangers to Going It Alone: Social Capital and the Origins of Community Resilience in the Philippines." *Continuity and Change* 22 (August 2007): 327–55.
———. "Wants, Wages, and Workers: Laboring in the American Philippines, 1899–1908." *Pacific Historical Review* 74 (2005): 59–86.
Beechert, Edward D. *Working in Hawaii: A Labor History.* Honolulu: University of Hawai'i Press, 1985.
Beito, David T. *From Mutual Aid to the Welfare State: Fraternal Societies and Social Services, 1890–1967.* Chapel Hill: University of North Carolina Press, 2000.
Bender, Thomas. *Rethinking American History in a Global Age.* Berkeley: University of California Press, 2002.
Bergad, Laird. *Coffee and the Growth of Agrarian Capitalism in Nineteenth-Century Puerto Rico.* Princeton: Princeton University Press, 1983.
Bhabha, Homi. "Of Mimicry and Man: The Ambivalence of Colonial Discourse." In *Tensions of Empire: Colonial Cultures in a Bourgeois World*, edited by Frederick Cooper and Ann Laura Stoler, 152–62. Berkeley: University of California Press, 1997.
Bodnar, John E. *The Transplanted: A History of Immigrants in Urban America.* Bloomington: Indiana University Press, 1985.
Bonilla, Frank, and Ricardo Campos. *Industry and Idleness.* New York: Centro de Estudios Puertorriqueños, 1986.
Bonus, Rick. *Locating Filipino Americans: Ethnicity and the Cultural Politics of Space.* Philadelphia: Temple University Press, 2000.
Boot, Max. "The Case for American Empire," *Weekly Standard*, October 15, 2001.
———. *The Savage Wars of Peace: Small Wars and the Rise of American Power.* New York: Basic, 2002.
Borrinaga, Rolando O. *The Balangiga Conflict Revisited.* Manila: New Day, 2003.
Bourdieu, Pierre. "Forms of Capital." In *Handbook of Theory and Research for the Sociology of Education*, edited by John G. Richardson, 241–58. New York: Greenwood, 1986.
———. *Outline of a Theory of Practice.* Cambridge: Cambridge University Press, 1977.
Bourgois, Philippe I. *Ethnicity at Work: Divided Labor on a Central American Banana Plantation.* Baltimore, Md.: Johns Hopkins University Press, 1989.
Bouvier, Virginia Marie. *Whose America? The War of 1898 and the Battles to Define the Nation.* Westport, Conn.: Praeger, 2001.

Brewer, Carolyn. "From Animist Priestess to Catholic Priest: The Re-Gendering of Religious Roles in the Philippines, 1521–1683." In *Other Pasts: Women, Gender and History in Early Modern Southeast Asia*, edited by Barbara Watson Andaya, 69–86. Honolulu: University of Hawai'i, 2000.

———. *Shamanism, Catholicism and Gender Relations in Colonial Philippines 1521–1685*. Aldershot, Eng.: Ashgate, 2004.

Briggs, Laura. *Reproducing Race: Race, Sex, Science, and U.S. Imperialism in Puerto Rico*. Berkeley: University of California Press, 2002.

Brooks, Lee M. "Hawaii's Puerto Ricans." *Social Process in Hawaii* 12 (1948): 46–57.

Burnett, Christina Duffy. "'They Say I Am Not an American . . . ': The Noncitizen National and the Law of American Empire." *Virginia Journal of International Law* 48 (2008): 660–718.

Burnett, Christina Duffy, and Burke Marshall. *Foreign in a Domestic Sense: Puerto Rico, American Expansion, and the Constitution*. Durham, N.C.: Duke University Press, 2001.

Cabán, Pedro A. *Constructing a Colonial People: Puerto Rico and the United States, 1898–1932*. Boulder, Colo.: Westview, 1999.

Cabranes, José A. *Citizenship and the American Empire: Notes on the Legislative History of the United States Citizenship of Puerto Ricans*. New Haven, Conn.: Yale University Press, 1979.

Campomanes, Oscar. "The New Empire's Forgetful and Forgotten Citizens: Unrepresentability and Unassimilability in Filipino American Postcolonialities." *Critical Mass* 2 (1995): 145–200.

Cannell, Fenella. *Power and Intimacy in the Christian Philippines*. Cambridge: Cambridge University Press, 1999.

Cariaga, Roman R. *The Filipinos in Hawaii: Economic and Social Conditions 1906–1936*. Honolulu: Filipino Public Relations Bureau, 1937.

Carr, Norma. "The Puerto Ricans in Hawaii: 1900–1958." PhD diss., University of Hawai'i, 1989.

Carter, Marina. *Voices from Indenture: Experiences of Indian Migrants in the British Empire*. London: Leicester University Press, 1996.

Chan, Sucheng. *Asian Americans: An Interpretive History*. Boston: Twayne, 1991.

———. *Hmong Means Free: Life in Laos and America*. Philadelphia: Temple University Press, 1994.

Chapin, Helen. *Shaping History: The Role of Newspapers in Hawai'i*. Honolulu: University of Hawai'i Press, 1996.

Cheng, Lucie, and Edna Bonacich. *Labor Immigration under Capitalism: Asian Workers in the United States before World War II*. Berkeley: University of California Press, 1984.

Chomsky, Aviva. *West Indian Workers and the United Fruit Company in Costa Rica, 1870–1940*. Baton Rouge: Louisiana State University Press, 1996.

Choy, Catherine Ceniza. *Empire of Care: Nursing and Migration in Filipino American History*. Durham, N.C.: Duke University Press, 2003.

Choy, Peggy Myo-Young. "Anatomy of a Dancer: Place, Lineage, and Liberation." In *Asian Settler Colonialism: From Local Governance to the Habits of Everyday Life in Hawaii*, edited by Candace Fujikane and Jonathan Okamura, 279–93. Honolulu: University of Hawai'i Press, 2008.

Clifford, Sister Mary Dorita. "Filipino Immigration to Hawaii." MA thesis, University of Hawai'i, 1954.

Clymer, Kenton J. *Protestant Missionaries in the Philippines, 1898–1916: An Inquiry into the American Colonial Mentality*. Urbana: University of Illinois Press, 1986.

Coman, Katharine, and Andrew William Lind. *The History of Contract Labor in the Hawaiian Islands.* New York: Arno, 1978.

Conniff, Michael L. *Black Labor on a White Canal: Panama, 1904–1981.* Pittsburgh: University of Pittsburgh Press, 1985.

Conroy, Hilary. *The Japanese Frontier in Hawaii, 1868–1898.* New York: Arno, 1978.

Cooper, Frederick. *Colonialism in Question: Theory, Knowledge, History.* Berkeley: University of California Press, 2005.

———. "Empire Multiplied: A Review Essay." *Comparative Studies in Society and History* 464 (2004): 247–72.

Cooper, Frederick, and Ann Laura Stoler. *Tensions of Empire: Colonial Cultures in a Bourgeois World.* Berkeley: University of California Press, 1997.

Couttie, Bob. *Hang the Dogs: The True and Tragic History of the Balangiga Massacre.* Manila: New Day, 2004.

Cullinane, Michael. "Ilustrado Politics: Filipino Elite Responses to American Rule, 1898–1908." PhD diss., University of Michigan, 1998.

Curtin, Philip. *The Rise and Fall of the Plantation Complex: Essays in Atlantic History.* Cambridge: Cambridge University Press, 1990.

Daniels, Roger. *The Politics of Prejudice: The Anti-Japanese Movement in California and the Struggle for Japanese Exclusion.* Berkeley: University of California Press, 1999.

Delgado, Richard, and Jean Stefancic. *Critical Race Theory: The Cutting Edge.* Philadelphia: Temple University Press, 2000.

Delmendo, Sharon. *Star-Entangled Banner: One Hundred Years of America in the Philippines.* New Brunswick: Rutgers University Press, 2004.

Domingo, Benjamin B. *The Philippines and Hawaii.* Manila: Foreign Service Institute, 1983.

Duany, Jorge. "A Transnational Colonial Migration: Puerto Rico's Farm Labor Program." *New West Indian Guide* 84 (2010): 225–51.

———. "Nation and Migration: Rethinking Puerto Rican Identity in a Transnational Context." In *None of the Above: Puerto Ricans in the Global Era*, edited by Frances Negrón-Muntaner, 51–63. New York: Palgrave MacMillan, 2007.

———. *The Puerto Rican Nation on the Move: Identities on the Island and in the United States.* Chapel Hill: University of North Carolina Press, 2002.

Duffey, Dennis. "The Northwest Ordinance as a Constitutional Document." *Columbia Law Review* 95 (1995): 929–68.

Emmer, P. C., and E. van den Boogaart. *Colonialism and Migration: Indentured Labour before and after Slavery.* Dordrecht, Neth.: Nijhoff, 1986.

Erman, Sam. "Meanings of Citizenship in the U.S. Empire: Puerto Rico, Isabel Gonzalez, and the Supreme Court, 1898 to 1905." *Journal of American Ethnic History* 27 (2008): 5–33.

España-Maram, Linda. *Creating Masculinity In Los Angeles's Little Manila: Working-Class Filipinos and Popular Culture, 1920s–1950s.* New York: Columbia University Press, 2006.

Espiritu, Augusto Fauni. *Five Faces of Exile: The Nation and Filipino American Intellectuals.* Stanford, Calif.: Stanford University Press, 2005.

Espiritu, Yen Le. *Home Bound: Filipino Lives across Cultures, Communities, and Countries.* Berkeley: University of California Press, 2003.

Ferguson, Niall. *Colossus: The Price of America's Empire.* New York: Penguin, 2004.

Figueroa, Luis. *Sugar, Slavery, and Freedom in Nineteenth-Century Puerto Rico.* Chapel Hill: University of North Carolina Press, 2005.

Findlay, Eileen. *Imposing Decency: The Politics of Sexuality and Race in Puerto Rico, 1870–1920*. Durham, N.C.: Duke University Press, 1999.

Flores, Juan. "The Diaspora Strikes Back: Nation and Location" In *None of the Above: Puerto Ricans in the Global Era*, edited by Frances Negrón-Muntaner, 51–63. New York: Palgrave MacMillan, 2007.

Follett, Richard. *The Sugar Masters: Planters and Slaves in Louisiana's Cane World, 1820–1860*. Baton Rouge: Louisiana State University Press, 2007.

Foster, John Bellamy, and Robert Waterman McChesney. *Pox Americana: Exposing The American Empire*. New York: Monthly Review, 2004.

Francia, Luis H. "The Rind of Things." In *Vestiges of War: The Philippine-American War and the Aftermath of An Imperial Dream, 1899–1999*, edited by Angel Shaw and Luis Velasco, xxi–xxviii. New York: New York University Press, 2002.

Fredrickson, George M. "From Exceptionalism to Variability: Recent Developments in Cross-National Comparative History." *Journal of American History* 82 (1995): 587–604.

Friday, Chris. *Organizing Asian American Labor: The Pacific Coast Canned-Salmon Industry, 1870–1942*. Philadelphia: Temple University Press, 1994.

Friend, Theodore. *Between Two Empires: The Ordeal of the Philippines, 1929–1946*. Ann Arbor: University of Michigan Press, 1978.

Fritz, Christian G. "A Nineteenth-Century 'Habeas Corpus Mill': The Chinese before the Federal Courts in California." *American Journal of Legal History* 32 (1988): 347–72.

Fu, Xuanning, and Tim B. Heaton. *Interracial Marriage in Hawaii, 1983–1994*. Lewiston, N.Y.: Mellen, 1997.

Fuchs, Lawrence H. *Hawaii Pono: "Hawaii the Excellent"; An Ethnic and Political History*. Honolulu: Bess, 1992.

Fujikane, Candace, and Jonathan Okamura. *Asian Settler Colonialism: From Local Governance to the Habits of Everyday Life in Hawaii*. Honolulu: University of Hawai'i Press, 2008.

Fujita-Rony, Dorothy B. *American Workers, Colonial Power: Philippine Seattle and the Transpacific West, 1919–1941*. Berkeley: University of California Press, 2003.

Gabaccia, Donna R. *Militants and Migrants: Rural Sicilians Become American Workers*. New Brunswick, N.J.: Rutgers University Press, 1988.

Gallagher, Mark Edward. "No More a Christian Nation: The Protestant Church in Territorial Hawai'i, 1898–1919." PhD diss., University of Hawai'i, 1983.

García-Colón, Ismael. "Buscando Ambiente: Hegemony and Subaltern Tactics of Survival in Puerto Rico's Land Distribution Program." *Latin American Perspectives* 33 (2006): 42–65.

Garfield, Seth. "Tapping Masculinity: Labor Recruitment to the Brazilian Amazon during World War II." *Hispanic American Historical Review* 86 (2006): 275–308.

Garrison, Vivian, and Carol I. Weiss. "Dominican Family Networks and United States Immigration Policy: A Case Study." *Center for Migration Studies* 7 (1989): 220–38.

Geertz, Clifford. "The Rotating Credit Association: A 'Middle Rung.'" *Development: Economic Development and Cultural Change* 10 (1962): 241–63

Genovese, Eugene D. *Roll, Jordan, Roll: The World the Slaves Made*. New York: Vintage, 1976.

Glasser, Ruth. *My Music Is My Flag: Puerto Rican Musicians and Their New York Communities, 1917–1940*. Berkeley: University of California Press, 1995.

Glenn, Evelyn Nakano. *Unequal Freedom: How Race and Gender Shaped American Citizenship and Labor*. Cambridge: Harvard University Press, 2002.

Go, Julian. *American Empire and the Politics of Meaning: Elite Political Cultures in the Philippines and Puerto Rico during U.S. Colonialism.* Durham. N.C.: Duke University Press, 2008.

———. "Chains of Empire, Projects of State: 'Political Education' and United States Colonial Rule in Puerto Rico and the Philippines." *Comparative Studies in Society and History* 42 (2000): 253–70.

———. *Patterns of Empire: The British and American Empires, 1688 to the Present.* Cambridge: Cambridge University Press, 2011.

Go, Julian, and Anne L. Foster. *The American Colonial State in the Philippines: Global Perspectives.* Durham: Duke University Press, 2003.

Goffman, Erving. *Asylums: Essays on the Social Situation of Mental Patients and Other Inmates.* New York: Anchor, 1961.

Gordon, Alec. "The Agrarian Question in Colonial Java: Coercion and Colonial Capitalist Sugar Plantations, 1870–1941." *Journal of Peasant Studies* 27 (1999): 1–34.

Goss, Jon, and Bruce Lindquist, "Placing Movers: An Overview of the Asian-Pacific Migration System." *Contemporary Pacific* 12 (2000): 385–414.

Grasmuch, Sherri, and Patricia R. Pessar. *Between Two Islands.* Berkeley: University of California Press, 1991.

Griffiths, Stephen L. *Emigrants, Entrepreneurs, and Evil Spirits: Life in a Philippine Village.* Honolulu: University of Hawai'i Press, 1988.

Grimshaw, Patricia. *Paths of Duty: American Missionary Wives in Nineteenth-Century Hawaii.* Honolulu: University of Hawai'i Press, 1989.

Guisti-Cordero, Juan. "*Compradors* or *Compadres*? 'Sugar Barons' in Negros (the Philippines) and Puerto Rico under American Rule." In *Sugarlandia Revisited: Sugar and Colonialism in Asia and the Americas, 1800 to 1940*, edited by Ulbe Bosma, Juan A. Guisti-Cordero, and G. Roger Knight, 177–200. New York: Berghahn, 2007.

———. "Labor Ecology and History in a Caribbean Sugar Plantation Region." PhD diss., SUNY Binghamton, 1994.

Guterl, Matthew, and Christine Skwiot. "Atlantic and Pacific Crossings: Race, Empire, and 'The Labor Problem' in the Late Nineteenth Century." *Radical History Review* 91 (2005): 40–61.

Gutman, Herbert George. *Work, Culture, and Society in Industrializing America: Essays in American Working-Class and Social History.* New York: Vintage, 1977.

Halpern, Rick. "The Iron Fist and the Velvet Glove: Welfare Capitalism in Chicago's Packinghouses, 1921–1933." *Journal of American Studies* 26 (1992): 171–83.

Halter, Marilyn. "Beyond the Continental USA: Local Culture and National Identity in Hawai'i and Puerto Rico." Paper presented at the Conference on Local Culture and National Identity in Hawai'i and Puerto Rico, San Juan, 2000.

Handlin, Oscar. *The Uprooted: The Epic Story of the Great Migrations That Made the American People.* New York: Grosset and Dunlap, 1971.

Haney-López, Ian. *White by Law: The Legal Construction of Race.* New York: New York University Press, 1996.

Hart, D. G. *That Old-Time Religion in Modern America: Evangelical Protestantism in the Twentieth Century.* Chicago: Dee, 2002.

Hau'ofa, Epeli. *We Are the Ocean: Selected Works.* Honolulu: University of Hawai'i, 2008.

Hawaiian Sugar Planters' Association, *Facts about Hawaii's Largest Industry: Sugar.* Honolulu: Hawaiian Sugar Planters' Association, 1959.

———. *Story of Sugar in Hawaii.* Honolulu: Hawaiian Sugar Planters' Association, 1926.

———. *Sugar in Hawaii: The Story of Sugar Plantations, Their History, Their Methods of Operations and Their Place in the Economy of Hawaii*. Honolulu: Hawaiian Sugar Planters' Association, 1949.

Hedman, Eva-Lotta E., and John Thayer Sidel. *Philippine Politics and Society in the Twentieth Century: Colonial Legacies, Post-Colonial Trajectories*. New York: Routledge, 2000.

Heinz, Don J. and Robert V. Osgood. "A History of the Experiment Station, Hawaiian Sugar Planters' Association: Agricultural Progress through Cooperation and Science 1946–1996." *Hawaiian Planters' Record* 61 (2009): 1–105.

Hempenstall, Peter. "Imperial Manoeuvres." In *Tides of History: The Pacific Islands in the Twentieth Century*, edited by K. R. Howe, Robert C. Kiste, and Brij V. Lal, 29–39. Honolulu: University of Hawaii Press, 1994.

Hernández, José. *Conquered Peoples in America*. Dubuque, Iowa: Hunt, 1997.

Hess, Carol. "John Philip Sousa's *El Capitan*: Political Appropriation and the Spanish-American War." *American Music* 16 (1998), 1–24.

Higham, John. *Strangers in the Land: Patterns of American Nativism, 1860–1925*. New Brunswick, N.J.: Rutgers University Press, 1998.

Hobsbawm, E. J., and T. O. Ranger. *The Invention of Tradition*. Cambridge: Cambridge University Press, 1992.

Hoganson, Kristin L. *Fighting for American Manhood: How Gender Politics Provoked the Spanish-American and Philippine-American Wars*. New Haven, Conn.: Yale University Press, 1998.

Hsu, Madeline Yuan-yin. *Dreaming of Gold, Dreaming of Home: Transnationalism and Migration between the United States and South China, 1882–1943*. Stanford, Calif.: Stanford University Press, 2000.

Hunter College, Centro de Estudios Puertorriqueños. History Task Force. *Sources for the Study of Puerto Rican Migration: 1879–1930*. New York: Centro de Estudios Puertorriqueños, Hunter College of the City University of New York, 1982.

Hunter College, Centro de Estudios Puertorriqueños. Oral History Task Force. *Extended Roots: From Hawaii to New York: Migraciones Puetorriqueñas a Los Estados Unidos, Conference Held March 22–24, 1984*. New York: Centro, 1986.

Hutchcroft, Paul D. "Colonial Masters, National Politicos, and Provincial Lords: Central Authority and Local Autonomy in the American Philippines, 1900–1913." *Journal of Asian Studies* 59 (2000): 277–306.

Ignacio, Abe. *The Forbidden Book: The Philippine-American War in Political Cartoons*. San Francisco: T'Boli, 2004.

Ileto, Reynaldo Clemeña. *Pasyon and Revolution: Popular Movements in the Philippines, 1840–1910*. Quezon City, Philippines: Ateneo de Manila University Press, 1997.

Jacobson, Matthew Frye. *Barbarian Virtues: The United States Encounters Foreign Peoples at Home and Abroad, 1876–1917*. New York: Hill and Wang, 2000.

Jasanoff, Maya. *Edge of Empire: Lives, Culture, and Conquest in the East, 1750–1850*. London: Vintage, 2006.

Johannessen, Edward L. H. *The Hawaiian Labor Movement: A Brief History*. Boston: Humphries, 1956.

Jones, Arun. *Christian Missions in the American Empire: Episcopalians in Northern Luzon, the Philippines, 1902–1946*. Frankfurt-am-Main, Germany: Peter Lang, 2003.

Joseph, G. M., Catherine LeGrand, and Ricardo Donato Salvatore. *Close Encounters of Empire: Writing the Cultural History of U.S.-Latin American Relations*. Durham, N.C.: Duke University Press, 1998.

Junasa, Bienvenido. "Filipino Experience in Hawai'i." *Ethnic Sources in Hawai'i, Social Process in Hawai'i* 29 (1996): 79–87.
Jung, Moon-Ho. *Coolies and Cane: Race, Labor, and Sugar in the Age of Emancipation*. Baltimore, Md.: Johns Hopkins University Press, 2006.
Jung, Moon-Kie. *Reworking Race: The Making of Hawaii's Interracial Labor Movement*. New York: Columbia University Press, 2010.
Kagan, Richard. "The Spanish Craze in the United States: Cultural Entitlement and the Appropriation of Spain's Cultural Patrimony, ca. 1890–ca. 1930" *Revista Complutense de Historia de América* 36 (2010): 37–58.
Kale, Madhavi. *Fragments of Empire: Capital, Slavery, and Indian Indentured Labor Migration in the British Caribbean*. Philadelphia: University of Pennsylvania Press, 1998.
Kalir, Barak. "Finding Jesus in the Holy Land and Taking Him to China: Chinese Temporary Migrant Workers in Israel Converting to Evangelical Christianity." *Sociology of Religion* 70, no. 2 (2009): 130–56.
Kameʻeleihiwa, Lilikalā. *Native Land and Foreign Desires: How Shall We Live in Harmony?* Honolulu: Bishop Museum Press, 1992.
Kaplan, Amy. *The Anarchy of Empire in the Making of U.S. Culture*. Cambridge, Mass.: Harvard University Press, 2002.
———. "'Left Alone with America': The Absence of Empire in the Study of American Culture." In *Cultures of United States Imperialism*, edited by Amy Kaplan and Donald E. Pease, 3–21. Durham, N.C.: Duke University Press, 1993.
Kaplan, Amy, and Donald E. Pease. *Cultures of United States Imperialism*. Durham, N.C.: Duke University Press, 1993.
Kaplan, Martha, and John Kelly. "On Discourse and Power: "Cults" and "Orientals" in Fiji." *American Ethnologist* 26 (1999): 843–63.
Karnow, Stanley. *In Our Image: America's Empire in the Philippines*. New York: Random House, 1989.
Kauanui, J. Kēhaulani. "Colonialism in Equality: Hawaiian Sovereignty and the Question of U.S. Civil Rights." *South Atlantic Quarterly* 107 (2008): 635–50.
———. *Hawaiian Blood: Colonialism and the Politics of Sovereignty and Indigeneity*. Durham, N.C.: Duke University Press, 2006.
Kennedy, Dale. "Essay and Reflection: On the American Empire from a British Historical Perspective." *International History Review* 29 (2007): 83–108.
Kerkvliet, Melinda Tria. *Unbending Cane: Pablo Manlapit, A Filipino Labor Leader in Hawai'i*. Mānoa: University of Hawai'i, 2002.
Kerr, James Edward. *The Insular Cases: The Role of the Judiciary in American Expansionism*. Port Washington, New York: Kennikat, 1982.
Kim, Jean. "Objects, Methods, and Interpretations: Imperial Trajectories, Haunted Nationalisms, and Medical Archives in Asian American History." *Journal of Asian American Studies* 14 (2011): 193–219.
Kramer, Paul A. *The Blood of Government: Race, Empire, the United States, and the Philippines*. Chapel Hill: University of North Carolina, 2006.
———. "Empires, Exceptions, and Anglo-Saxons: Race and Rule Between the British and United States Empires, 1880–1910." *Journal of American History* 88 (2002): 1315–53.
———. "Power and Connection: Imperial Histories of the United States in the World," *American Historical Review* 116 (2011): 1348–91.
Krauss, Bob. "California Mo' Bettah, Says Family." *Honolulu Advertiser*, June 24, 1978.
Kurth, James. "Migration and the Dynamics of Empire," *National Interest* 71 (2003): 5–16.

LaFeber, Walter. *The New Empire: An Interpretation of American Expansion, 1860–1898.* Ithaca, N.Y.: Cornell University Press, 1998.
Lai, Kum Pui. "Fifty Aged Puerto Ricans," *Social Process in Hawaii* 2 (1936): 24–27.
Lake, Marilyn, and Henry Reynolds. *Drawing the Global Colour Line: White Men's Countries and the International Challenge of Racial Equality.* Cambridge: Cambridge University Press, 2008.
Lal, Brij. *Girmitiyas: The Origins of the Fiji Indians.* Canberra: Journal of Pacific History, 1983.
Lal, Brij V., Doug Munro, and Edward D. Beechert. *Plantation Workers: Resistance and Accommodation.* Honolulu: University of Hawai'i Press, 1993.
Lapp, Michael. *Managing Migration: The Migration Division of Puerto Rico and Puerto Ricans in New York City, 1948–1968,* PhD diss., Johns Hopkins University, 1991.
Lasker, Bruno. *Filipino Immigration to Continental United States and to Hawaii.* New York: Arno, 1969.
Lasman, Lawrence. *Filipino Immigrants: A Study of Attitudes of Filipino Immigrants about Hawaii.* Honolulu: University of Hawai'i, 1971.
Lee, See Caroline. "Cultural Factors of Desertion in Hawaii." *Social Process in Hawaii* 6 (1939): 55–61.
Lieven, Dominic. *Empire: The Russian Empire and Its Rivals.* New Haven: Yale University Press, 2000.
Lind, Andrew William. *Hawaii's People.* Honolulu: University of Hawai'i Press, 1955.
Linnekin, Jocelyn. *Sacred Queens and Women of Consequence: Rank, Gender, and Colonialism in the Hawaiian Islands.* Ann Arbor: University of Michigan Press, 1990.
Lomnitz-Adler, Claudio. *Deep Mexico, Silent Mexico: An Anthropology of Nationalism.* Minneapolis: University of Minnesota Press, 2001.
Look Lai, Walton. *Indentured Labor, Caribbean Sugar: Chinese and Indian Migrants to the British West Indies, 1838–1918.* Baltimore, Md.: Johns Hopkins University Press, 1993.
Lowe, Lisa. *Immigrant Acts: On Asian American Cultural Politics.* Durham, N.C.: Duke University Press, 1996.
Mabalon, Dawn. *Little Manila is in the Heart: The Making of the Filipina/o Community in Stockton, California.* Durham, N.C.: Duke University Press, 2013.
MacDonald, John S., and Leatrice D. MacDonald. "Chain Migration, Ethnic Neighborhood Formation and Social Networks." *Millbank Memorial Fund Quarterly* 4 (1964): 82–97.
Maier, Charles S. *Among Empires: American Ascendancy and Its Predecessors.* Cambridge: Harvard University Press, 2007.
Maldonado, Edwin. "Contract Labor and the Origins of Puerto Rican Communities in the United States." *International Migration Review* 13 (1979): 103–21.
Mandell, Nikki. *The Corporation as Family: The Gendering of Corporate Welfare, 1890–1930.* Chapel Hill: University of North Carolina Press, 2001.
Mapes, Kathleen. *Sweet Tyranny: Migrant Labor, Industrial Agriculture, and Imperial Politics.* Champaign: University of Illinois Press, 2009.
Mar, Lisa. *Brokering Belonging: Chinese in Canada's Exclusion Era, 1885–1945.* Oxford: Oxford University Press, 2010.
Martínez-Fernández, Luis. *Torn between Empires: Economy, Society, and Patterns of Political Thought in the Hispanic Caribbean, 1840–1878.* Athens: University of Georgia Press, 1994.

Matrana, Marc R. *Lost Plantation: The Rise and Fall of Seven Oaks*. Jackson: University Press of Mississippi, 2006.
Maurer, Bill. *Recharting the Caribbean: Land, Law, and Citizenship in the British Virgin Islands*. Ann Arbor: University of Michigan Press, 1997.
May, Glenn Anthony. *Inventing a Hero: The Posthumous Re-Creation of Andres Bonifacio*. Madison: University of Wisconsin Center for Southeast Asian Studies, 1996.
McClintock, Anne. *Imperial Leather: Race, Gender, and Sexuality in the Colonial Contest*. New York: Routledge, 1995.
McCoy, Alfred W. *An Anarchy of Families: State and Family in the Philippines*. Madison: University of Wisconsin Center for Southeast Asian Studies, 1993.
McCoy, Alfred W., and Francisco A. Scarano, *The Colonial Crucible: Empire in the Making of the Modern American State*. Madison: University of Wisconsin Press, 2009.
McFarland, Daniel, and Aimee Eng. "The Japanese Question: San Francisco Education in 1906." Stanford, Calif.: Stanford University School of Education: 2006.
McGowan, William P. "Industrializing the Land of Lono: Sugar Plantation Managers and Workers in Hawaii, 1900–1920." *Agricultural History* 69 (1995): 177–200.
McGregor, Davianna Pomaika'i. "Statehood: Catalyst of the Twentieth-Century Kanaka 'Ōiwi Cultural Renaissance and Sovereignty Movement." *Journal of Asian American Studies* 13 (2010): 311–26.
McKeown, Adam. *Melancholy Order: Asian Migration and the Globalization of Borders*. New York: Columbia University Press, 2008.
McWilliams, Carey. *Factories in the Field: The Story of Migratory Farm Labor in California*. Hamden, Conn.: Archon, 1969.
Medina, Nitza C. "Rebellion in the Bay: California's First Puerto Ricans." *CENTRO Journal* 13 (2001): 84–95.
Meinig, D. W. *The Shaping of America: A Geographical Perspective on 500 Years of History*. New Haven, Conn.: Yale University Press, 1986.
Menjívar, Cecilia. *Fragmented Ties: Salvadoran Immigrant Networks in America*. Berkeley: University of California Press, 2000.
Merry, Sally Engle. *Colonizing Hawai'i: The Cultural Power of Law*. Princeton, N.J.: Princeton University Press, 2000.
Mintz, Sidney Wilfred. *Caribbean Transformations*. Chicago: Aldine, 1974.
———. *Worker in the Cane: A Puerto Rican Life History*. New York: Norton, 1974.
Mize, Ronald, and Alicia C. S. Swords. *Consuming Mexican Labor: From the Bracero Program to NAFTA*. Toronto: University of Toronto Press, 2010.
Mizuta, Iwao. "Some Aspects of Public Welfare in Hawaii." *Social Process in Hawaii* 6 (1940): 62–70.
Montgomery, David. *The Fall of the House of Labor: The Workplace, the State, and American Labor Activism, 1865–1925*. Cambridge: Cambridge University Press, 1987.
Morales Carrión, Arturo, and María Teresa Babín. *Puerto Rico: A Political and Cultural History*. New York: Norton, 1983.
Moreno Fraginals, Manuel. *The Sugarmill: The Socioeconomic Complex of Sugar in Cuba, 1760–1860*. New York: Monthly Review, 1976.
Moreno Fraginals, Manuel, Frank Moya Pons, and Stanley L. Engerman. *Between Slavery and Free Labor: The Spanish-Speaking Caribbean in the Nineteenth Century*. Baltimore, Md.: Johns Hopkins University Press, 1985.
Muncy, Robyn. *Creating a Female Dominion in American Reform, 1890–1935*. Oxford: Oxford University Press, 1994.

Nakasato, Earl T. *75th Anniversary 1912–1987 Puna United Church of Christ*. Puna, Hawai'i: United Church of Christ, 1987.
Nakonz, Jonas, and Angela Wai Yan Shik. "And All Your Problems Are Gone: Religious Coping Strategies among Philippine Migrant Workers in Hong Kong." *Mental Health, Religion and Culture* 12 (2009): 25–38.
Negrón-Muntaner, Frances. *None of the Above: Puerto Ricans in the Global Era*. New York: Palgrave McMillan, 2007.
Negrón-Muntaner, Frances, and Ramón Grosfoguel. *Puerto Rican Jam: Rethinking Colonialism and Nationalism*. Minneapolis: University of Minnesota Press, 1997.
Negrón-Portillo, Mariano. "Puerto Rico: Surviving Colonialism and Nationalism." In *Puerto Rican Jam: Rethinking Colonialism and Nationalism*, edited by Frances Negrón-Muntaner and Ramón Grosfoguel, 39–56. Minneapolis: University of Minnesota Press, 1997.
Nellist, George F. *Men of Hawaii: A Biographical Record of Men of Substantial Achievement in the Hawaiian Islands*. Honolulu: Honolulu Star-Bulletin, 1930.
———. *The Story of Hawaii and Its Builders*. Honolulu: Honolulu Star Bulletin, 1925.
Ngai, Mae M. "From Colonial Subject to Undesirable Alien: Filipino Migration, Exclusion, and Repatriation, 1920–1940." In *Re-Collecting Early Asian America: Essays in Cultural History*, edited by Josephine Lee, Imogene L. Lim, and Yuko Matsukawa, 111–26. Philadelphia: Temple University Press, 2002.
———. *Impossible Subjects: Illegal Aliens and the Making of Modern America, Politics and Society in Twentieth-Century America*. Princeton: Princeton University Press, 2004.
Nolan, Mary. "Against Exceptionalisms." *American Historical Review* 102 (1997): 769–74.
Okamura, Jonathan Y. *Filipino American History, Identity and Community in Hawai'i: In Commemoration of the 90th Anniversary of Filipino Immigration to Hawai'i*. Mānoa: University of Hawai'i, 1996.
———. *Imagining the Filipino American Diaspora: Transnational Relations, Identities, and Communities*. Studies in Asian Americans. New York: Garland, 1998.
Okamura, Jonathan Y., Amefil Agbayani, and Melinda Tria Kerkvliet. *The Filipino American Experience in Hawai'i: In Commemoration of the 85th Anniversary of Filipino Immigration to Hawaii*. Mānoa: University of Hawai'i, 1991.
Okihiro, Gary Y. *Cane Fires: The Anti-Japanese Movement in Hawaii, 1865–1945*. Philadelphia: Temple University Press, 1991.
Omi, Michael, and Howard Winant. *Racial Formation in the United States: From the 1960s to the 1990s*. New York: Routledge, 1994.
Osorio, Jon Kamakawiwo'ole. *Dismembering L'ahui: A History of the Hawaiian Nation to 1887*. Honolulu: University of Hawai'i Press, 2002.
———. "Ku'e and Ku'oko'a: History, Law, and Other Faiths," In *Law and Empire in the Pacific: Fiji and Hawaii*, edited by Sally Engle Merry and Donald Brenneis, 213–37. Santa Fe: School of American Research Press, 2003.
Pagden, Anthony. *Peoples and Empires: A Short History of European Migration, Exploration, and Conquest from Greece to the Present*. New York: Modern Library, 2001.
Palloni, Alberto, Douglas S. Massey, Miguel Ceballos, Kristin Espinosa, Michael Spittel. "Social Capital and International Migration: A Test Using Information on Family Networks." *American Journal of Sociology* 106 (2001): 1262–95.
Paredes, Ruby R. *Philippine Colonial Democracy*. Quezon City: Ateneo de Manila University Press, 1989.
Parkin, David. "The Categorization of Work." In *Social Anthropology of Work*, edited by Sandra Wallman, 317–35. New York: Academic, 1980.

Parreñas, Rhacel Salazar. "'White Trash' Meeting the 'Little Brown Monkeys': The Taxi Dance Hall as a Site of Interracial and Gender Alliances between White Working Class Women and Filipino Immigrant Men in the 1920s and 30s." *Amerasia* 24 (1998): 115–34.

Patterson, Wayne. *The Korean Frontier in America: Immigration to Hawaii, 1896–1910.* Honolulu: University of Hawai'i Press, 1988.

Peck, Gunther. "Divided Loyalties: Immigrant Padrones and the Evolution of Industrial Paternalism in North America." *International Labor and Working-Class History* 53 (1998): 49–68.

———. *Reinventing Free Labor: Padrones and Immigrant Workers in the North American West, 1880–1930.* Cambridge: Cambridge University Press, 2000.

Perea, Juan. "Fulfilling Manifest Destiny: Conquest, Race, and the *Insular Cases.*" In *Foreign in a Domestic Sense: Puerto Rico, American Expansion, and the Constitution,* edited by Christina Duffy Burnett and Burke Marshall, 140–66. Durham, N.C.: Duke University Press, 2001.

Pérez, Gina M. *The Near Northwest Side Story: Migration, Displacement, and Puerto Rican Families.* Berkeley: University of California Press, 2004.

Pérez, Louis A. *The War of 1898: The United States and Cuba in History and Historiography.* Chapel Hill: University of North Carolina Press, 1998.

Picó, Fernando. *History of Puerto Rico: A Panorama of Its People.* Princeton, N.J.: Wiener, 2006.

Pinheiro, John C. "Extending the Light and Blessings of Our Purer Faith: Anti-Catholic Sentiment among American Soldiers in the U.S.-Mexican War." *Journal of Popular Culture* 35 (2001): 129–52.

Poblete, JoAnna. "The S.S. Mongolia Incident: Medical Politics and Filipino Colonial Migration in Hawai'i." *Pacific Historical Review* 82 (2013): 248–78.

Porter, A. N. *Religion Versus Empire? British Protestant Missionaries and Overseas Expansion, 1700–1914.* Manchester: Manchester University Press, 2004.

Pruitt, Bernadette. "For the Advancement of the Race: The Great Migrations to Houston, Texas, 1914–1941." *Journal of Urban History* 31 (2005): 435–78.

Quintero Rivera, A. G. *Workers' Struggle in Puerto Rico: A Documentary History.* New York: Monthly Review, 1976.

Rafael, Vicente L. *Contracting Colonialism: Translation and Christian Conversion in Tagalog Society under Early Spanish Rule.* Durham, N.C.: Duke University Press, 1993.

———. *Discrepant Histories: Translocal Essays on Filipino Cultures.* Philadelphia: Temple University Press, 1995.

———. *White Love and Other Events in Filipino History.* Manila: Ateneo de Manila University Press, 2000.

Ralston, Caroline. *Grass Huts and Warehouses: Pacific Beach Communities of the Nineteenth Century.* Honolulu: University Press of Hawai'i, 1978.

Ravenal, Earl. "What's Empire Got To Do with It? The Derivation of America's Foreign Policy." *Critical Review: A Journal of Politics and Society* 21 (2009): 21–75.

Reidy, Joseph P. "Mules and Machines and Men: Field Labor on Louisiana Sugar Plantations, 1887–1915." *Agricultural History* 72 (1998): 183–96.

Reinecke, John E. *The Filipino Piecemeal Sugar Strike of 1924–1925.* Honolulu: Social Science Research Institute, 1996.

Rivera, Raquel Z. "Will the 'Real' Puerto Rican Culture Please Stand Up? Thoughts on Cultural Nationalism." In *None of the Above: Puerto Ricans in the Global Era,* edited by Frances Negrón-Muntaner, 217–31. New York: Palgrave McMillan, 2007.

Rivera Ramos, Efrén. *The Legal Construction of Identity: The Judicial and Social Legacy of American Colonialism in Puerto Rico*. Washington D.C.: American Psychological Association, 2001.

Rodgers, Daniel T. "Exceptionalism." In *Imagined Histories: American Historians Interpret the Past*, edited by Anthony Molho and Gordon S. Wood, 21–40. Princeton, N.J.: Princeton University, 1998.

Rodriguez, Clara E., and Virginia Sánchez Korrol. *Historical Perspectives on Puerto Rican Survival in the U.S.* Princeton: Wiener, 1996.

Rodriguez, Robyn. *Migrants for Export: How the Philippine State Brokers Labor to the World*. Minneapolis: University of Minnesota Press, 2010.

Rodriguez, Victor M. "Boricuas, African Americans, and Chicanos in the 'Far West': Notes on the Puerto Rican Pro-Independence Movement in California, 1960s–1980s." *New Political Science* 20 (1998): 421–39.

Rodríguez-Silva, Ileana. *Silencing Race: Disentangling Blackness, Colonialism, and National Identities in Puerto Rico*. New York: Palgrave Macmillan, 2012.

Roland, Charles. *Louisiana Sugar Plantation during the American Civil War*. Leiden, Neth.: Brill, 1957.

Roopnarine, Lomarsh. *Indo-Caribbean Indenture: Resistance and Accomodation, 1838–1920*. Kingston, Jamaica: University of the West Indies Press, 2007.

——. "Return Migration of Indentured East Indians from the Caribbean to India 1838–1920." *Journal of Caribbean History* 40 (2006): 308–24.

Root, Maria P. P. *Filipino Americans: Transformation and Identity*. Thousand Oaks, Calif.: Sage, 1997.

Rosenberg, Emily S., and Eric Foner. *Spreading the American Dream: American Economic and Cultural Expansion, 1890–1945*. New York: Hill and Wang, 1982.

Said, Edward W. *Orientalism*. New York: Vintage, 1994.

Salyer, Lucy E. *Laws Harsh as Tigers: Chinese Immigrants and the Shaping of Modern Immigration Law*. Chapel Hill: University of North Carolina Press, 1995.

San Buenaventura, Steffi. "Nativism and Ethnicity in a Filipino-American Experience." PhD diss., University of Hawai'i, 1990.

San Juan, E. *Beyond Postcolonial Theory*. New York: St. Martin's, 1998.

Santiago-Valles, Kelvin A. *"Subject People" and Colonial Discourses: Economic Transformation and Social Disorder in Puerto Rico, 1898–1947*. Albany: State University of New York Press, 1994.

Saranillio, Dean Itsuji. "Colliding Histories: Hawai'i Statehood at the Intersection of Asians 'Ineligible to Citizenship' and Hawaiians 'Unfit for Self-Government.'" *Journal of Asian American Studies* 13 (2010): 283–309.

Sarat, Austin, and Thomas R. Kearns. *Law in Everyday Life*. Ann Arbor: University of Michigan Press, 1993.

Scarano, Francisco A. "The Jibaro Masquerade and the Subaltern Politics of Creole Identity Formation in Puerto Rico, 1745–1823." *American Historical Review* 101 (1996), 1398–431.

——. *Sugar and Slavery in Puerto Rico: The Plantation Economy of Ponce, 1800–1850*. Madison: University of Wisconsin Press, 1984.

Schiller, Nina Glick, and Georges Eugene Fouron. *Georges Woke Up Laughing: Long-Distance Nationalism and the Search For Home*. Durham, N.C.: Duke University Press, 2001.

Schmidt-Nowara, Christopher. "Spanish Origins of American Empire: Hispanism, History, and Commemoration, 1898–1915." *International History Review* 30 (2008): 32–51.

Schoofs, Robert. *Pioneers of the Faith: History of the Catholic Mission in Hawaii, 1872–1940.* Honolulu: Sturgis, 1978.

Scott-Smith, Giles. "From Symbol of Division to Cold War Asset: Lyndon Johnson and the Achievement of Hawaiian Statehood in 1959." *History* 89 (2004): 256–73.

Senior, Clarence. "Patterns of Puerto Rican Dispersion in the United States." *Social Problems* 2 (1954), 93–99.

Sharma, Miriam. "Labor Migration and Class Formation among the Filipinos in Hawaii, 1906–1946." In *Labor Immigration under Capitalism: Asian Workers in the United States before World War II,* edited by Lucie Cheng and Edna Bonacich, 579–615. Berkeley: University of California Press, 1984.

——. "The Philippines: A Case of Migration to Hawaii, 1906 to 1946." In *Labor Immigration under Capitalism: Asian Workers in the United States before World War II,* edited by Lucie Cheng and Edna Bonacich, 337–58. Berkeley: University of California Press, 1984.

——. "Pinoy in Paradise: Environment and Adaptation of Pilipinos in Hawaii." 1906–1946." *Amerasia Journal* 7(1980): 91–117.

Siddall, John William. *Men of Hawaii: A Biographical Reference Library Complete and Authentic, of the Men of Note and Substantial Achievement in the Hawaiian Islands.* Honolulu: Honolulu Star-Bulletin, 1921.

Sidel, John Thayer. *Capital, Coercion, and Crime: Bossism in the Philippines.* Stanford, Calif.: Stanford University Press, 1999.

Silva, Noenoe. *Aloha Betrayed: Native Hawaiian Resistance to American Colonialism.* Durham, N.C.: Duke University Press, 2004.

Smith, Tony. *The Pattern of Imperialism: The United States, Great Britain, and the Late-Industrializing World Since 1815.* Cambridge: Cambridge University Press, 1981.

Sorensen, Ninna Nyberg, and Karen Fog Olwig. *Work and Migration: Life and Livelihoods in a Globalizing World.* London: Routledge, 2002.

Soriano, Fred. "Filipino Hawaiian Migration and Adaptation: New Paradigms for Analysis." *Ethnic Sources in Hawai'i* 29 (1996): 139–54.

Souza, Blase Camacho. "The Puerto Rican Born in Hawai'i." In *Change and Continuity: Puerto Rico and Hawai'i, Viewer's Guide.* Honolulu: The Puerto Rican Heritage Society of Hawai'i, 1992.

——. "Puerto Ricans: Past and Present." *Plantation Village News* November–December (1981): 3, 9.

——. "Trabajo y Tristeza–'Work and Sorrow': The Puerto Ricans of Hawaii, 1900–1902." *Hawaiian Journal of History* 18 (1984): 156–73.

Souza, Blase Camacho, Alfred P. Souza, and Puerto Rican Heritage Society of Hawaii. *De Borinquen a Hawaii Nuestra Historia: from Puerto Rico to Hawaii.* Honolulu: Puerto Rican Heritage Society of Hawai'i, 1985.

Stasiulis, Daiva and Nira Yuval-Davis. *Unsettling Settler Societies: Articulations of Gender, Race, Ethnicity and Class.* London: Sage, 1995.

Steinmetz, George. "Return to Empire: The New U.S. Imperialism in Comparative Historical Perspective." *Sociological Theory* 23 (2005): 339–67.

Stoler, Ann Laura. *Carnal Knowledge and Imperial Power: Race and the Intimate in Colonial Rule.* Berkeley: University of California Press, 2002.

Takai, Yukari. "The Family Networks and Geographic Mobility of French Canadian Immigrants in Early-Twentieth-Century Lowell, Massachusetts." *Journal of Family History* 26 (2011): 373–94.

Takaki, Ronald T. *Pau Hana: Plantation Life and Labor in Hawaii, 1835–1920*. Honolulu: University of Hawai'i Press, 1983.

———. *Strangers from a Different Shore: A History of Asian Americans*. New York: Penguin, 1990.

Thompson, E. P. *The Making of the English Working Class*. London: Gollancz, 1980.

Thompson, Winfred Lee. *The Introduction of American Law in the Philippines and Puerto Rico, 1898–1905*. Fayetteville: University of Arkansas Press, 1989.

Tomlins, Christopher L. *The State and the Unions: Labor Relations, Law, and the Organized Labor Movement in America, 1880–1960*. Cambridge: Cambridge University Press, 1985.

Trask, Haunani-Kay. *From a Native Daughter: Colonialism and Sovereignty in Hawai'i*. Honolulu: University of Hawai'i Press, 1999.

Tu, T. Huynh. "From Demand for Asiatic Labor to Importation of Indentured Chinese Labor: Race Identity in the Recruitment of Unskilled Labor for South Africa's Gold Mining Industry." *Journal of Chinese Overseas* 4 (2008): 51–68.

Vellema, Sietze, Saturnino M. Borras Jr., and Francisco Lara Jr. "The Agrarian Roots of Contemporary Violent Conflict in Mindanao, Southern Philippines." *Journal of Agrarian Change* 11 (2011): 298–320.

Ward, R. Gerard. "Contract Labor Recruitment from the Highlands of Papua New Guinea, 1950- 1974." *International Migration Review* 24 (1990): 273–96.

Weber, Max. *The Protestant Ethic and the Spirit of Capitalism*. Los Angeles: Roxbury, 1998.

Wenzlhuemer, Roland. "Indian Labour Immigration and British Labour Policy in Nineteenth-Century Ceylon" *Modern Asian Studies* 41 (2007): 574–602.

Wexler, Laura. *Tender Violence: Domestic Visions in an Age of U.S. Imperialism, Cultural Studies of the United States*. Chapel Hill: University of North Carolina Press, 2000.

Whalen, Carmen Teresa, and Víctor Vázquez-Hernández. *The Puerto Rican Diaspora: Historical Perspectives*. Philadelphia: Temple University Press, 2005.

Whitehead, John S. *Completing the Union: Alaska, Hawai'i, and the Battle for Statehood*. Albuquerque: University of New Mexico, 2004.

Williams, Frederick D. *The Northwest Ordinance: Essays on Its Formulation, Provisions, and Legacy*. East Lansing: Michigan State University Press, 1989.

Winks, Robin. "The American Struggle with 'Imperialism:' How Words Frighten." In *The American Identity: Fusion and Fragmentation*, edited by Rob Kroes, 143–77. Amsterdam: Universiteit van Amsterdam, 1980.

Woods, Lindsay Shelton. "American Protestant Fundamentalism in an Ilocano Town: A Case Study." PhD diss., University of California at Los Angeles, 1993.

Yaremko, Jason M. *U.S. Protestant Missions in Cuba: From Independence to Castro*. Gainesville: University Press of Florida, 2000.

Yu, Bin. *Chain Migration Explained: The Power of the Immigration Multiplier*. New York: 2008.

Yu, Henry. *Thinking Orientals: Migration, Contact, and Exoticism in Modern America*. Oxford: Oxford University Press, 2001.

Ziker, Ann. "Segregationists Confront American Empire: The Conservative White South and the Question of Hawaiian Statehood, 1947–1959." *Pacific Historical Review* 76 (2007): 439–66.

Zwick, Jim. "The Anti-Imperialist League and the Origins of Filipino-American Oppositional Solidarity." *Amerasia Journal* 24 (1998): 64–86.

Zwiep, Mary. *Pilgrim Path: The First Company of Women Missionaries to Hawaii*. Madison: University of Wisconsin Press, 1991.

INDEX

Abinales, Patricio, on patronage in the Philippines, 99
Abril, Bernabella, 51, 67
Abril, Sen. Mariano, 75, 81; receives worker complaint petition, 82
Adams, Gerald, on bells of Balangiga, 168
Aducayan, Ambrocio, 62
Aguilar, Filomeno, on sugar industry, 52
alien citizens, 6
Allen, Charles H., 30, 39
American Legion, 80–81
American Samoa, U.S. jurisdiction in, 2
Amoroso, Marcella Queypo, 52
Ancheta, Lope, 53, 57
Anderson, Tommy F., 122, 131, 142
Anglo anxieties over incorporation, 97
Anglo laborers, 84–85
Ang Sandata (newspaper), 103
Antaran, Policarpio, 57
anti-Filipino attitudes, 61
Armesquita, Vincente, 34, 36
arrests, Puerto Rican in Hawai'i, 81
assimilation: policies promoting, 6–7; stereotypes, 41
Ayala, César, on plantation development in Puerto Rico, 18

Baker, Newton D., 82
Balangiga, bells of. *See* bells of Balangiga
Balangiga Research Group, 171
Baldoz, Rick, on Filipino workers on West Coast, 72
Balmori, Joaquin, 100
bangos (work ID numbers), 63
Bankoff, Greg, on U.S. denial of imperialism, 8

banks: Filipino deposits in, 53; HSPA assistance with, 68
Belen, Patricio, 126
Bell, Maj. Gen. Franklin, 168
bells of Balangiga, 24, 168–71; ownership, 168; return authorized, 171
Bergad, Laird, on coffee laborers, 33, 90
Binay, Jejomar, 171
blacklisting, labor, 90
blacksmiths, plantation, 86
border control, 8
Bureau of Insular Affairs (BIA), 26, 41, 48, 76, 82, 85, 96, 97, 159; power to Philippine Bureau of Labor, 97–98; referral process, 76–77
Bureau of Labor and Statistics (for HSPA), 58, 79
Bush, George H. W., declares Puerto Rico equivalent to a state, 166
Butler, J. K. 58, 68, 71109, 126

Cabalo, Munico, 69
California, Puerto Rican migration from Hawai'i to, 92
Cariaga, Roman, on returning Filipino laborers, 62
Carr, Norma: on Puerto Rican women and food in Hawai'i, 29; on cultural nationalism, 38; on Puerto Rican arrests in Hawai'i, 81
Casino, Teodoro, sponsors Balagiga Bells return bill, 171
Catholic church, 131–32; disrupts Protestant services, 134; position on bells of Balangiga, 170
Catholicism in Puerto Rico, 13
Cavino, Jose, 86

217

218 Index

chain migration, 50, 53, 54, 69, 70
Cheney, Dick, on bells of Balangiga, 168–69
Cheyenne, Wyo., 168–69
childbirth, en route to Hawai'i, 30
children, HSPA policies toward, 67–68
churches. *See* Protestant church
citizenship: challenges to Puerto Rican, 79; debates over Filipino and Puerto Rican, 5, 41; Hawai'i Supreme Court decision on, 79–80; Supreme Court ruling on, 1–2; U.S. plenary power over, 4; voting and, 78
civil service jobs, Puerto Ricans in, 92
Clinton, Bill, on bells of Balangiga, 169
coffee: crop destroyed by hurricane, 25; decline of market, 25
coffee plantations: labor relationships on Puerto Rican, 33, 90; permanent laborers on, 33; worker independence on, 33
Colondre, Jacinto, 157
colonial communication, 77, 83, 86; directives on, 83; map, 77; restrictions on official, 83
colonial subjects, status of Spanish, 26
colonialism, U.S., 163; consistency of, 3; denial of concept of U.S., 164; policies, 10
Commonwealth Party, 166
Congress of Industrial Organizations (CIO), 130
consular offices, foreign in Hawai'i, 83; handling worker complaints, 84
consul generals, labor issues handled by, 22
contract labor, ban in Hawai'i, 4
Correa, Antonio G., 80
Cortezan, C. C., 67
cultural nationalism, Puerto Rican, 38

Dagdag, Gaspar, 69
Dagdag, Juan, 69
Dagdag, Leon and Bernardino, 69
Dagdag, Victoriano, 69
dancing, religious opposition to, 135
Danlag, Claudio, 63
Davila, Felix Cordova, 82

day laborers (*jornaleros*), 33
Daza, Eugenio, 168
Deacon, H., 144–45
de Fiesta, Federico, 69
de Fiesta, Severino, 69
de la Rosa, Eufemio, 86
Delmendo, Sharon, on bells of Balangiga, 168
Department of Labor, reports on labor conditions, 32
Desha, Stephen L., Sr., 80
de Soto, Aurelie, 29
Dias, Tanilau, 78
Dillingham, B. F., 152
Dimas Alang, 126
Dinson, Severo, 62
diseases, spread in pre-expansion Hawai'i, 11
Dizon, N. C., 117
Downes v. Bidwell, 10
Draytom, Juan, 34
Duany, Jorge: on Puerto Rican nationalism, 38; on stereotypes, 42

Eckart, C. F., 84
Elective Governors Act, 165
Elizarry, Marlin, 157
España-Maram, Linda, on single-male Filipinos, 61
Eugenio, Macario, 135, 136
Evangelista, Antonio, 100
Evardone, Ben, 171
exceptionalism, U.S., 163

family issues, Progressive focus on Puerto Rican, 14
family reunions, 66–68; formalized process for, 66; limited support for, 67; on Ola'a plantation, 66
Farrington, Wallace, 107, 111, 116
Filipinization, 12, 96, 97–99, 105, 106, 109, 113; officials as elites, 99; religious orders promote, 123; sovereignty promised through, 97
Filipino Evangelical Church, 124
Filipino labor: anti-tuberculosis campaign, 114–15; citizenship issues, 4; complaints, 103, 114; dormitories,

100; in Hawai'i, 3, 4, 19; interaction with Puerto Ricans, 94; mobility, 4–5, 7; passage home, 102, 103; petitions, 105–6; protests, 114; quality of housing, 100; recruitment by HSPA, 20; strikes, 121–22; wages cut, 121
Filipino Labor League, 130
Filipino Labor Union, 103
Filipino Protestant Church (Ola'a), 131, 134
Filipinos: barred from U.S. citizenship, 12; from wards to foreigners, 5; in Hawai'i, 6; made subject to immigration restrictions, 13; most successful laborers, 21
Filipino upper class, 107; Ligot associations with, 110; reliance on U.S., 96
Filner, Rep. Bob, 171
Flores, George, 78
Flores, Juan, on cultural nationalism, 38
food: furnished by HSPA to Puerto Rican laborers, 32; Puerto Rican labor complaints about, 29
Foraker Act (1900), 14
Foronda, Leon, 122–23
Fort D. A. Russell (Cheyenne, Wyo.), 168, 169
Fortuño, Gov. Luis, 166
Foster, Anne, on interconnected empires, 8–9
Fraginals, Manuel Moreno, on politics of sugar in Caribbean, 18
Fransinete, Felipe Cruz y, 40
Fraticelli, Charles, 89
free labor, 5
free return passage, 61–63; requirements for, 63
Fujikane, Candace, on recruiting sugar cane labor, 16
Fujita-Rony, Dorothy, on family recruitment, 69–70

Gaba, Epifanio, 67
Gallagher, Mark, on HEA influence, 127
García-Colón, Ismael, 26, 40
Garfield, Seth, on migratory flows determined by market forces, 21
Gil, Luis, 84

Gillette (Wyo.) *News-Record*, 169
Go, Julian, on interconnected empires, 8–9
Gonzales v. Williams, 26
Gonzalez, Jose Marques, 84
Gonzalez, Pedro, 86
Good, Stanley W., 108
Goss, Jon, on temporary labor, 57, 65
grievance process, 21, 82–83, 86, 96; government agency motivation for, 85
Guisti-Cordero, Juan, on plantation discipline, 17
Guzman, Pedro, 75, 78, 81, 94; complaint dismissed, 87; files complaint, 81–82, 86, 87; results from complaint, 87–88

Hakalau plantation, 145
Hallowell, John W., 82
Harrison, Francis Burton, encourages Filipinization, 12–13
Hau'ofa, Epeli, on colonialism, 164
Hawai'i: application of U.S. laws to, 11–12; as borderland, 10; as colony, 11; becomes U.S. territory, 11; cane industry in, 16; expectations for statehood, 10; governor, 12; labor links with Puerto Rico, 2; map, 20; migration to California from, 92–93; as military base, 12; monarchy, 10, 11; perceptions of Filipinos in, 51–52, 54; Puerto Rican migration to, 26, 77–78; stereotypes of Puerto Ricans in, 80–81; as sugar source, 11
Hawaiian Board, 133, 136
Hawaiian Business Agency, 144
Hawaiian Evangelical Association (HEA), 23, 67, 122, 123, 125, 128, 129, 130, 131, 140; hires Pagan, 140, 141–42; influence with plantation management, 126–27; on purchase of car, 136
Hawaiian government: dismisses Puerto Rican grievances, 85; investigates working conditions, 35; reports on labor recruitment, 42; requests for investigations, 39, 85; resists recruitment of Puerto Rican laborers, 42–43; responds to complaints, 85

Hawaiians, 6, 10–11; rights of Native, 6; citizenship, 11; social relations among, 10; stereotype Puerto Ricans, 43

Hawaiian Sugar Planters Association (HSPA), 3–4, 16–17; age-limit policies, 59; allows for Filipino laborer transfers, 70; banking system, 53; blacklist rule, 90; company stores, 34; complaint process, 83; complaints against retracted, 36; conducts complaint investigations, 86; contracts with Filipino laborers, 62; cost of free-passage policies, 65; costs of recruitment for, 31; demand for labor stability, 34; dictates travels of labor commissioner, 100–101; donates to anti-tuberculosis campaign, 114–15; discourages reentry, 58; employment of older workers, 58–59; employment policies, 58; employment programs, 4, 18–19; encourages permanent relocation, 60; encourages positive messages to Philippines, 50; family reunification program, 66, 70; Filipino embrace of policies, 47, 52; financial support for Protestant churches, 127, 133; forced to provide transport home, 103; foremen, 33; frustration with Puerto Rican mobility, 89; grievances against, 21, 36, 44–45, 96; handles labor remittances, 53–54; history, 16; ignores continental fears against recruitment, 61; importation of Japanese and Korean laborers, 48; interference in investigations, 35; labor policies, 17, 20, 34, 36, 45; letters of recommendation issues, 57–58; Ligot relations with, 109, 111–12, 113; negotiates labor agreements, 46; Paid Transport Application program, 68–69; pays for return home, 62; Philippine Bureau of Labor work with, 54; policies on hiring strikers, 113; portrayal of conditions, 36; presence as unique factor in Hawaiian sugar industry, 18–19; and Puerto Rican labor, 26, 28, 30, 44–45, 140; and Puerto Rican mediators, 141; qualifications for return passage, 62; recruitment of Filippinos, 20, 140; recruitment of Puerto Ricans, 30–34, 40–41, 44–45, 46; recruitment policies in the Philippines, 49–50, 54–55, 59–60, 73; recruits Filipino laborers, 48, 49–50, 54–55; respond to travel complaints from Puerto Ricans, 31; resumes Puerto Rican recruitment, 44–45; retention strategies, 56–57, 66–68, 73; return passage programs for Filipinos, 48, 57, 61–63; seeks non-Native Hawaiian labor, 16; support from government on petitions, 87; supports government overthrow, 17; tracking laborers, 71; transfer policies, 71; wages and benefits, 32, 45

Hawai'i Supreme Court, on voting rights for Puerto Ricans, 79

Haxthausen, Manuel Romero, 29, 37

Hayward, Calif., Puerto Rican migration from Hawai'i to, 92

Haywood, William, 48

health, recruits en route, 31

health complaints, 84

health inspections, 27

Hess, Carol, on U.S. and Spanish imperialism, 9

Honoka'a plantation, 75, 82

Hopkins, S. G., 82

housing, 32; Filipino labor, 100; provided by HSPA, 32

hurricane destroys Puerto Rico coffee crop, 25

Ibera, Simeon, 122, 125, 126–37; on absence, 135–36; builds church, 129–30; buys car, 136; compared to Santa Ana, 135; as community leader, 138; conflicts with congregation, 136–37; on dancing, 135; as middleman, 126–28, 131–33, 136, 137; motives questioned, 132–33; as pastor to Ola'a, 128, 129, 132–34, 136; as source of information on labor, 126; as union organizer, 130–31

identity, residency status and, 38

Iglesias, Santiago, 35

Ilocos, Philippines, 50, 52, 55

Imperialism, 164; common features of Spanish and U.S., 9; consistency of U.S., 9; contrasting U.S. and empire views, 8; distance from center of power, 6; Philippines and Puerto Rico as signs of minimal U.S., 8; process and function of U.S., 5; in Puerto Rico, 15; U.S. denial of, 8, 163–64; U.S. following British, 9
income taxes, Puerto Rico exempted, 15
incorporation, Anglo anxieties over, 97
Indian British colonials, 7; lack of mobility, 7, 19; legal ties to plantations, 7, 19
intra-colonial communication, 21
intra-colonialism, 7, 172; lack of representation, 21, 86
intra-colonial mobility, end of, 40
investigations, BIA, 82
Irwin, Harry, 82, 86, 87, 88; report, 90–91; view of Puerto Ricans, 87, 88

Japanese strike (1909), 48
jornaleros (day laborers), 33
Jones Act (1917), 14, 78, 165
Jose, Filemon, 63
Judd, H. P., 142

Kalauokalani, David, 79
Kalir, Barak, on evangelical churches, 129
Kamehameha III, 11
kangany labor system, 7
Kaplan, Amy, on U.S. nativism, 97
Kennedy, C. C., 89
kinship networks, 89
Kramer, Paul, on U.S. following English imperialism, 9

labor: importation into Hawai'i, 11; protection for Anglo and Native Hawaiian, 84; recruitment in British and U.S. colonies, 18; recruitment in Puerto Rico, 26–29; recruitment worldwide for Hawai'i sugar, 16; replacement in Hawai'i after strikes, 17; sugar plantation needs in Hawai'i, 15–16; temporary, 33, 57, 61; unskilled, 85

labor agents, Puerto Rican reliance on, 23, 139–44; as interpreters, 144; as mediators, 140
labor commissioner, Philippine: in Hawai'i, 22, 100–105; as community leaders, 105; permanent, 105
labor complaints, 22, 75, 81, 86, 101, 105; Philippine government control over, 97, 100, 105
labor contracts, 102
laborers, Filipino: age-limit policies, 59; in Alaska canneries, 72; attitudes of Anglos to single male, 61; contracts, 57, 62, 63–64, 70–71; contracts as a requirement for free return, 62; embrace HSPA policies, 48; expectations, 52–53; families accompanying, 60; family reunions, 66–68, 70; family separations, 67; free transport home for, 61, 62–63; Hawaiian population numbers, 48; material success, 62; medical inspections before recruitment, 56; migration to the West Coast, 72; mobility, 60, 61–62, 70–72, 73; Paid Transport Application program, 68; recruitment, 54–56; reentry requirements, 58; retention, 56–57, 59, 66–68; return passage policies for, 63–65; seeking return to Hawai'i, 57–58; send money home, 53; single males in Hawai'i, 60–61; stereotypes of single male, 60–61; successful recruitment of, 49, 59; transfers among plantations, 70
laborers, Puerto Rican, 1, 26–27: autonomy, 89; circumventing immigration restrictions, 26; complain about conditions, 29, 33, 34–35, 39, 78, 86; complaint, 75, 81–83, 86–87; costs to return home, 40; deaths en route, 31; deceptive contracts given to, 29; deprivation of rights, 34–35; end of migration to Hawai'i, 27; family ties, 89; grievance process for, 22, 76–77; in Hawai'i, 19; isolation on plantations, 34; journey to Hawai'i, 30; lack of local leadership in Hawai'i, 22, 75–76; leadership roles, 143; leave plantations, 91; letters complaining of conditions, 34, 86, 87;

laborers, Puerto Rican (*continued*): living conditions in Hawai'i, 32; migration to mainland, 92; mobility, 4–5, 7, 88, 149; move to cities, 91; needs ignored, 76; numbers in Hawai'i, 39; occupation changes, 91–92; perceptions of national identity, 38–39; petitions to U.S. government, 35, 82, 86; portrayals of, 14; promises made to, 29; protest conditions, 35, 75; quitting agricultural work, 91; recruitment, 20, 27, 29–30, 36, 44–45, 159; recruits, 27, 30–31; relations with Filipinos, 94; reliance on mediators, 4, 141–44, 160; repatriation requests, 40, 82; reports on conditions, 29, 39; requests for return, 39–40, 78; revolts en route to Hawai'i, 31; Souza and, 147–49; travel conditions, 30–31; wages and benefits, 32, 34, 144, 145, 154; workday regulation by HSPA, 33
labor grievances, 95
labor history, 3
labor mediators, 23, 100, 122, 126–27, 128, 138, 141, 143, 160–61; language interpreters, 23
labor migrants: influence of legal structures on, 21; Puerto Ricans protest conditions, 29; reliance on community leaders, 23; work and living conditions, 19
labor mobility, migration patterns shaped by, 18, 90–91
labor organizers, 100, 103; harassed, 127; status, 104
labor protests, 114
labor recruiters, 50
labor recruitment, 7, 26–45, 141; efforts to prevent future, 82; failures, 19, 25–26, 45; of families, 27; government expectations for, 26, 42; Hawaiian government reports on, 42, 43; local government resistance to, 41; in the Philippines, 47, 48–49, 52, 56–57, 59–60; practices in the Philippines, 49–50, 54–56, 62; process in Puerto Rico, 27; promises, 20, 28, 29; Puerto Rican government role in, 44–45; remittance role in, 54; U.S. government encouragement for, 40–41

labor strikes, Filipino, 100, 103, 106, 116, 133; against Hawai'i sugar, 17; maintaining order during, 1; strike of 1924, 116–17, 126, 128; strike of 1925, 121
labor union, 132; organized, 130–31
Labrador, Baldomera Pervera, 50–51
Labrador, Licario, 63
Labrador, Sixto, 63
La Correspondencia, 1, 156–58
Lai, Walton Look, on politics of Caribbean plantations, 18
Laino, Victorino, 95: Ligot doubts claims, 99, 111
land reform, 11
Lane, Franklin P., 82
leadership: lack of labor, 24; Puerto Rican migrant, 22
legal rights, contrasted with social discrimination, 6
legal structures, analysis of, 21
letters: HSPA encourages positive, 50, 59; positive to Philippines, 52
letters of recommendation, 56–57, 58; as problem for HSPA, 57–58
Ligot, Cayetano, 95, 98, 106, 107–8, 109–13; anti-tuberculosis campaign, 114; control over newspaper, 118; death, 119; ineffectiveness for U.S. colonials, 99, 110, 119; and labor strike of 1924, 116–17; as labor commissioner for Hawai'i, 98–99, 107–8, 118–19; as leader of Philippine elite, 98, 113; class bias, 111, 112–13; opinions about Filipino laborers, 111, 112; petitions to remove, 115–16, 119–20; powers, 108; priorities, 107, 119; reports, 109–11; removed, 118; supports HSPA policies, 99, 108, 111–12, 119–20; visits plantations, 109, 113
Lili'uokalani, overthrow of Queen, 11
Lindquist, Bruce, on temporary labor, 57, 65
Lionson, Vincente, 123
Lomnitz-Adler, Claudio, on power brokers, 141

Maier, Charles, on manifest destiny, 163

Makiki Experiment Station, 142
Maldonado, Daniel, 78
Maldonado, Edwin, on migration to California, 92
management, Anglos in, 85
manifest destiny, 163
Manlapit, Pablo, 103–6, 108, 126; arrested, 117; reputation challenged, 104
Marcella, Trinidad, 33
Mariano, Candido, 59, 71
Marín, Luis Muñoz, 165
marriage, free passage requirements for, 63
Martinez, Antonia, 158
Matrana, Marc R., on plantation labor discipline, 17
McCarthy, C. J., 82
McIntyre, Frank, 41, 45, 159
McKeown, Adam, on border control, 8
McKinley, William, on Philippine self-government, 98
McStocker, F. B., 144–47, 152–55, 160
Mead, Royal D., HSPA official, 83, 86, 102
medical inspections, recruitment requirement for, 56
Merry, Sally, on government structures, 21
Mexicans as potential laborers, 150
migration: flows determined by market forces, 21; history, 3; into Hawaiian cities, 91; as population cure, 159
Miguel, Matias, 47, 57, 61; family, 47
Mintz, Sidney, on plantation development in Puerto Rico, 18
Minvielle, Alberto E., 1, 2, 23, 151–60; compared to Souza, 159–60; as community leader, 143; as mediator, 4, 140, 151–54, 156, 157; as labor agent, 23, 140–54, 158; on migration to Hawai'i, 159; in Puerto Rico, 156–60; presents Puerto Ricans in best light, 155; prevents walkout, 154; as recruiter, 152; on social customs, 154; as translator, 152, 153; working for HSPA, 140, 151, 152–53, 158; writes for *La Correspondencia*, 156–58

missionaries, in Hawai'i, 11
mobility: as escape from plantation conditions, 88; HSPA frustration with Puerto Rican, 89
money: dependence on remittances, 57; sent home by Filipinos, 53
Murphy, Frank, attempts to remove Ligot, 118
mutual benefit socieites, Puerto Rican, 148

Nab, Bob, on bells of Balangiga, 170
Nakonz, Jonas, on evangelical churches, 134
names, confusion over similar, 63
Naquin, W. P., 83
national identity, Puerto Rican, 38–39
Native Hawaiians: contrasted with U.S. colonials, 6; independence demands, 15; land dispossession of, 11; support for complaints, 84
nativism, U.S. colonials facing, 7
Negrón, Policarpo Ulises, 31
Negrón-Portillo, Mariano, 36
New Orleans as embarkation point for laborers, 30
New Progressive Party (NPP), 167
newspapers: on national identity, 39; reports on conditions for Puerto Rican laborers, 29, 36–37, 156–57; reports on deceptive contracts, 29
Ngai, Mae, on alien citizens, 6
Nicolas, Tito, 55–56
Nine Mile Camp, 124
Northwest Ordinance, territorial expansion in, 9

Obama, Barack, on Puerto Rican status, 165, 171
Office of Resident Labor Commissioner to Hawai'i, 105
Okamura, Jonathan, on Hawai'i labor recruiting, 16
Ola'a plantation, 1, 50, 58, 60, 84, 90, 95, 145, 151, 156; as baseline for study, 19; church, 124, 129–30, 131–32; employs Minvielle, 152; employs Souza, 147; ethnic mediator, 140; Filipino use of RTA system, 66, 68–69;

Ola'a plantation (*continued*): kinship relations of laborers, 69–70; labor strike, 121; leaders, 126; pastor service, 125, 128; petition for pastor, 122–23; religious services, 123; support for anti-TB campaign, 114
Ola'a sugar agency, 102
Olwig, Karen Fog, on mobility of workers, 19
Ombon, Domingo, 57–58
Oms, Ramón, 31
Ongais, Danny, 91–92
open colonial mobility: defined, 3; lack of leadership for, 4
Osorio, Jonathan, on government structures, 21
overview, 19–24

Pa'auilo plantation, 35
Pacific Mail Steamship Company, Ligot complaint against, 108
Pacific Sugar Mill, 83
Padilla, Alejandro Garcia, 167
Pagan, Fermin, 92–93
Pagan, Joseph, 140–42
Pagan, Raymond, 80
Paid Transport Applications (PTA), 68, 69 70, 124; costs, 69
Palloni, Alberto, on social networks, 53
Parangan, Emilio, 117, 118
Paxton, Elmer E., 90, 152
Pearl Harbor Navy Yard, 92
Peck, Gunther, on padrones, 110, 114, 125, 156
Pepeekeo plantation, 144–45, 148
Pflueger, W., 58, 62
Philippine Bureau of Labor, 54, 96, 104; formed, 97; Hawaiian correspondence, 98; work with HSPA, 54
Philippine government: appoints labor commissioners in Hawai'i, 100; assists laborers, 96; controls labor complaints, 97; Office of Resident Labor Commissioner to Hawai'i, 105; promised sovereignty, 97
Philippine Independence Act, 72
Philippine Mission, 123
Philippine Normal School, 98

Philippines: anti-imperialism, 12; ceded to U.S., 12; independence from Spain, 12; independence from U.S., 13; living conditions, 50–52; map, 51; revolt against Spain, 12; as sugar source, 12; as U.S. military base, 12, 13
plantation house, 32
plantation labor: contrasts between coffee and sugar, 34; destroys property, 90; needs tempering nativism, 7; Puerto Rican in Hawai'i, 26; shortages, 5; working conditions for, 16
plebiscite, Puerto Rico, 165–66, 167; vote totals, 166, 167
Pol, Pablo Vilella, on impact of hurricane, 25
Popular Democratic Party (PDP), 167
Porto Rico Association, 148, 149, 150, 160
Protestant church, 122, 129–30, 138; conversions, 131–34, 138; and Filipinization, 123; as part of U.S. colonial project, 127; teachings, 134
Protestant ministers, multiple roles of, 23
Protestant pastors, as Filipino community leaders, 122, 124–30; influence, 122; labor petitions for, 122–23
protests: Puerto Rican, 36–37; business leaders on recruitment, 37
Puerto Rican bureau of labor, 46, 159
Puerto Rican elites, 21; and cultural nationalism, 38; fear labor shortages, 37; nationalism, 38; opposition to Hawaiian labor recruitment, 37
Puerto Rican government: dependence on BIA, 82; involvement in recruitment, 54–55; legislative support for investigations of Hawai'i labor, 82; requests for investigations of Hawai'i labor conditions, 39–40, 85; resistance to Hawai'i recruitment, 43; support for laborers in Hawai'i, 81, 85; takes active role in labor recruitment, 44–45
Puerto Rican labor agents, 143
Puerto Rican laborers. See laborers, Puerto Rican
Puerto Rican Revolutionary Party, 13–14; asks for U.S. citizenship, 14

Puerto Ricans: negative perceptions of Hawai'i, 36, 43; stereotypes, 78, 80, 88; views of U.S. government, 35
Puerto Rico: as commonwealth, 14–15, 165; crime, 28; cultural nationalism, 38; map, 28; outmigration, 38; poverty in, 28; race, 14; reactions to U.S. rule, 5; rebellion against Spain, 13; representation in U.S. Congress, 15; referendums, 15; slaves imported to, 13; as Spanish colony, 13; as U.S. colony, 14; U.S. citizenship, 2, 5, 14, 79–80; U.S. economic control over, 14; U.S. supervision over, 76
Puerto Rico Democracy Act of 2010, 168
Puerto Rico Federal Relations Act, 165

quarantine, recruit, 31
Quarles, J., 79–80
Quezon, Manuel, 105

Rabe, Amb. Raul, 169
racial divisions among laborers in Hawai'i, 94
Rafael, Vicente, on Philippine ruling class, 110
Ramos, Fidel, on bells of Balangiga, 168, 169, 170
Ramos, Ramona, 78
Reciprocity Treaty (1875), 16
Recruit Transport Application, HSPA, 66, 124; policy limitations, 66
referendum, Puerto Rico, 165–66
recruiters: complaints about, 34–35, 46; false information from, 29; government oversight, 30, 46; newspaper opposition to, 37; opposition to, 36–37; pay by number, 27
recruitment: HSPA programs for, 59–60; of families, 60
recruitment agents: Philippines, 54–56, 59; license requirements, 54
Reidy, Joseph, on labor relations on sugar plantations, 17
Remigio, Prudencio A., 101; relations with HSPA, 101
remittances, 53, 57; dependence on, 57, 67

return-passage programs, 62–65; limitations, 66; problems, 65
Rios, Tana, 89
Rivera, Manuel Soto, 46
Rivera, Raquel, on cultural nationalism, 38
Roble, Vicente Maldonado, 158
Rodrigues, Miguel, 91
Rodriguez, Victor, 92
Rodríguez-Silva, Ileana, on Puerto Rican portrayals of race, 14
Roopnarine, Lomarsh, on intra-colonialism, 7
Roosevelt, Theodore, Jr., 43; abolishes labor commissioner position, 118
Rosario, Juanito, 140; as community leader, 140, 143; influence with HSPA, 143
Rosario, Vicente, 143
Ross, George, 145
Ruiz, Alex, 52, 100

Sanchez, Manuel Olivieri, 78–79, 80
San Ciriaco hurricane, 25
Santa Ann, Flaviano M., 1, 2, 23, 121, 123, 124–30, 152–53; as community leader, 124–25, 138; as community mediator, 4, 23; conflicting roles, 127–28; as mediator, 127, 128; motives questioned, 132–33; as negotiator, 125; as strike opponent, 121; service as pastor, 23, 123, 126, 132; service to laborers, 124–29, 131; as translator, 126
Santana, John 33, 80, 91
Santiago, Alfred, 80–81
Santiago-Valles, Kelvin, on working class troubles, 25, 91
Schenck, Norman C., 128–29, 130, 134, 135, 136, 137
Sestak, Joe, on bells of Balangiga, 169
Sharma, Miriam, on returning Filipino laborers, 62
Shik, Angela Wai Yan, on evangelical churches, 134
single-male labor communities, 60–61; stereotypes of, 61
Smith, W. C., 91
socio-legal labor history, 5–6

Sorensen, Ninna Nyberg, on mobility of workers, 19
Souza, Blase Camacho, 26, 88–89
Souza, Florentin, 139, 144–51; applies to work for HSPA, 145–46; as business agency manager, 144; as community leader, 143; compared to Minvielle, 159–60; earnings, 147, 148, 150; establishes association, 148; as ethnic mediator, 139, 144, 145, 147, 159–60; as independent agent, 150, 153; as interpreter, 146–47; as labor agent, 140, 144, 145, 146, 147; as mediator, 151
Spanish consul, complaints to, 84
Spanish imperialism, common features of U.S. and, 9
Spanish language, complaints of absence of, 29
statehood: ambiguities for Puerto Rico, Philippines, Guam, 10; promises for Hawaiian, 10
Stimson, H. L., 118
sugar industry: Hawai'i as center for, 11, 16; paternalism in, 18; production, 26; recruitment, 3
sugar plantations: employment of older workers on, 58–59; existence in other regions, 18; Filipino familiarity with, 52; housing for workers, 17–18; labor needs, 15–17; manager preference for older workers, 59; reliance on cheap labor, 17; reports from, 86; significance in American history, 163; tensions between central and local managers, 71; transfer policies, 71; visits by Ligot to, 109; wealth generation from, 18

Taíno Indians, 13
Takai, Yukari, on chain migration, 69
Territorial Filipino Council, 118
Thomas, Sen. Craig, 170
Thompson, Frank E., 104
Ti Bagno (newspaper), 98
Ti Silaw (newspaper), 118
Torres, Maria, 39
Towner, Horace, 45
transfer request policy, 71

transnationalism, intra-coloniality and, 7
Treaty of Paris, 9, 79; citizenship in Article 9, 4
Trochez, Andalecio, 91, 92–93
Tung Du Chon, South Korea, 168
Tydings-McDuffie Act (Philippine Independence Act), 72

United States: expansionism and jurisdiction, 2–3; overseas empire, 9, (map, 10)
United States government: accepts findings from HSPA, 87; encourages labor recruitment to Hawai'i, 47; faith of Puerto Rican workers in, 35; investigates labor complaints, 84; supports Puerto Rican recruitment to Hawai'i, 43
University of Hawai'i, academic reports on Puerto Ricans, 43
U.S. colonials (legal-political category), 2; ambiguous status of Puerto Rican, 26; attempts to recall Ligot, 115; category defined, 3; complaint process, 96; contrasted with Native Hawaiians, 6; circumvented border control, 8; distinguished from people in earlier acquisitions, 9; as cheap labor source, 5; exemption from immigration restrictions, 3; government regulation of, 5; military views of, 42; mobility, 7–8, 19; needs disregarded by government, 97; personal experiences of, 6; petitions to remove Ligot, 116
U.S. Department of the Interior, 85

Varona, Francisco, 64, 101, 117; files complaints, 102–3
Vegas, John, 92
Villaneuva, Gus, 143
Virgin Islands, U.S. jurisdiction in, 2
Visayas, 50, 52, 167–68
voting rights, Puerto Rican drive for, 78–79; Hawai'i Supreme Court decision on, 79–80; suit filed for, 79

wage laborers, sugar cane, 17
Wagner, George, 50

Walcutt, Charles C., Jr., 82
Walker, H. A., 66
Walker, R. C., 102
Wall, Jean, 171
Ward, R. Gerard, on labor contracts, 48
War Department, view of Puerto Ricans in Hawai'i, 41
wards, U.S. colonials as U.S., 5
Warren Air Force Base, Wyoming, 168
Wasserburger, Jeff, 169
Watt, A. J., 57, 64–65, 95, 111, 114, 116, 126; trusts middlemen, 126
Watt, John, 50, 60
Wolters recruitment agency, 152
Wood, Leonard, 106, 109, 110, 111, 115, 116
working class, Puerto Rico: criminality among, 25; hurricane effect on, 25. See also laborers, Puerto Rican
workers, sugar-cane: dissatisfaction with jobs, 17; relationships with employers, 17
Wyoming Veterans Affairs Council, 169

JOANNA POBLETE is an assistant professor of history at the University of Wyoming.

THE ASIAN AMERICAN EXPERIENCE

The Hood River Issei: An Oral History of Japanese Settlers
 in Oregon's Hood River Valley   *Linda Tamura*
Americanization, Acculturation, and Ethnic Identity:
 The Nisei Generation in Hawaii   *Eileen H. Tamura*
Sui Sin Far/Edith Maude Eaton:
 A Literary Biography   *Annette White-Parks*
Mrs. Spring Fragrance and Other Writings
 Sui Sin Far; edited by Amy Ling and Annette White-Parks
The Golden Mountain: The Autobiography
 of a Korean Immigrant, 1895–1960   *Easurk Emsen Charr;
 edited and with an introduction by Wayne Patterson*
Race and Politics: Asian Americans, Latinos,
 and Whites in a Los Angeles Suburb   *Leland T. Saito*
Achieving the Impossible Dream:
 How Japanese Americans Obtained Redress
 Mitchell T. Maki, Harry H. L. Kitano, and S. Megan Berthold
If They Don't Bring Their Women Here:
 Chinese Female Immigration before Exclusion
 George Anthony Peffer
Growing Up Nisei: Race, Generation, and Culture
 among Japanese Americans of California, 1924–49   *David K. Yoo*
Chinese American Literature since the 1850s   *Xiao-huang Yin*
Pacific Pioneers: Japanese Journeys to America
 and Hawaii, 1850–80   *John E. Van Sant*
Holding Up More Than Half the Sky:
 Chinese Women Garment Workers
 in New York City, 1948–92   *Xiaolan Bao*
Onoto Watanna: The Story of Winnifred Eaton   *Diana Birchall*
Edith and Winnifred Eaton: Chinatown Missions
 and Japanese Romances   *Dominika Ferens*
Being Chinese, Becoming Chinese American   *Shehong Chen*
"A Half Caste" and Other Writings   *Onoto Watanna;
 edited by Linda Trinh Moser and Elizabeth Rooney*
Chinese Immigrants, African Americans,
 and Racial Anxiety in the United States, 1848–82   *Najia Aarim-Heriot*
Not Just Victims: Conversations with Cambodian Community Leaders
 in the United States   *Edited and with an introduction by Sucheng Chan;
 interviews conducted by Audrey U. Kim*
The Japanese in Latin America   *Daniel M. Masterson
 with Sayaka Funada-Classen*
Survivors: Cambodian Refugees in the United States   *Sucheng Chan*
From Concentration Camp to Campus: Japanese American Students
 and World War II   *Allan W. Austin*

Japanese American Midwives: Culture, Community,
    and Health Politics   *Susan L. Smith*
In Defense of Asian American Studies:
    The Politics of Teaching and Program Building   *Sucheng Chan*
Lost and Found: Reclaiming the Japanese American
    Incarceration   *Karen L. Ishizuka*
Religion and Spirituality in Korean America
    Edited by David Yoo and Ruth H. Chung
Moving Images: Photography and the Japanese American
    Incarceration   *Jasmine Alinder*
Camp Harmony: Seattle's Japanese Americans
    and the Puyallup Assembly Center   *Louis Fiset*
Chinese American Transnational Politics   *Him Mark Lai,*
    edited and with an introduction by Madeline Y. Hsu
Issei Buddhism in the Americas   *Edited by Duncan Ryûken Williams*
    and Tomoe Moriya
Hmong America: Reconstructing Community
    in Diaspora   *Chia Youyee Vang*
In Pursuit of Gold: Chinese American Miners and Merchants in the American
    West   *Sue Fawn Chung*
Pacific Citizens: Larry and Guyo Tajiri
    and Japanese American Journalism in the World War II Era
    Edited by Greg Robinson
Indian Accents: Brown Voice and Racial Performance
    in American Television and Film   *Shilpa S. Davé*
Yellow Power, Yellow Soul: The Radical Art
    of Fred Ho   *Edited by Roger N. Buckley and Tamara Roberts*
Fighting from a Distance: How Filipino Exiles
    Helped Topple a Dictator   *Jose V. Fuentecilla*
In Defense of Justice: Joseph Kurihara
    and the Japanese American Struggle for Equality   *Eileen Tamura*
Asian Americans in Dixie: Race and Migration
    in the South   *Edited by Jigna Desai and Khyati Y. Joshi*
Undercover Asian: Multiracial Asian Americans
    in Visual Culture   *Leilani Nishime*
Islanders in the Empire: Filipino and Puerto Rican Laborers
    in Hawai'i   *JoAnna Poblete*

*The University of Illinois Press
is a founding member of the
Association of American University Presses.*

---

*Composed in 9.5/12.5 Palatino Linotype
by Lisa Connery
at the University of Illinois Press
Manufactured by Sheridan Books, Inc.*

*University of Illinois Press
1325 South Oak Street
Champaign, IL 61820-6903
www.press.uillinois.edu*